MOVING UP, MOVING OUT

MOVING UP, MOVING OUT

THE RISE OF THE BLACK MIDDLE CLASS IN CHICAGO

WILL COOLEY

NIU PRESS / DEKALB IL

Northern Illinois University Press, DeKalb 60115
© 2018 by Northern Illinois University Press
All rights reserved

27 26 25 24 23 22 21 20 19 18   1 2 3 4 5
978-0-87580-787-4 (paper)
978-1-60909-243-6 (e-book)
Book and cover design by Yuni Dorr

A portion of chapter two appeared as "Moving On Out: Black Pioneering in Chicago, 1915–1950,"
Journal of Urban History 36, no. 4 (July 2010): 485–506.

Library of Congress Cataloging-in-Publication Data is available online at http://catalog.loc.gov

To Melissa and Ella Pearl

CONTENTS

ACKNOWLEDGMENTS

A book such as this has one name on the cover but many people contributed in its winding journey to publication. My dissertation adviser and mentor, James Barrett, provided comments, revisions, and not-so-subtle reminders to finish up. David Roediger, Clarence Lang, and Adrian Burgos were also invaluable guides. Reading forums such as the Working-Class Reading Group, Dissertation Chapter Group, and Walsh Works-in-Progress provided constructive feedback. John Hoffmann made available a graduate assistantship in the sterling University of Illinois History and Lincoln Collection. Fellowships and grants from the Illinois Department of History, the King V. Hostick Award from the Illinois State Historical Society and the Illinois Historic Preservation Agency, and support from the Business History Conference supplied needed funds for research and conference participation. Walsh University also awarded me a sabbatical, affording crucial time for making final changes for submission. Peter Rachleff, Eric Schneider, and Edward Larkin challenged me to put in the work.

Chris Agee, Brian Ingrassia, Julilly Kohler-Hausmann, Jason Kozlowski, and Catherine Connor read portions of this manuscript and offered insightful suggestions. The anonymous readers at Northern Illinois University Press had invaluable comments. Amy Farranto, Nathan Holmes, Yuni Dorr, and Debby Vetter shepherded it to completion. Robert Johnston told some harsh truths about paring down the scope. Librarians and archivists assisted me greatly in finding research material. Alyssa Arciello, Katie Hutchison, and Melissa Bauer used their sleuthing skills to track down sources. Locating the material was one thing, having a place to stay was another. Robert and Susan Simmons, Russ and Kristen Ellis, Aaron Metzger, Kristen Nash, Larry and Diane Zavadil, Joshua Zavadil, Anthony Sigismondi and Melissa Prentice, Mark Kummerer, and Virginia Kummerer imparted first-rate lodging and companionship.

My parents, Allen and Ivalene Cooley, imparted lessons in intellectual inquiry and social justice. I am forever in debt to their guidance and love. Melissa Kath and Ella Pearl Kath Cooley are patient, inquisitive, and supportive. I hope this book makes them proud.

MOVING UP, MOVING OUT

INTRODUCTION

In 1954, George Johnson left a sales job to start a hair-care products company with his wife, Joan. The Johnsons made quality hair-relaxer creams, but as an African American couple in Chicago, they could not land financing from white banks to produce and market their brands. After a loan officer told him their idea was "ridiculous," George fibbed to receive his initial funding. He went to another branch of the same firm and received $250 for a "family vacation." In the following years, the business flourished but banks still denied the Johnsons loans. Despite the impediments, they distributed their merchandise through beauty shops and customers snapped it up. By 1960, sales ran at $425,000 a year.[1]

The proceeds propelled the Johnsons to relocate to Chatham, a prestigious neighborhood on the city's South Side that saw an influx of African Americans in the late 1950s. The community had long been an area where European Americans assimilated into the white middle class, but most residents could not imagine black Americans as part of this process. Despite some sincere efforts at welcoming the newcomers, panic-stricken whites usually sold their homes and left. One casualty was the local Chatham Bank, where Johnson Products had substantial sums deposited. On August 22, 1963, the bank closed its doors and the Federal Deposit Insurance Corporation liquidated it, citing financial malfeasance by controlling stockholders.[2]

For black residents of Chatham, the bank's closure seemed like the final, crippling act of animosity by retreating whites. "I recognized that this was really going to be a terrible blot on the entire community," Johnson recalled. "A bank is the business center of any community, and when a bank goes under, then people begin to leave, and the community starts to go down and fall apart."[3] Johnson, mindful of his previous disappointments in securing credit, collaborated with seven other businessmen to start a new bank in the same location. Independence Bank rose from the ashes as the first black-owned bank to open its doors in Chicago since the Great Depression.[4] After weathering early challenges, Independence Bank became the country's largest black-owned bank, and Johnson Products emerged as the first company headed by African Americans to be listed on the American Stock Exchange.[5] Through their tenacity and resourcefulness, the black middle class rallied to save an entire community from falling victim to neglect and disinvestment.

The Johnsons' story illustrates the main themes of this book. The twentieth century produced unprecedented socioeconomic mobility for large numbers of Americans. As the writer Nelson Algren remarked, Chicago was a "city on the make," filled with dreamers and schemers.[6] While black Chicagoans engaged in collective workplace, community, and political struggles, they also used individualistic means to secure the American Dream. The Johnsons became affluent but struggled to earn access to the mainstream. They made products serving the black market, lived in a segregated area, and helped form a bank mainly for black customers. Like many African Americans that obtained prosperity, they did so on a different track, and only after overcoming hurdles placed by obstinate whites.

Moving Up, Moving Out presents the damage racism and discrimination exacted on black Chicagoans and their communities while accentuating the resilience, struggles, and the often-compromised positions of upwardly mobile African Americans. Many historians have wondered why African Americans, as their hopes for the Great Migration dimmed in Northern ghettoes, did not turn to more radical means. Indeed, African American activists and intellectuals offered a host of alternative routes to empowerment, including nationalism, communism, social democracy, and community-based political liberalism.[7] These movements all had a deep impact but the pull of economic climbing within the system held strong, despite its flaws and hypocrisies, especially when African Americans could point to people who had made it against the odds. Black middle-class sensibilities were shaped by their individual and collective encounters with discrimination, structural disparities in housing and employment, and critiques from within the race.

Class is a relationship, and historians often discuss the black middle class in terms of its relations with the masses, critiquing it for what members did or did not do to the "uplift" the race. Some scholars credit their egalitarian efforts to reach down and assist with political mobilization, civil rights activities, and "giving back."[8] Indeed, the middle class often forthrightly believed they were setting the best example for other African Americans and saw themselves as envoys to the white establishment. They took on leading roles in the freedom struggle, particularly when the objectives served their interests. The black masses regularly looked to elites for leadership and inspiration and hoped that their accomplishments would change white attitudes in regard to race, citizenship, and integration.[9] Critics, however, faulted the middle class as rootless, powerless, and lacking awareness of their social responsibilities.[10] They charged that they were far too comfortable in their cramped political and economic realms and used the poor as a dependent power base in a system of clientage exchange.[11] As they moved up, detractors argued that they abandoned the community and left these "clients" to fend for themselves.[12]

There are many paths to resistance, though, and black strivers should be examined on their own terms.[13] Many were focused on personal achievement, a motivation that did not necessarily exclude other pursuits, including racial uplift. As the book details, the black middle class expressed more concern and did far more for the less fortunate than its white counterpart. Yet as Kevin Gaines notes, uplift was not an "independent black perspective"; rather, it was formed by prevailing cultural currents and power structures. The contradictions between uplift ideals tied to personal ambitions and the stifling reality of discrimination made uplift ideology a "faulty construction" unsuited to meet the enormous challenges posed by white supremacy.[14] The elite and middle class often internalized the "lift as we climb" ideology, but they did so under heavy pressures to discipline and pacify the supposedly unruly members of the race. When scholars and intellectuals hold the black middle class to these standards for progressive, radical, or conservative ends, they feed white hopes for racial peace on-the-cheap.[15]

Though it was the land of hope, African Americans faced systemic encumbrances in the urban North. The black middle class developed not only in terms of its relationship to poor and working-class African Americans, but by overcoming a white superstructure that usually opposed its aims. African

Americans came to Chicago in large numbers beginning in the mid-1910s as conditions worsened in the Jim Crow South. Chicago's bustling, diverse economy and political freedoms made it the Midwestern city that seemed to offer the best chances for migrants. Drawing mainly from the states with train routes to the city—Texas, Arkansas, Mississippi, Louisiana, and Tennessee—by the late 1910s the South Side rivaled Harlem as the capital of the "New Negroes." Blacks from peasant-style conditions in the South arrived and saw what the New Orleans–born and –bred Mahalia Jackson called a "Negro city" with black police and firefighters, black professionals, and a brawny political submachine. "Never before had Negroes lived so well or had so much money to spend," she recalled.[16]

African Americans like Jackson who came to Chicago arrived under conditions that should have led to easy assimilation. Modest numbers settled early in the city's development, their population underwent gradual growth, and they were mainly native-born, English-speaking Protestants. However, the factor that proved to matter most was the color of their skin, relegating them to segregated living conditions and closing them off from the majority of economic opportunities.[17] Chicago's rigid boundaries paved the way for the American-style apartheid in a dual housing market, as whites could live wherever they could afford, while placing restrictions on freedom of movement for African Americans. Whites used racial covenants and violence to sequester blacks to a narrow strip of territory running down the city's South Side and a limited area on the West Side. While the city excited her, Jackson also noted that her domain was limited, and "you could go for miles and miles without seeing a white person."[18] This provided blacks with a sense of ease—they did not have to bother with whites. As they soon learned, though, Chicago constricted their ambitions. Blacks expanded this living space block by block, but their neighborhoods were beset by overcrowding and substandard conditions that worsened over the twentieth century as jobs and capital left.[19] Most disturbingly, the city was routinely ripped apart by a series of ugly, violent ordeals that ranged from all-out riots to small-scale disturbances. In nearly all these cases, white elites leaned heavily on the black middle class to pull Chicago back from the brink. They complied by not giving up on the city, but also adeptly used their elevated positions to negotiate advancement for themselves, while usually hoping that these personal steps forward would also improve the lot of the race.

Though racism was the root cause of most of these conflagrations, African Americans' consistent contestation of the city's color lines sparked them through the defiant belief that whites possessed no monopoly on the good life. African Americans joined in movements that pushed for broad gains. The vehicles for change included unions, civil rights groups, political parties, and community organizations.[20] While those actions have been well covered by scholars, this book concentrates on the impacts of individual strivings. As historian Michele Mitchell finds, members of the "aspiring class" that emerged during Reconstruction had a major effect on the black mind-set. They concentrated on hard work and economic advancement as the keys to progress.[21] Racial barriers severely hampered this mobility, but by the late 1910s certain blacks attained advantages in income, education, and status. The migration boosted prospects, and in cities such as Chicago, the aspiring class sought personal gains while endeavoring to distinguish and distance themselves from poor African Americans. Discrimination undoubtedly changed the meanings of "middle class" for these African Americans. Unlike European ethnics, who could change their names and "whiten" their résumés to blend into the middle class, discrimination barred blacks from achieving skilled work, foremen jobs, white-collar posts, and many professional positions. In this situation, higher-status blacks often distinguished themselves through cultural standards such as respectability, behavior, and dress. As the Black Metropolis expanded, money eclipsed these yardsticks as the primary defining characteristic of middle-class life, particularly as they used this wealth to move out into desirable areas. Unlike their white peers, though, they continued to wrestle with their responsibilities to the entire race. The black middle class, W. E. B. Du Bois noted in 1947, had long been torn by the dilemma as to whether its strivings should strengthen racial solidarity and the push against the caste system, or if it should "seek escape" through assimilation.[22]

This study details how class differences bared fissures in the black community and produced quandaries for black Chicagoans interested in racial welfare but concurrently trying to make personal gains. The affluent emerged as community leaders, but despite calls for uplift, they could not substantially change the fortunes of the poor and working class. As Preston Smith notes, they were not Chicago's structural architects, but their insistence that their own achievements were evidence of societal headway helped legitimize discriminatory capitalism.[23] Yet they were not social democrats and cared little for alternative forms of organizing society. They were individualists within a segregated milieu and did much to shape their circumstances. Shut out of many mainstream pursuits, black strivers creatively fashioned white-collar positions in the first half of the twentieth century. Instead of acceding to residential containment, these pioneers set about breaking through into areas befitting their attainments. While they often pursued integration with enlightened whites, when these hopes faded, they set out forming and protecting middle-class enclaves. As the civil rights movement began to pay dividends in the 1960s and 1970s, they initiated integration into often-hostile corporate workplaces. Through their personal experiences, the black middle class encountered the full wrath of racism firsthand. They pressed forward, though, hoping to simultaneously open opportunities for African Americans willing to follow their path. Black strivers were not egalitarians and did not think they were bound to take on extra responsibilities if they interfered with individual rewards. They knew that American society had produced these inequalities, and it was unjust and impractical for the black middle class to fix them.

The chapters that follow focus on the sites where Chicago's African Americans forged a middle class. Chapter 1 details the experiences of the thousands of African Americans who journeyed to Chicago in the 1910s and 1920s, seeking refuge from Southern atrocities and pursuing the "Promised Land." The migration included scores of ambitious, talented, and credentialed newcomers prepared to make a rapid ascent. Yet unlike Europeans, who found grudging acceptance, white gatekeepers nearly completely disqualified blacks from consideration. In response, black Chicagoans set up a "Black Metropolis" through entrepreneurship and careers in black-owned businesses.[24] Though African Americans created a vibrant city-within-a-city, small businesses could not satisfy the employment needs of black Chicagoans. Stymied by racism, African Americans developed alternative ways to make a living through formal and informal aspects of the economy such as real estate speculation, storefront preaching, and gambling operations. These pursuits attracted the go-getting while generating controversy within the community. Black Chicagoans often viewed the successful as victims of a system that capped their advancement, heroes pressing to make gains for the race, and exploiters of fellow blacks. That these three descriptions could exist concurrently illuminated Chicago's racialized political economy. The accomplishments of African Americans in unconventional fields also showed the hypocrisy of a society that claimed to value skill and aspiration while severely constraining black Chicagoans' chances, engendering a warily cynical black version of the American Dream.

Chapter 2 details the wretched housing conditions for blacks in the Windy City during the period of the First Great Migration. This abject situation is well-covered historical territory, but few scholars have examined extraordinary measures taken by African Americans to find suitable living spaces and break down residential boundaries.[25] For African Americans, upgrading housing was a tortuous process. Though clashes over territory included friction and brutal incidents between European groups, by the late 1910s borders were most pronounced along black/white lines. African Americans pushed through these obstacles, simultaneously rallying racial pride while revealing class tensions. The prosperous took particular umbrage at the indiscriminate mixing of people in their neighborhoods as they watched successful white-ethnics move out of slums and blend into the middle class. Yet many also understood that moving out was not an act of snobbery, but a necessary tactic to create space for a home-starved people, and pioneers made steady expansions by pressing into self-styled "white" districts, braving obstacles ranging from the annoying to the life-threatening.[26] Housing did not trickle down to African Americans; rather, they consistently claimed the right to live where they chose despite ferocious resistance.

Chapter 3 examines the optimism over integration in the 1950s and 1960s by focusing on Chatham, a neighborhood built on swampy land on the Far South Side not fully developed until after World War II. In Chicago and across the nation, liberal academics, journalists, and average citizens touted that middle-class blacks and whites, secure in their status, were ready to mix in places such as Chatham and serve as a new national pattern.[27] As well-off African Americans boldly moved into the area, residents tried to coalesce around shared concerns for upkeep, crime prevention, and school quality. Gradually, however, most white residents fled, exhibiting the shortcomings of postwar liberalism. Residential turnover was a common occurrence in the postwar era, and most studies of these neighborhoods conclude as whites exit, neglecting the importance of the aftermath.[28] Disappointed but not surprised, middle-class African Americans preserved their enclaves as the city's shortage of decent housing threatened to decimate their hard-won gains. Chatham was not part of the "second ghetto," but was among the much-prized "gilded ghettoes."[29] Middle-class neighborhood protection was controversial as critics contended that the affluent had deserted the less advantaged, leaving them bereft of role models, and privileged local matters over civil rights struggles.[30] The reality was more complex. A "golden age" of the ghetto had never really existed, as the black middle class had a long tradition of moving out to find hospitable living arrangements. Likewise, most middle-class black Chicagoans did not abandon fellow African Americans, but rather took active roles in the civil rights movement in the 1960s and 1970s.[31] At the same time, they pushed back against white efforts to solve citywide issues through black middle-class sacrifices. Housing discrimination and white flight left the black middle class to deal with the legacies of segregation and the escalating urban crisis.

Chapter 4 shifts from the neighborhood to the managerial workplace, showing how blacks pushed into the corporate mainstream in the affirmative action era. In the 1960s, after decades of protests and the arrival of government action, African Americans entered corporate careers, greatly expanding the middle class.[32] While many scholars have studied this process, few examine how black Americans instigated integration and did its unpredictable work on a daily basis in the salaried ranks.[33] Work and economics were an integral part of the civil rights story, as these quotidian concerns drove the agenda of the freedom movement.[34] For blacks in white-collar careers, pioneering was an onerous task. While the positions often came with monetary and status rewards, integration was a grind as white leaders looked to them to perform on the job and to mollify Chicago's restive black population.

This is a study of the American Dream, but it is far from romantic. It shows that white Northerners paid lip service to equality of opportunity while creating inequality in the educational institutions, workplaces, and neighborhoods that produced the middle class. Black Chicagoans demonstrated their talent and ambitions, but they entered through the narrow gate, preventing them from enjoying the fullness of the country's bounty. African Americans resisted these restrictions at nearly every turn by moving up into better careers and moving out into higher-quality communities, but their continued marginalization helped create a deeply dysfunctional city. White society made grudgingly small concessions to black strivers and then saddled them with major obligations for easing the city's racial conundrums.

Black Chicagoans were not merely acted on, though. Migrants came to the city for decades, inspired by visions of prosperity. Though this belief was strained and appeared at several points to be on the verge of collapse, the black middle class kept it from completely falling apart. Chicago, in all its glory and faults, was held together by black dreams of progress.

HUSTLERS AND STRIVERS

Giles Johnson
had four college degrees
knew the whyfore and this
and the wherefore of that
could orate in Latin
or cuss in Greek
and, having learned such things
he died of starvation
because he wouldn't teach
and he couldn't porter.

—Frank Marshall Davis, "Giles Johnson, PhD"[1]

In 1917, Edward Jones and his family joined the exodus from Mississippi to Chicago. The Jones family was prominent—Ed's father was Reverend Edward Jones Sr., president of the National Baptist Convention from 1915 to 1923. Ed Jones attended Howard University, but had to stop when his father became ill and died. Back in Chicago, he could only find work as a waiter. Disgusted, he entered the business of taking policy gambling bets. With a substantial investment from his mother, he and his two brothers steadily built an illicit empire, raking in millions of dollars by the late 1930s.[2] Flush with cash, the Joneses diversified into legitimate businesses. The leases on real estate on the main thoroughfares in Bronzeville precluded blacks, so they bought property and opened the country's first black-owned department store.[3] Ed also purchased a large home, farms in Michigan, substantial real estate on the South Side, a villa in France, and a ranch in Mexico.[4] Jones was flamboyantly rich, but also a leading employer of black Chicagoans. Most importantly, he was a symbol of success for African Americans in a city where everything seemed to be run by whites.

For years, Jones and other "policy kings" safeguarded their illicit operations by making hefty payoffs to law enforcement and politicians. Jones and his brothers became so intermeshed with the Democratic machine that they served as ward precinct captains and used their sprawling organizations to reliably deliver votes on election day. Though Chicago's organized crime syndicate, the Outfit, long coveted the abundant policy proceeds, the operators and their well-compensated political patrons rebuffed these efforts.[5] In addition, the syndicate governed a remarkably honest and peaceable racket, which fostered customer loyalty—black and white—and general community acceptance of what many regarded as a harmless amusement.[6]

Jones was a powerful organized crime figure, but he was not a player in Chicago's Outfit. Italians were predominant in the syndicate, but it also included Jews, Greeks, Poles, and others with European backgrounds.[7] Much like the city's mainstream businesses, Outfit members did not extend full partnerships and equal opportunities to African Americans. Instead, in the late 1930s, the Outfit began an aggressive campaign against black gangsters. White hoodlums murdered Walter Kelly, the numbers boss in nearby Gary, Indiana, in 1939.[8] The next year, they delivered tiny coffins with black dolls in them to the Jones brothers as a warning. The messages on the dolls stated, "Rest in peace. If you pull even one drawing in northern Indiana you'll catch up with what Walter Kelly got."[9]

The situation worsened as policy kings lost their political cover. Chicago mayor Edward Kelly had been a reliable ally, handing out patronage positions, elevating black officeholders, and supporting opening neighborhoods to home-starved African Americans. He received generous contributions from policy kings in return for shielding them from prosecution and competitors. In 1946, Jacob Arvey replaced Kelly as chair of the Democratic Party. Arvey opposed open housing and counted among his associates several Outfit figures. Within days white gangsters kidnapped Ed Jones.[10] After a week in captivity, the Jones family paid a $100,000 ransom, and the kidnappers dropped a haggard Ed on a side street. Frightened but alive, the gambling chief retreated to his ranch in Mexico.[11] As the *Chicago Defender* feared, the snatching was the opening salvo by "other racial groups" with "gun and bomb" to take over the racket and "utilize the South Side for only pillage and plunder."[12] The Outfit killed off and scared off the remaining policy kings, culminating with the murder of Ed's lieutenant and successor Ted Roe in 1952.[13]

Ed Jones had a spectacular rise and fall, but his travails reveal the challenges faced by African Americans seeking to get ahead in the Windy City. Though he was educated, discrimination impeded his search for a suitable occupation. Undeterred, he achieved entrepreneurial riches and respect in the underground economy. Even there, Jim Crow in organized crime cut the careers of policy kings short. The Outfit continued to pay Jones $200,000 a year to stay away, but otherwise held a firm grip over what was formerly the largest and most lucrative black-owned business in the city.[14]

This chapter examines how segregation and discrimination forced black Chicagoans to generate inventive routes to upward mobility. Though most of the African American migrants were unskilled and lacked formal education, plenty came with the requisite proficiencies, talents, and educational credentials to achieve socioeconomic gains. Most found only frustration, joining the mass of migrants that had their hopes dashed. While European immigrants and their children advanced through unions, corporate capitalism, entrepreneurship, and education, white gatekeepers blocked African Americans from these avenues. Given the execrable conditions endured by most blacks in the segregated city, some historians view the migration as a failed experiment.[15]

Yet, confronted with what Richard Wright called the "hopeless limits" of Chicago, black Chicagoans still hoped and, in some cases, succeeded.[16] From the First Great Migration to the Great Depression, the city's African American population mushroomed. Over this period, one factor remained constant: black men and women in Chicago needed to be creative to get ahead. With most traditional routes of mobility closed to them, they expanded delineations of respectability through unconventional advancements. There were some white-collar careers open to African Americans in government, politics, and black-owned business, but not nearly enough to satisfy demand.[17] In response, innovators created remunerative employment in gambling organizations, storefront preaching, and real estate speculation. These posts conferred dignity, status, and chances for advancement, rare things for African Americans in the first decades of the twentieth century. They also help explain why black Chicagoans, while certainly skeptical about American platitudes on equality of opportunity, did not turn against the democratic-capitalist system en masse.

In their own distinct ways, these pursuits also generated controversy within the community. Critics charged that gambling operators, preachers, and landlords preyed on desperate migrants. Yet most African Americans also understood that economic marginalization limited their options. Men and women in these roles regularly took a keen interest in racial advancement, making them community leaders. Their accomplishments not only signified determined progress but were important examples of upward mobility for the poor and working class. However, these cases also reveal how racism consigned African Americans to separate and unequal paths to advancement. As the Outfit made clear to Ed Jones, Chicago's version of white supremacy was all-encompassing.

THE MIGRANT PUSH

In the mid-1910s, the migrations of Southern-born African Americans forever changed Chicago's demographics, culture, and politics. A series of factors spurred this exodus north. Blacks faced the intolerable social, political, and economic conditions of the Jim Crow South following the failure of Reconstruction, as white supremacists targeted African Americans in an onslaught of bigoted lawmaking, lynching, and pogroms.[18] The outbreak of World War I stemmed immigration from Europe and created a labor shortage. Employers responded by opening factories to black workers and sending labor agents to canvass the South. By the end of the 1910s, millions of restive feet were moving north and west. From 1916 to 1919 alone, the African American presence in the Windy City increased 86 percent.[19]

Chicago offered higher wages, increased independence, better educational opportunities, and legally enshrined civil rights. More than anything, it was a place of *possibility*. When Richard Wright came on a train in 1927, he was "full of a hazy notion that life could be lived with dignity."[20] Knowledge of these opportunities spread across the South through the newspapers, contacts with kin and friends, and labor agents. "America is not always going to deny the privileges of its Republican government to its dark-hued sons and daughters," the *Chicago Whip* confidently stated in 1922. "Chicago is the place to start from; it is the keynote of America."[21] Through the 1920s most black Chicagoans were optimistic about the future. Vibrant jazz and blues clubs, black-owned businesses, well-dressed professionals, improved schooling, and the emergence of a political submachine of the Republican Party all contributed to the faith that they were on the way up.[22] This hopefulness made Chicago a magnet. Over the thirty years from 1910 to 1940, the black population in Chicago multiplied by a factor of nearly seven, to 277,731 people.[23]

Not all African Americans greeted the newcomers warmly. Detractors depicted migrants as country bumpkins "totally unprepared" for their new urban environs. Higher-status residents, seeking to solidify their positions through negative comparisons, labeled the detached men who ventured north "drifters," "floaters," and "ne'er do wells" easily attracted away from Dixie by "the stories of easy work at high wages."[24] The *Chicago Defender* regularly lectured migrants on proper behavior, admonishing Southerners with harangues such as "Don't talk so loud, we're not all deaf" and "Don't wear handkerchiefs on your head."[25] This portrayal of Southern immigrants became a standard narrative. Playwright August Wilson's Boy Willie arrives in the North with a truckload of watermelons and is brash, impulsive, and loud, still a "boy" at age thirty. His companion, Lymon, is slow-witted and easily separated from his hard-earned wages by fast men and faster women. Their country ways embarrass their more established and refined cousins, who lament, "You can't come like normal folks. You got to bring all that noise with you."[26] According to some, migrants not only needed jobs and shelter, but tutorials on proper behavior. According to E. Franklin Frazier, old settlers "scarcely regarded themselves as members of the same race" as migrants.[27] In this oft-repeated scenario, Chicago before the mass migration was a place where blacks lived relatively free from prejudice in almost all parts of the city and were invited into white homes as "ordinary neighbors."[28]

Subsequent scholars showed that while the mass migration fundamentally rehsaped Chicago's black community and increased racial tension as ethnic groups fought for resources, jobs, and space, the hegira did not signal the tragic end of a golden age of race relations in Chicago. Segregation and discrimination, often enforced through violence, were evident in Chicago prior to the migration, if on a smaller scale.[29] African Americans had already established several significant institutions such as the Provident Hospital, the Wabash Avenue YMCA, and *Chicago Defender*. They had also elected "race men" to the state legislature and city council. Yet whites established the color line in employment and housing long before the Great Migration.[30] While the famed sociologists Horace Cayton and St. Clair Drake asserted that population increase and the race riot of 1919 "profoundly altered relationships" between the races, black-white interactions mostly continued the precedents in place before the migration.[31]

Meager attempts at demarcation like the "Old Settler's Club" were soon over-whelmed by migrants with the talent, ambition, and the means to make a rapid adjustment to city life. While some old settlers had been "the first in establishing class distinctions" and constituting an "upper crust" based on manners, color, and ancestry, the *Chicago Whip* editorialized in 1923, they were quickly being joined by upstarts who were making wealth and achievement the most import-ant status factors. Light skin, straight hair, and Northern birth were socially advantageous, one Chicagoan noted, but over time "money counts most."[32] Although the old settlers clung tenaciously to a manufactured sense of suprem-acy, in the 1920s social status in Chicago's black community shifted from eti-quette and duration in the city to wealth, occupational rank, and power. When black Chicagoans envisioned the meanings of making it, they turned their jaun-diced eyes to the men and women who achieved these markers.

A MULTIFARIOUS MIGRATION

The migration north was diverse, bringing skilled and unskilled, educated and illiterate. In his contemporary study of the migration, Emmett Scott remarked that a "most striking feature of the northern migration was its individualism."[33] The bulk of migrants were landless farmworkers arriving with cardboard suit-cases, apprehensions, and hope.[34] But the exodus also included more than a few who arrived in Northern cities with a myriad of advantages.[35] People like William Latham, a migrant from Mississippi, capitalized on this when he founded Underwriters Insurance Company in 1918 and hired other newcom-ers with experience in Southern-based insurance companies. The talent helped Underwriters prosper throughout the 1920s.[36]

With circumstances in the South growing "more grewsome [*sic*] and fiend-ish with each succeeding day," more and more higher-status African Americans found the violent terrorism of white supremacists unbearable.[37] Artisans faced increased discrimination and white competition and emerged as the vanguard of migration. Skilled and educated workers wrote to the *Chicago Defender* seeking advice on moving to the North.[38] According to NAACP leader Walter White, Southerners frequently targeted the affluent for the "crime" of "being too prosperous for a Negro."[39] As Ida B. Wells argued, lynching in the South was frequently "an excuse to get rid of Negroes who were acquiring wealth and property," a forceful route to "keep the nigger down."[40] One Mississippi minister planned his move to Chicago because at the very least black people "had the privilege of dying a natural death there. That is much better than the rope and torch. I will take my chance with the northern winter." A doctor from the same state closed his practice in 1919 and headed north, declaring the local situation to be "a little short of suicide," and a place where "no man can still respect himself while the white south hunts us down with as much vigor as one digs rats out of a hole." Similar testimonials in the late 1910s and 1920s came from barbers, automobile mechanics, and schoolteachers. Professional people reported that whites were making life uneasy for them because they imagined the growing discontent could be traced to the race's more advanced element. The mass departure also left professionals without customers and clients. A Memphis insurance agent stated that "on account of the race people leaving here so very fast my present job is no longer a profitable one." A *Defender* correspondent in Birmingham wrote that while average blacks were way ahead in moving, even the elites were "now considering the advisability of going north to better their condition."[41]

The ambitious, the educated, and the adventurous were often more willing to seek a new beginning.[42] Some newcomers were not accustomed to big-city life, Carl Sandburg observed, but he recorded that the new arrivals also included a banker, a newspaper editor, a schoolteacher, and several successful businessmen. Tuskegee and Hampton graduates abounded, and they enthusiastically bantered back and forth over the theories of Booker T. Washington and W. E. B. Du Bois.[43] Population growth accelerated the development of the city's professional and commercial classes. Prior to the migration, "frustrated professionals" were without a client base and often ended up in service occupations. Robert Abbott, the publisher of the *Chicago Defender*, received his law degree in 1898 and made three exasperating attempts to practice before turning to the newspaper business, an undertaking that flourished because of the migration.[44]

The upsurge in the black population produced opportunities for upward mobility, and capable and determined newcomers filled these elevated stations. However, discrimination limited the size and scope of the playing field. Many African Americans were equally or better positioned than rural, native-born whites or European immigrants to achieve their dreams. Yet as these newcomers discovered, employers ensured that their color meant more than their smarts and their credentials. Given that black Americans were citizens, spoke English, and arrived in places like Chicago with high aspirations, the middle class should have grown more racially diverse. This was not the case.

HIGH HOPES IN THE BLACK METROPOLIS

The move north was more than just flight from violent oppression or an answer to the industrial want ads. Black Americans invested in the American republican ideals of equality before the law, and migrants had substantial expectations for the "Promised Land." They came north already immersed in the cultural virtues of thrift, self-discipline, and temperance, and the increased educational and employment opportunities fostered high hopes for migrants and their children. In addition, some arrivals, especially the young, came with a swaggering self-assurance. The poet Frank Marshall Davis remembered that he and other newcomers were ready to take on the world. "You got the world in a jug, Lawd, stopper in your hand," he recalled. "You got the River Jordan flowing through your veins, and the gals oughta stand in line waiting to be baptized. You've got confidence oozing through your pores."[45]

The migration's peasant-to-proletarian character often led to an underestimation of newcomers' bolder objectives. In his study of the First Great Migration, James Grossman argues that migrants had "modest goals—a job in a Chicago packinghouse or steel mill" and looked to Northern factories and cities to "obtain what other Americans supposedly had—the opportunity to better their condition by hard work."[46] Although migrants sought security and a higher standard of living through industrial occupations, they also had rapidly expanding aspirations. Many industrial and domestic workers, not merely satisfied with their paychecks, had even greater long-term expectations than their Eastern and Southern European counterparts, who often had an "antimobility work ethos" that valued family, community, and the return to their homelands over individual goals.[47] Numerous black migrants came to Chicago looking for "eny [sic] kind of work," but often did not settle for this once they arrived.[48]

Long deprived of decent schooling, migrants regarded educational opportunities as the "key to freedom." One Mississippian vowed to give "my children an advantage that I never had." A Louisiana packinghouse worker migrated because he wanted "to go somewhere I could educate my children so they could be of service to themselves when they gets [sic] older, and I can't do it here." John Johnson, the future publishing magnate, left his Arkansas hometown because there was no black high school and his mother insisted he get his diploma. A female migrant from the Deep South came in the 1930s to attend a "big university to make a name for myself" like other "great Negro women." In Chicago, she reasoned, she could "make a contribution to the Negro race" and "be socially prominent and economically independent."[49] Once in the city, men and women flocked to night schools, even after putting in full days of labor. Migrants "positively swarmed" to Wendell Phillips public night school, the largest in Chicago, where four thousand black men and women enrolled in 1921 and 15 percent of the teaching force was African American.[50]

Young blacks also held lofty aspirations. A study of eighth graders in Chicago found that 90 percent of black students were headed to high school, equaling Jews as the ethnic group with the highest matriculation rates. The researcher noted that these schoolchildren realized they must be better educationally equipped than whites to compete for careers, and their future plans "showed more thought and originality than did those of any other children"[51] Nationally, black pupils had high expectations for their futures.[52] African Americans were not naïve about the racism their children were sure to encounter. As Langston Hughes's poem "Mother to Son" related, life would be "no crystal stair." However, the mother tells her son that she has been "a-climbin' on" and "turnin' corners," and her son must do the same.[53] Parents needed to brace their young for prejudicial hardships to come, but at the same time could point to their own advances as evidence of headway. For black Americans, the North was enigmatic, simultaneously a place of unbounded possibilities and unmistakable boundaries.

African Americans knew that they would have to seize opportunities to fight for equality. Many believed that fairness could be had, and oftentimes the initial impressions of the city contributed to migrants' ascendant orientation. Migrants marveled at the impressive Overton Building on State Street, housing numerous businesses owned by entrepreneur Anthony Overton, and the five-story Binga Arcade commissioned by banker Jesse Binga.[54] Though rare, the "physical presence" of black teachers and administrators "was more important than the lessons they taught," John Johnson remembered. "I'd never seen so many well-dressed and well-educated blacks in one place." Johnson was also inspired by insurance men, who were "moving paper and talking big money talk just like White folk."[55] The *Chicago Defender*, which circulated widely in the South via railroad employees, commonly featured the rise of wealthy African Americans, but also detailed success stories of average migrants like Robert Wilson, who came to Chicago from Atlanta with "one nickel and a Lincoln penny" but obtained work in a foundry and now had a car, a house, a bank account, and had been able to bring his family from the South.[56]

Although segregation forced migrants into squalid living conditions, this assured that the poor and working class interacted daily with thriving men and women. As scholars argue, the achievements of the well-heeled in the ghetto made "bourgeois symbolism" and "middle-class ideals" take a solid hold in the imagination of black Chicagoans.[57] Journalist Warner Saunders remembered that "people of almost every ilk lived in the same community. . . . You saw the 'best' and the 'worst' all in one neighborhood." While many middle-class Africans Americans resented living next to the "worst" of the race, others believed it helped the poor visualize a better future. "For me, life was interesting in the neighborhood and there were always people who were making it and were successful," historian and real estate magnate Dempsey Travis recalled. "Famous people lived close by, and that meant there was hope."[58] African Americans, despite encountering discrimination, were not immune from a national culture that stressed personal attainment. Even Booker T. Washington and W. E. B. Du Bois, whose ideological battles shaped much of black thought in the first half of the twentieth century, had a vision of uplift, self-help, and support of black businesses.[59]

Optimists hoped that African Americans were just the latest racial group to come to Chicago and that they would be given opportunities for upward mobility and assimilation. "The Irish had their day, then the Greek, the Pole and the Jew each in their turn. Each has passed on to the better tasks in industry but not without an encounter with race prejudice," one commentator wrote in the Urban League journal *Opportunity*. "Anti-race sentiment has not been directed at the Negro alone."[60] In this formulation, black city dwellers would soon move up socioeconomically as they gained a foothold in the economy. "Money is a wonderful thing," an editorial in *Half-Century Magazine* declared in 1922. "If you have enough of it, the world voluntarily places a coat of white wash over your blackest crimes. Money opened the doors for some of the most exclusive places to the Jews. Enough money would blind the eyes of the white race to our own color."[61] Another writer noticed that as African Americans became more fortunate, "white" firms increasingly solicited their business. He believed this was an encouraging sign, as "money is the one thing in the world that doesn't lose one iota of its value because a Colored man possesses it."[62] Idealists stubbornly held onto these sentiments long after it became clear that whites would not afford blacks the same chances.[63]

"VACANCIES FOR NEGROES IN INDUSTRY WERE MADE AT THE BOTTOM"[64]

Instead of following the immigrant pattern, black Chicagoans encountered stark discriminatory patterns in employment and promotions. Employers segmented the labor market and relegated black workers to lower-wage and less-secure jobs regardless of their qualifications, hampering factory hands, skilled trade workers, and the college educated alike.[65] Not only did whites deny blacks promotions, many migrants experienced downward mobility. The Department of Labor reported in 1917 the phenomenon of carpenters and cabinetmakers returning South, as they resented being shut out of unions and unable to find suitable work. Migrant professionals also discovered that the change of address came with increased competition and more stringent accreditation requirements. Schools were slow to hire qualified black instructors and administrators—there were no black principals until 1928—even when they became overwhelmingly African American. Skilled and educated Southerners had to be content with factory and service work in the North because of discrimination, and youths saw no point in training for trades that unions barred them from practicing.[66]

Black women's prospects were even more limited. An investigation of graduates of Wendell Phillips High School in the late 1920s found that young women qualified as clerical and office workers were only offered employment as "ordinary workers in factories."[67] After the manager of a hotel queried why a high school graduate was looking for work as a maid, the woman's frustrations poured forth. "Yes, I can type. I can write 50 words a minute in shorthand. I can keep books, but my face is black. Do you hear me, my face is black! So I must do the drudge work!"[68] A 1927 study confirmed that there were plenty of African Americans qualified for white-collar work, but few positions open to them. "The problem of the educated Negro seeking employment is a serious one," the author concluded. "Many well-educated Negroes must work at vocations where their training cannot be utilized."[69] The nation extolled education and training as the keys to the good life, but for blacks this was a false promise.

Workers came to Chicago and usually started at the bottom, but discrimination doomed blacks to stay there. For African Americans in factories, the elation of obtaining work was short-lived as employers relegated them to inhumane conditions. Laborers experienced deafening machines, overpowering smells, insufficient ventilation, intense heat or bitter cold, the reckless rate of the assembly and disassembly lines, and industrial ailments such as "brown lung" and "hog itch."[70] Black laborers were regularly dissatisfied with their treatment by petty bosses, the distance to plants from their homes, unequal pay, and promotions reserved for whites. They realized that employers had consigned them to the flu holes, hide cellars, gut shanties, bone houses, and fertilizer rooms for life. "We go right in the furnace where it is so hot no man can stand it for more than twenty minutes at a time," a steelworker testified. "When we come out the buttons on our coats are so hot they will burn you if you touch them. My eyes are ruined from the work."[71] African Americans were caught in the triple whirlwind of employer discrimination, union coldness, and hostility from white coworkers.[72] Migrants were not unwary of the limits of the North, but still perplexed at how their expectations met bitter reality. As the Chicago bluesman Big Bill Broonzy remarked, "All over the USA it's the same soup, just served in a different way."[73]

Due to these conditions, many African Americans sought more dignified occupations. "Clean work" often brought greater freedoms, more perquisites, higher chances for promotion, and healthier bodies.[74] Few workers remained satisfied with menial stations and ventured out to try to better their lot and their lives. All over Chicago there were porters trying to hustle up the money for college, tradesmen on their way to a law degree, peddlers with visions of expansion, and domestics singing gospel with dreams of stardom. For optimistic new arrivals, the first thing on their minds after securing a job was to find something better.

Yet virtually every occupation utilized by European immigrants and native whites for upward mobility excluded black Chicagoans. White-collar jobs in almost all private corporations were unattainable, and during economic recessions or slack business, the few African Americans who had found employment were the first to be let go.[75] Despite organized struggles like "Don't Buy Where You Can't Work," black job seekers were continually denied employment at businesses they patronized. In 1929 two Chicago banks reported that blacks were more than 90 percent of their savings depositors and about 25 percent of commercial deposits, but the Industrial Bank engaged one black woman in the savings department and the Bankers Bank only employed one black chauffeur and one janitor. Three other banks had black customers but no African Americans above the rank of janitor. Employers reasoned that they were not interested in "sociological experiments" or that they feared negative reactions from white coworkers and patrons.[76] In 1939 the *Chicago Whip* indignantly reported that blacks paid over $40 million to white insurance companies and "received the sum total of no jobs in return."[77]

Discrimination at all levels of employment meant that educational achievements magnified frustrations. In comparison to those in the laboring classes, black college graduates usually had an economic advantage that translated into a higher quality of life. However, when compared to whites, the labor market differentials were gaping at the top of the economic ladder in terms of wages and occupations, mainly because corporations excluded blacks from munificent white-collar careers.[78] As the sociologist Clifford Shaw documented,

Chicagoans breathed "in a cultural atmosphere filled with the heady ozone of individualism," but the black man was "forced, literally, to act out the drama of his life career upon a stage shrunken to the proportions of the racial ghettos of our cities."[79] Many learned African Americans ended up in service; a union official in the early 1940s stated that in his Chicago station seventy-two of ninety porters had college degrees. After a Dartmouth-educated Pullman porter died in a wreck with his Phi Beta Kappa key on his chest, the *Chicago Whip* called him "another martyr to American hatred." If he "had been given a man's chance he would have been in a position to help the world, but being nipped in the bud while blacking boots is an end that leaves us bitter and sick at heart."[80] Although employers supposedly sought aptitude and initiative in their salaried employees, they obstinately refused to see blacks as individuals.

The hypocrisy of the so-called "Promised Land" bred cynicism among African Americans. One researcher, noting the ambition of black children, urged Chicagoans to give them a chance "on basis of their education and personal ability to enter their chosen fields and to stand or fall on their merits as individuals."[81] The chance did not come. For some African Americans, the barriers took an extreme psychological toll. "Think of the feelings in the hearts of boys and girls of my race who are clean, intelligent and industrious," a self-described "new negro" wrote, "who apply for positions only to meet with the polite reply that, 'We don't hire niggers.'"[82] For these youths, the American Dream revealed itself as a cruel joke.

With all these obstructions in place, blacks had to look outside the mainstream for opportunity. Efforts to "move on up" included involvement in pursuits such as gambling rackets, real estate speculation, and storefront preaching. These occupations created controversy because these entrepreneurs often exploited fellow African Americans, but most also acknowledged that the combination of free-market capitalism and racist limits warped economic prospects. African Americans often afforded a degree of understanding to shady practices because they had common experience with racism and discrimination and an admiration for the hustler ethic.

TAKING A CHANCE ON "POLICY"

In 1921 an African American woman came to Chicago from Oklahoma with her two children. After two days searching for employment, she obtained a dishwashing job, but four years with her hands submerged in soapy water took its toll, and her doctor instructed her to quit. Left with few other employment options, she turned to numbers running. In this job she "wrote" twenty dollars daily, keeping five dollars for her share. "I'm forty-five years old and have lived in five states," she said, "but that's the best job I ever had."[83]

The Chicago variant of numbers, called "policy," provided thousands of jobs for black Chicagoans. Multiple wheels existed in the city, competing for bettors in the "poor man's stock market." A daily lottery that involved picking three numbers, at its height in the late 1930s it included an estimated 4,200 gambling stations employing ten thousand people who handled one hundred thousand players per day. Policy operators paid protection fees to law enforcement to turn a blind eye or actively shield their wheels.[84] The safest place in the city, some said, was the policy drawing, as police, often in uniform, served as "tellers" and escorted the daily receipts. Few efforts were made to conceal policy depots; signs in windows such as "We Write All Books" hung visibly. One researcher claimed, "children born in Chicago within the past fifteen years are unaware of the fact that the operation of policy is illegal."[85] There were occasional crackdowns on numbers' businesses, but they were usually politically motivated rather than in the name of law and order.[86] The game did engender occasional criticism and soul-searching in the community. Social reformers charged that policy preyed on the "poor and superstitious" and discouraged work. Others held a more tolerant view. As the historian Humbert Nelli explains, most Chicagoans abhorred poverty more than crime, and the shadow economy was a ready method for overcoming a lack of money.[87] For those squeezed by unemployment, underemployment, and discrimination, it offered dignity and remuneration.[88]

Numbers operations were highly structured organizations, with "policy kings" earning their way to the top of the hierarchy. They were a varied bunch, with some members of the "overdressed underworld" clad in flashy suits and diamonds. These "sports" engaged in conspicuous consumption and lived lavishly—a journalist recalled that a policy king's wife paved the vestibule of her mansion with silver dollars.[89] Others tried to fit into middle-class society, eschewing glamour for decorum. Regardless of their bearing, policy kings elicited thrills, envy, and admiration from black residents. "There was nothing I wanted more than to run policy," Warner Saunders recalled, "like any other boy in that community." The future reporter knew that gambling was technically illegal, but policy kings were his "greatest heroes," and as he grew up, he realized that discrimination made it hard for his neighbors to concretely define "illegitimate" activity.[90]

A tacit approval of policy developed because, unlike other forms of vice and gambling, organizers ran an orderly game and put themselves forth as responsible citizens by contributing to churches and civil rights groups, financing politicians, and making loans. Although there were some crooked writers and policy operators, the drawings were usually held in a large room with from two hundred to five hundred employees present, keeping the game honest and orderly, and the syndicate strictly disciplined operators who failed to pay winners. Neighbors protested dice, craps, and card games that created disorder, but rarely raised a ruckus about policy.[91] One finicky citizen who resided in the Lilydale community, an area of "people of higher ideas and people of self-respect," bragged that his neighbors had facilitated the closing of a local nightclub casino, yet tolerated the two policy stations that operated nearby. "Almost everybody plays policy," he reasoned, "but our organizations don't bother the policy station because that is the only form of gambling that most people think is all right."[92] Some vociferous critics spoke out against the game, yet most blacks understood that rampant discrimination forced go-getters to fall back on vice as an occupation, and policy was a relatively clean racket. As one informant contended, the Jones brothers "appear to be businessmen first. It is not their fault that the law considers policy to be a racquet [sic]. They are not racketeers. Only colored boys who cannot enter legitimate business because of the color barrier, & must turn to illegitimate policy." The Jones brothers' middle-class background was not unique inside gambling organizations as outlaw capitalism offered more prospects than mainstream businesses.[93]

Black Chicagoans were fully aware that the game was in the house's favor, but at least the beneficiaries were local men made good, a source of pride when nearly everything appeared to be white-owned and -operated. "Policy barons peeled and ate the South Side like a ripe banana," Frank Marshall Davis conceded. "But they were black; Al Capone, Bugs Moran and the others did not muscle in on this rich racket."[94] Even the upper crust of society regularly interacted with policy kings, though they preferred not to admit it. Reverend Harold Kingsley of the prestigious Good Shepherd Church outspokenly disparaged the numbers game but eased his opposition after gambling entrepreneur Julian Black donated $50,000 to Kingsley's community house.[95]

Similarly, the South Side Community Committee, a distinguished civic organization, sought to impress upon youths that the "swaggering racketeer" was not the local "big shot" in comparison to the hard-working, legitimate businessman "who had the confidence and respect of his neighbors." Yet the chair of the women's committee was Mrs. James Knight, whose husband rose up from being a Pullman porter to a policy king, owner of the famous Palm Tavern jazz club and first mayor of Bronzeville, a ceremonial post sponsored by the *Chicago Defender*. "Some of the women on my committee obtain their money from businesses which cannot be called exactly uplifting," a member admitted. "But that's all right. We don't mind. As long as they are willing to contribute money we are glad to receive it." An observer of the group perceived that many black Chicagoans made few distinctions between the criminal and the conventional, but because elites were embarrassed by the intermixing, they made a big show of attacking the illicit pursuits. "This, however, is strictly a type of play acting which has little reality so far as the residents themselves are concerned." The bosses of illicit enterprises were "well integrated in the total pattern of dominance in the community." However, the observer recommended that the South Side Community Committee should "refrain from mentioning the fact" in public, because the "outside world" would not understand.[96]

Policy kings took on leadership roles on the South Side. Among the six candidates for the first mayor of Bronzeville in 1934, four made their money in the informal economy.[97] They also reinvested in their communities. By the 1930s nineteen Chicago policy-wheel operators had at least twenty-nine different legitimate businesses. Racketeers like Dan Gaines, owner of the only black Ford Motors dealership, and Robert Cole, president of Chicago Metropolitan Insurance Company and owner of the Negro League's Chicago American Giants baseball team, secured personal fortunes through gambling operations but used their capital to branch out into legal businesses that provided employment.[98] A Chicago Urban League official stated that while he was "not in favor of the policy game," he was glad to see blacks managing it and reinvesting in local businesses such as taverns, funeral homes, and shoe stores.[99] Without the investment capital generated by gambling, black enterprise in the first half of the twentieth century would have been extremely bleak. The profits from policy were built on the dreams of men and women who wagered their nickels and dimes looking for a big break, but the game also generated jobs, venture capital, and a class of wealthy, civic-minded entrepreneurs.

For African Americans seeking decent employment, the industry required thousands of functionaries. Men and women worked as door-to-door solicitors (called "writers"), fielders, doormen, checkers, stampers, bookkeepers, and supervisors. The exertions of "writers" at the bottom of the pyramid were akin to insurance salespeople working on commission, and the slots higher up in organizations were increasingly lucrative, with managers drawing weekly salaries of up to $320.[100] Salaries during the Depression for checkers, pickup men, and guards ranged from $25 to $45 a week, and unlike white-owned firms, gambling operations had a merit system where talented, diligent employees secured choice positions. By comparison, stockyards workers earned from $20 to $30 a week during times of regular employment in the 1920s, while the lucky few who kept their jobs during the Depression took home around $11 weekly. In the 1930s, most employers cut domestic worker pay from $4 a day to $4 a week. Though policy included the perils of organized crime and occasional harassment from the police, it was significantly less dangerous than the killing floor or the foundry, and unlike the laundry or kitchen it allowed workers to use their initiative. Additionally, blacks enjoyed the thrill of defying white strictures on their ambitions and earnings.[101]

Policy workers were a mixed lot. In the late 1920s a researcher estimated that six to seven thousand black men and women on the South Side earned their living from the game, and while some writers could only sign their names with difficulty, others were well educated. One policy king employed eight hundred writers in 1928, half of whom were women. "Their chief assets were nerve and integrity," an investigator argued. "The former being necessary to 'take the rap' if caught by the police, and the latter, in enabling them to build up a large clientele."[102] Another contemporary researcher believed that policy writers in the Depression "would probably make good salesmen, but what are they going to sell? . . . Most of them never received any training and less opportunity."[103] As the economic slump deepened and black banks and insurance businesses failed, college-trained African Americans entered gambling operations, applying rationalized principles of business organization including advertising to promote betting. Policy kings added lawyers, bookkeepers, and experienced accountants to the payrolls, easing any remaining stigmas attached to the industry.[104] "Many men have given up the legitimate pursuits of insurance collecting, Pullman portering and waiting to engage in number writing," policy critic J. Saunders Redding remarked. "They are not all stupid men. They feel that the income from the racket is permanent."[105] For these workers, policy was dignified and rewarding labor.

Participation in the informal economy was often a strategy to meet fundamental needs. In their economically disadvantaged communities, blacks viewed policy not as a legal transgression, but as an appealing alternative to protracted deprivation. This did not mean they had a higher tolerance for crime, but rather saw shades of gray in capitalism. African Americans spoke out about the crime problem, but also pointed out racial double standards in the justice system, decried the poor and often predatory police performance, and offered solutions that attacked root causes.[106] Meanwhile, city authorities actively quarantined vice activities in black areas, and the media ignored the reasons for crime and sensationalized the results. As Richard Wright worried, the "violently reactionary and vicious nature of the *Chicago Tribune*," with its "lurid stories of so-called Negro crime, written in a wildly sensational manner," was "provocative enough to spur a race riot in Chicago every twenty-four hours."[107]

Gallingly, blacks faced overt discrimination in organized crime as well, as Chicagoland's syndicates excluded them from full partnerships. Through their political connections and payoffs, policy kings were able to keep white mobsters at bay. But from the late 1930s to the 1950s, whites murderously took over policy wheels and established a profitable dominance over the rackets, signaled most clearly through Ed Jones's kidnapping and exile.[108] For black Chicagoans, the reign of the policy kings had demonstrated how cunning operators had subverted racist structures, but their downfall indicated the potency of racism in nearly every aspect of political and economic life.

STOREFRONTS TO SUCCESS

Black Chicagoans also took sacred paths to white-collar work. The tremendous influx of African Americans to the city inundated existing churches and created the mushroom growth of "storefront" churches. Storefront churches often attracted poor and working-class Southerners who felt out of place in the more restrained, decorous houses of God. Many Southern migrants clung tenaciously to their religious rituals that accentuated human struggle, African values, and an ecstatic style of worship. For congregants, soul met body through religious expression, and euphoric worship regained control over one's essence while seeking God's blessings. Ministers spoke of the God of justice who had delivered them from slavery and would be there for them in their current struggles, fortifying feelings of a joint destiny. One woman testified she made twice-weekly pilgrimages to Olivet Baptist to thank God for providing a "place where colored folks worship and ain't pestered with white folks." Chicago's grind spawned the blues, but the city's plebeian churches also produced gospel music. "Blues are songs of despair," gospel innovator Mahalia Jackson contended. "Gospel songs are songs of hope. When you sing gospel, you have a feeling that there is a cure for what is wrong."[109]

Ministers long occupied an esteemed and vital role in black culture. "The Preacher," W. E. B. Du Bois observed, "is the most unique personality developed by the Negro on American soil. A leader, a politician, an orator, a 'boss,' an intriguer, an idealist,—all these he is, and ever, too, the centre of a group of men, now twenty, now a thousand in number."[110] As Chicago's black population swelled, ambitious men and women sought to fill these roles, and youths aspired to ordination. For a young Melvin Van Peebles, being a preacher had a "fireman-like, tarzanlike romantic appeal."[111] Churches with imaginative names like the Willing Workers Spiritualist, Spiritual Love Circle, Crossroads to Happiness, and Church of Lost Souls appeared in abandoned buildings furnished with only rudimentary benches and crate altars. Tiny but determined congregations painted their windows in imitation of the stained-glass panes of more ostentatious houses of worship.[112] Not all migrants headed for the storefronts—the congregants swelled established Baptist and African Methodist Episcopalian churches as well—but some men and women sought professional occupations through fulfilling spiritual needs.

The mainstream clergy and middle-class Chicagoans typically considered the presence of so-called "jackleg" storefront preachers as an alarming development. A poll of 341 black professionals in 1937 found that 94 percent vehemently objected to storefront churches, believing that they were "rackets" maintained for the support of fraudulent ministers who preyed on the religiosity of the ignorant and damaged the sacredness of the church. A social worker stated that storefront churches were simply facades for "ministers who go out to get money for the church which never gets to the church."[113] A writer in *Opportunity* referred to storefront clerics as "cast-offs," "religious criminals," and members of the "piker class" who engaged in the "prostitution of the church."[114] Critics maintained that storefront clerics violated the biblical warning against serving two masters, charging that their quest for money equaled and occasionally surpassed their mission to save souls.

Detractors deemed upstart preachers as charlatans who had not earned their station. Conventional ministers resented uneducated evangelists elbowing into stations that professional clergy secured through painstaking study. University-educated African Methodist Episcopal minister J. Langston Poole stated that storefront preachers were "almost illiterate and so ignorant and appeal only to those people's emotions and make no appeal to their intelligence."[115] A scribe for the Illinois Writers Project argued that most of them were "false prophets, imposters, and exploiters" and complained that "the ministry among Negroes is the only profession which is overmanned while the other professions are undermanned." In 1930, blacks made up only 7 percent of the Second City's population, but were 15 percent of all clergymen, and by the 1940s, there were an estimated 700 preachers for 500 pulpits in the Black Metropolis, with 75 percent of all churches the storefront variety.[116]

The preaching profession was "overmanned" for good reason. The church was one of the primary paths for social mobility, especially since no formal training was required for the job, only "the call" from God. A national study of 591 urban black ministers in the North and South in the 1930s found that 427, just over 72 percent, had no degree of any kind, college or seminary.[117] The minister role offered clean, dignified labor and was one of the few white-collar careers readily available to African Americans.

Despite accusations that storefront preachers sought to avoid labor, becoming an evangelist took a high degree of hard work. With so much competition among churches and denominational mobility by parishioners, preachers had to refine their oratorical talents and recruit congregants, often while holding second jobs. Crafting sermons, forming choirs, and delivering inspiration at prayer meetings and church services required flair and consistency, and storefront churches commonly failed to attract patrons or raise adequate funds to pay the rent.[118] Maintaining a congregation involved the entrepreneurial knack, and the faithful within the "Spiritualist" and "Holiness" milieu thought that ministers' and gospel artists' use of the commercial market was an acceptable way to spread the word. Preachers recorded music-laden sermons such as "Jonah and the Whale," "Lord's Army Marches On," and "Where Will You Be Next Christmas Day?" and sold them in stores. Ministers used weekly radio shows to spread the word and promote their churches.[119] Inspired congregants felt that their spiritual guides should be rewarded for their talents and that their affluence was a sign of God's bounty.

Though critics accused storefront preachers of entering the vocation for "selfish purpose[s]," aspirants knew that religious callings could lead them to distinction.[120] In Chicago, certain "Holiness" or "Spiritualist" churches grew to large and popular houses of worship. Clarence H. Cobbs, the stylish preacher of the First Church of Deliverance, built his flock from a storefront to a massive congregation housed in a grand, art moderne–style structure.[121] Elder Lucy Smith started a prayer meeting in her own house in 1916; by 1926 her All Nations Pentecostal congregation built a $65,000 church.[122] In addition, a large number of mainline churches in Chicago had humble beginnings in storefronts or homes before purchasing or building respectable edifices.[123] The Good Shepherd Church, which attracted the "elite of the Negro race," began with intimate meetings in the front of a home in 1925. Although Reverend Kingsley of Good Shepherd stated that storefront preachers were a "case of the blind leading the blind," incipient ministers could look to his church as an example of what was possible.[124]

Certain storefront clerics rose from modest origins to earn esteemed positions. The Protestant tradition accepted schisms, and congregants believed that storefronts were temporary locations.[125] Cobbs began by holding spiritualist meetings in a small room and attained notoriety by charging admission to view the body of an executed murderer; by the late 1930s he had a congregation of nine thousand.[126] His influence forced open doors to the establishment as organizations looked to him as someone who truly represented the poor, including serving on the executive committee of the NAACP.[127] As Horace Cayton observed, the prevalence of churches and funeral homes in Chicago were no accident, because "these two activities afforded Negroes their limited possibilities of making big money."[128]

Class differences in religious rituals exposed community fissures. Many middle-class blacks looked down on the emotionalism practiced by the poor and working class and believed that spiritualist preachers were leading their flocks astray while reinforcing stereotypes. As historian Wallace Best finds, though, African American religious establishment "had to gradually yield preeminence to a dynamic and class-diverse religious culture, as these churches found in their midst growing numbers of southern migrants, who were overwhelmingly poor and working class."[129] Storefront preachers also subverted these critiques by attracting congregants, pushing into the mainstream, and democratizing religious authority. Some particularly gifted ministers rose from humble beginnings to become key political forces with large, loyal followings. The blending of sacred messages and secular fortunes reflected both the personal desires to get ahead and the communal acceptance of strivers.

HUSTLING SPACE: THE REAL ESTATE GAME

While storefront preachers sold eternal salvation, other determined blacks peddled space on earth. The Black Belt's housing shortage, exacerbated by segregation, left anyone who owned a house or large apartment with the potential for profit. Most landlords in the ghetto were white, but African Americans recognized that they could also turn property into considerable income. By 1907 at least ten black real estate operators were active on the South Side.[130] Prominent African Americans such as Oscar DePriest and Jesse Binga made substantial fortunes by approaching the owners of rental buildings and guaranteeing a year's return. They evicted all the white tenants, raised rents by 25 to 50 percent, and subdivided the building.[131] The large returns spurred investments in the segregated residential market. "All over the south side," an observer noted, "one will find postmen and stockyards laborers with annual incomes of less than $2,000 feverishly struggling to keep up the payments on a four- or six-flat building."[132] The excessive rents and shoddy accommodations became a crisis, but collective action against this predicament was blunted by the African Americans, including a host of community stalwarts, who earned their living as landlords.

Segregation fostered deplorable living conditions, and renters especially begrudged the practice of subdividing dwellings into smaller and smaller "kitchenette" apartments. Migrant tenants were often forced to "double up" to make rent, and kitchenettes proliferated across the Black Belt. Reformers roundly denounced the "evils" of kitchenettes as a "moral and physical hazard of first importance" that contributed to high mortality rates, delinquency, sexual deviance, illegitimate children, and community deterioration.[133] For Gwendolyn Brooks, kitchenettes were where dreams clashed with the smell of "yesterday's garbage ripening in the hall." Richard Wright described them as "our prison, our death sentence without a trial, the new form of mob violence that assaults not only the lone individual, but all of us, in ceaseless attacks."[134] Gallingly, African Americans paid a much higher price than whites for their shoddy domiciles, a practice that came to be known as the "color tax."[135] As the *Chicago Whip* seethed, "We live like dogs and pay like princes."[136] Most Africans Americans understood that discrimination was the root cause of this misery, but their landlord was often a rich black man like Carl Hansberry, the "King of the Kitchenettes."[137]

Despite strong resentments toward subdividing and outrageous rents, black elites saw opportunity. The Negro Chamber of Commerce advocated bringing more apartments and houses under the control of black agencies but made no calls to lower rent levels. "Cases were found of colored landlords whose exploitation was fully as extreme as that of white landlords," one investigator reported in 1928. "With the increase in the purchase of apartments by Negroes as an investment it seems probable that neither lower rents nor improved conditions in Negro neighborhoods will result from Negro ownership of rental properties."[138] Landlords claimed that tenants, especially uncultured migrants, caused the problems. "Kitchenettes are not bad," a proprietor stated. "It's the people who are bad."[139] During the Depression the mass evictions of tenants included black renters put out by black property owners, demonstrating the limits of racial solidarity. When city officials cracked down on policy gambling in 1931 at the behest of Mayor Anton Cermak, the Chicago NAACP protested the raids vigorously, objecting to the "Cossack"-style abuses of business owners. Yet the NAACP remained almost silent on the rash of home evictions, some of which were carried out by African American proprietors and management companies.[140]

Though black landlords generally escaped scrutiny in the 1910s and 1920s, the Depression brought class conflict into the open. Black laborers suffered disproportionately as the first fired and last hired.[141] In 1929, the Chicago Urban League reported, "Every week we receive information regarding the discharge of additional Race workers who are being replaced by workers of other races."[142] By 1932, almost half of Chicago's black workforce was unemployed, causing a wave of evictions.[143] The only thing worse than a kitchenette, it seemed, was losing it, and anger boiled over in 1931. The Negro Tenants' Protective League especially targeted Congressman DePriest for turning out the unemployed and "fleecing his own race." On August 1, 1931, DePriest, dubbed the "millionaire Negro landlord" by his critics, met with other property owners and demanded that Chicago's chief of police halt anti-eviction actions by the Communist-led Unemployed Councils. On August 3, during a melee over an eviction, police killed three African American men. The following November DePriest lost his reelection bid, in part because he was unable to escape his reputation as a rapacious slumlord.[144]

Likewise, indignant black Chicagoans turned on Jesse Binga, who had been the largest black real estate owner in Chicago in the 1920s. Schooled in the real estate business by his mother, Adelphia, young Jesse made his first sizable real estate deal when the government opened an Indian reservation near Pocatello, Idaho, to the public. Binga bought twenty lots and then sold them at a considerable profit.[145] He moved to Chicago in the early 1890s, and after dabbling in a series of ventures, he returned to real estate, buying slum property at rock-bottom prices, renovating and subdividing units, and then renting to home-starved migrants. Binga also became a "blockbuster"—breaking the segregationist residential patterns through real estate deals—a hazardous but lucrative practice.

White assailants frequently attacked Binga—in one six-month stretch they bombed his property five times.[146] Binga was undeterred. When terrorists hit his $30,000 home in an exclusive neighborhood for the fifth time, a newspaper quoted Binga saying, "This is the limit; I'm going." He quickly denied the account, announcing, "Statements relative to my moving are all false. . . . I will not run." The banker fought attempts to foreclose on black homeowners who moved into white areas by taking over their mortgages. In resisting such efforts, he also situated himself as a "race man." "The race is at stake and not myself," he proclaimed. "If they can make the leaders move, what show will the smaller buyers have?"[147] Binga's courage and savvy elevated him from back alley huckster to the foremost black capitalist on the main line. In the 1920s, he could boast that he owned more footage on State Street, Chicago's major thoroughfare, than any other man. His "Binga Block" between Forty-Seventh and Forty-Eighth Streets was the longest tenement row in Chicago.[148]

Boosters portrayed Binga as interested in racial advancement through capitalism and uplift. Housed in a magnificent granite edifice and flanked by the Gothic-style Binga Arcade, the Binga State Bank was the "pride of the racial group of Chicago," a manifestation of race progress in the 1920s. Robert Abbott, the editor and publisher of the *Chicago Defender*, owned stock in the bank and burnished the businessman's image.[149] Binga positioned himself as a role model and believed his bank was a step toward relieving "conditions that are said to be making our people the undesirable citizens of Chicago." Through instruction and community institutions, he stated, the influential could "develop a thrifty and desirable person out of an indolent, reckless spendthrift."[150] He argued that his blockbusting had freed up more living space and that blacks should follow his example of using ingenuity and hard work to overcome hurdles.

Yet Binga's version of uplift included some harsh assessments of fellow African Americans. "I'm an Irishman," he stated in 1916. "You won't find any other colored people like me."[151] A black journalist charged that the laconic capitalist was "not worried about the Race problem," but in "solving an individual problem."[152] Any racial benefits his largesse produced—jobs in his bank or more residential space in Chicago—were merely residuals to his pursuit of wealth. He was simultaneously admired for his accomplishments and resented as a landlord with an inexorable drive for profit who talked down to his employees and other blacks, boasting, "Jesse Binga knows how to deal with Negroes."[153] The *Chicago Whip* doggedly disparaged Binga, calling him an "arrogant individual" and a "Black Capitalist ... very much disliked by the black constituency."[154] Even as whites targeted him with racially motivated violence, critics scolded him for distancing himself from the masses.[155]

Suspicions over Binga's ethics were confirmed in 1930, when his bank and fortune collapsed, and investigators revealed that the autocrat ran the bank as his "personal wallet." Tens of thousands of black Chicagoans lost their small but hard-earned savings.[156] Few elite African Americans lost their investments, though, as reports revealed that the bank had only two accounts over $10,000, and the average deposit was only $66.12. "We are being urged to support our own institutions in preference to those of the other race," wrote one Chicagoan, "yet it has become public knowledge that many of our race leaders, who do this exhorting, have been, and are depositing the bulk of their savings in [downtown] Loop banks."[157] The formerly adulatory *Chicago Defender* turned censorious, noting that Binga exploited his "own people" by raising rents $10 and $15 per month above the rates whites paid, a method replicated by other dealers. In 1938, a black politician tabbed him as "one of the most vicious Negroes when he was in power" and related that "his present circumstances make him an outcast and menace."[158] The Depression intensified the criticism directed toward wealthy men such as Binga, as those who had listened to the maxims of the elite to work hard, save, and be thrifty recognized that, though they had played by the rules, the economic downturn and bank failures left them penniless and without prospects.

Like policy men and storefront preachers, landlords met criticism for exploiting black Chicagoans' precarious social and economic situation. These real estate investors and managers, though operating legally, were often more divisive among black residents than other hustlers. African Americans appreciated that they were functioning in a segregated marketplace distorted by racism, but they begrudged real estate managers for inflating the price of a basic need. Unlike gambling, which was a luxury, housing was a necessity, and residents bitterly resented their unhealthy, cramped, and overpriced quarters. Even as pioneers made more space for themselves by braving mobs and winning court cases to overturn racially restrictive covenants, poor and working-class African Americans worried that these gains would mainly benefit elites, while the price gouging and poor conditions for ghetto dwellers continued.[159]

HUSTLER'S TOWN

Due to discrimination, black Chicagoans had difficulty demarcating the lines between legitimate and illegitimate occupations. Folklorists referred to it as being "put in a trickbag," as whites tasked African Americans with making the best of bad options. As the Depression deepened, civic leader Irene McCoy Gaines lamented that young women in Chicago "have come to consider all vocations (whether legal or illegal) as rackets" and "we have observed promising boys from respectable families leave school to find 'a profitable racket' and in a few short years become heroes of the underworld, heralded for their prominence as 'big shots.'"[160] From the vantage point of some African Americans, however, the "big shots" were resisting the stifling forces of racism through attainment, regardless of how they earned their cash. "You get sick and tired of depending on the other fellow for bread and butter, wearing the same old thing," a black male in boy's court stated. "My idea of a 'big shot' is this. You don't have to depend on nobody for nothing."[161] The lauding of the hustle, even when it was illegal, reflected rising cynicism. Although elites continued to moralize, their authority was severely damaged by the Depression and the realization that many had made their money through real estate speculation and gambling. A college-educated policy racketeer related the skepticism of operating in fundamentally inequitable racist/capitalist terrain:

> Dishonesty is the key to all wealth. Many of the great fortunes of the present day were accumulated by methods which might be open to question. People forget very easily. Should I die, leaving my children a million dollars, no one will question the source of their wealth, and they—the second generation—will be the financial, social, and cultural leaders of their day. Only by attaining economic security however gained, will the Negro in Chicago, or anywhere in America, ever get ahead.[162]

This policy king grasped the unique position of African Americans as marginal actors in the national economy and made clear that "white wealth" was not and had never been "pure wealth," something the ancestors of former slaves knew well.

Chicago, as the writer Leon Forrest observed, was a "hustler's town." "The word was if you couldn't make it in Chicago," he wrote, "you couldn't make it anywhere."[163] The imposition of racism and discrimination combined with corruption fostered a situation where the realities of survival overwhelmed standard notions of propriety. Policy, storefront preaching, and the real estate game were all routes of upward mobility that skirted the lines of respectability, yet they were also part of adaptation to city life. When *Our World*, a black glossy, boasted that Chicago was the "money capital of Negro America" in 1951, the magazine featured impresarios such as Judge Parker, the "Sausage King," and the insurance magnate Truman Gibson, as well as Reverend Clarence Cobbs, the former storefront preacher who picked up two $400 vases for his $50,000 house in two Cadillacs, and Ted Roe, the "millionaire policy boss of the South Side." The article suggested that there was no line between the respectable business owner and the outlaw capitalist; only money mattered.[164] Many African Americans admired the hustler ethic when they all felt the sting of prejudice, segregation, and discrimination.

Blacks came to Chicago seeking the land of hope, but instead ran into widespread and nearly pervasive discrimination in employment, education, and residence. Their narrowed opportunities made intraracial class relations more intimate, as the poor and working class lived close to the more well-off members of the race. For some, these moneyed men and women served as examples of making it against the odds, but others saw them as exploitative. The myriad of interests also diminished collective action, as some strivers either ignored calls for "race solidarity" or refashioned them to suit their needs. In Chicago, upward mobility often involved complex interactions with members of one's own racial or ethnic group. For black capitalists, this negotiation was particularly difficult because segregation made fellow blacks their only clients. Hustlers understood the harshness of city life and turned it to their advantage. Despite recurrent calls for racial unity, the jaded commonly expressed variations of author James D. Corrothers's "Chicago Golden Rule": "Do de other feller, befo' he do you."[165] One Chicagoan excused Oscar DePriest's overcharging rents, saying if he "hadn't gotten it, someone else would have."[166] African Americans knew that they lacked the same opportunities as whites, and to thrive they would have to make hard choices. Blacks, regardless of their backgrounds, simply were not on a level playing field. As the next chapter details, this was not only true in what they could do, but where they could do it.

CHAPTER 2

MOVING ON OUT

"Oh my house may have its east or west
Or north or south behind it.
All I know is I shall know it,
And fight for it when I find it."

—Gwendolyn Brooks, "The Ballad of Rudolph Reed"[1]

On the Sunday morning of April 12, 1914, Frederick Jefferson awoke to the milkman frantically ringing the doorbell. The smell of benzine filled the house, and Jefferson ran downstairs to find his front and back porches on fire. Grabbing his rifle, he recalled the threats made against his family by local whites relayed to him by friendly neighbors. Both exits were ablaze, so he directed his wife and his nine-year-old daughter out through the windows. The Oak Park fire department was newly equipped with an auto hose and chemical wagon, and the innovations proved their value as firefighters made the run in less than five minutes and saved the cottage.[2]

The Jeffersons had purchased their charming home four years earlier when the nearest neighbor was a block away, but as whites bought lots in the immediate area they resented the presence of a black family. Real estate agents marketed nearby properties with the promise that the "Niggers wouldn't be there more than a year." But the Jeffersons resolved to stay in their home, even after the local Jackson Improvement Association ran off a black neighbor and "prominent women" of Oak Park openly declared that "somebody should get rid of the Jeffersons if they had to use matches or dynamite."[3] On that Sunday morning someone—the Oak Park police believed it was a hired incendiary—finally acted.[4]

Oak Park was a fashionable suburb of Chicago, an ideal dwelling away from the dust and smoke of the big city. Leading residents made their homes there, seeking a garden spot in the expanding metropolis and wanting to surround themselves with neighbors who were mainly Protestant and native-born. The growing area also comprised several strivers, including the Jeffersons. Frederick and his wife had both graduated high school and attended college; now they were homeowners in a well-to-do suburb. Yet due to the color of their skin, locals considered the family interlopers, and regardless of their educational accomplishments, Frederick was only able to find work as a chauffeur while Mrs. Jefferson did domestic service. As the village grew, their mere existence in a "near great" area made them a source of angst, notwithstanding the esteem they had cultivated among some community members.[5]

The assault dismayed racial liberals. The *Daily Jewish Courier* compared the incident to Polish pogroms and stated that Jefferson's house "was burned for no other reason than that the Negro chose to make his home in Oak Park in a neighborhood of white aristocracy."[6] The incident perplexed the *Chicago Defender*. Oak Park, the newspaper noted, was a "settlement of refinement and culture," but the attempted murder "would have done credit to Lynchburg, Miss." The editors labeled the perpetrators the "scum of the village," "poor whites," and a "band of Georgia 'crackers,'" but reminded readers that "as this is Illinois and not South Carolina, justice will be meted out."[7] As the subsequent strikes against black residents mounted, the *Defender's* prediction of justice proved to be wishful thinking.

Instead, the episode reflected an emerging precedent. African Americans asserted their right to freedom of residence in the city and its suburbs but were met by enmity and ultimately violence. Despite a collective hope for the North as a place of possibility and the stubborn belief that the "better element" of whites would accept upwardly mobile blacks as neighbors, African Americans encountered fierce resistance in their efforts to move on up and move on out. When African Americans advanced into so-called "white" neighborhoods, they risked their lives, and each move was a forceful declaration of their demands for equal citizenship. Whites consistently resisted black newcomers, and municipal authorities repeatedly declined to uphold their duties to protect them, so pioneers defended themselves, their families, and their investments. When Oak Park whites made a second attempt in 1916 to burn the Jeffersons out, Frederick was prepared with two guns and a huge watchdog. Aiming his revolver, he shot at the assailant five times, wounding him as he fled.[8]

In the first half of the twentieth century many African Americans placed their hopes in republican conventions such as property ownership and upward mobility to claim individual rights, political liberty, and full citizenship. However, black urban dwellers were caught between an unwelcoming white world and declining conditions in a jam-packed ghetto. While the story is usually told from the vantage point of whites who reacted to "invasions" with hostility and flight, this chapter centers on the experiences of pioneers who were agents of spatial and socioeconomic expansion and initiators of integration.[9] Despite the legal and extralegal barriers, pioneers consistently demonstrated that they would not be restrained by these artificial fences. Most often they were Chicagoans with the means and the business connections to purchase homes in white areas. As with the political, social, and economic status of African Americans, rights to freedom of residence included definite changes along with racist continuities. In the late 1910s, black Chicagoans attempted to turn their improved economic status into homeownership out of the ghetto confines. Whites responded with severe violence and legally binding restrictive covenants. This push renewed after World War II, and whites reacted with the same disturbingly familiar patterns.

Prior to the civil rights movement, black inner-city communities included a mixture of people of different classes, in part due to Northern residential segregation. Blacks all sent children to the same schools, used the same public facilities, and shopped in the same stores. Professionals serviced ghetto areas and were a visible community presence. However, with more housing available to African Americans, those that could moved out, leaving the most disadvantaged groups in inner-city areas where jobs were scarce and opportunities meager. William Julius Wilson stresses that this middle-class flight not only was a drain of capital and talent but removed role models.[10]

Wilson's influential assertions have achieved wide cultural currency and affluent African Americans regularly wrestle with the contention that they deserted their communities and abandoned the less fortunate members of the race.[11] Instead of celebrating risk takers for knocking down the walls of residential segregation and working toward the goals of integration, nostalgic

observers laud the "golden age of the ghetto" when African Americans emphasized community over individualism.[12]

This chapter historicizes the debate on black middle-class flight, showing
that class and race struggles over space were a reality from the earliest days
of the formation of a substantial African American community in Chicago.
Blacks had considerable motivations to improve their residential situation. Due
to white-dominated political structures, vice functioned virtually unchecked in
Chicago's Black Belt. As more African Americans arrived in the city and whites
hardened racial lines, overcrowding, substandard living conditions, and health
issues became more acute. Residents deemed these circumstances undesirable
for their well-being and, importantly, for raising children. Class position was
not static, and poor and working-class blacks who enhanced their economic
standing also attempted to better their housing.[13] Few were willing to stay in
deteriorating neighborhoods, and the yearning to improve their residence
was an ordinary and generally accepted fact of life. However, stabilization
proved difficult when segregation and large-scale migration overwhelmed class
boundaries. The fight for suitable housing produced decades of high-profile
struggles against discrimination, but also bared concerns over whether these
battles were benefiting all black Chicagoans. African Americans rallied to the
cause, but while their efforts produced more living space, it also furthered intraracial divides. Pioneers shouldered the burden of breaking down residential
barriers and felt the added weight that they could and should lift the entire race
with them.[14]

THE PERILS OF OVERCROWDING

Black Chicagoans had pressing motives for moving, including health hazards.
Congestion was not a problem unique to African Americans. One study in 1923
found that Poles, Bohemians, Italians, and Jews were even more packed into
dwellings; these ethnic groups, however, had space opening up to them as the
city grew.[15] Blacks did not. Tenants inhabited domiciles with broken doors and
windows, unsteady flooring, leaking roofs, pest infestations, and plumbing troubles. Landlords put meager effort into repairs and maintenance; owners considered their buildings fast-depreciating assets and bled them for every penny
before they reached complete dilapidation. Owners could always find desperate

home seekers, regardless of the condition of the units. Tenants strained to pay inflated rents; some sought workers on the night shift as lodgers because the "hotbeds" they occupied during the day could also be rented at night. For black Chicagoans, homes were places for working, eating, and sleeping. Life was lived in the outdoors.[16]

In addition, residents could not help but notice that when their neighborhoods became predominantly black, municipal services declined precipitously and city officials stopped enforcing zoning laws. Muck and filth made alleys in the poorer South Side districts virtually impassable, and ashes and garbage accumulated in yards and overflowed into the streets. Though critics chalked this up to migrant unfamiliarity with cities, it had more to do with neglect by city departments.[17] This negligence was a recurrent problem as living space expanded, even in middle-class areas. One block club reported waging "relentless war" with city officials just to get garbage hauled away once a week, while streets were only cleaned right before elections. Though black votes often determined the balance of political power in the city, an African American resident ruefully observed in 1927 that "our power doesn't do us much good when we want to get an alley cleaned up or a disorderly house closed."[18]

Poor sanitation, congestion, and discrimination in access to medical care increased mortality in the Black Belt as residents suffered disproportionately from a myriad of otherwise preventable health problems. While mortality rates for whites were decreasing in the 1920s, statistics published in 1925 indicated that the death rate of Chicago blacks was comparable to that in Bombay, India, and life expectation rates for nonwhites remained strikingly lower in the 1930s and 1940s (see table 1).[19] While tuberculosis was generally associated with poverty, in the cloistered confines of the South Side it claimed lives from all social strata, including *Chicago Defender* publisher Robert Abbott.[20] If parents needed yet another reason to locate to more favorable surroundings, a 1927 study showed that tuberculosis death rates for blacks under age twelve were ten to twenty times higher than for whites of the same age range, while in 1926, 41 percent of the total deaths of children under age eleven were among black Chicagoans who made up just 3 percent of the total population of this age group.[21] Disease and death sharpened the conviction that the ghetto was "no place for children."[22] Some observers even wondered whether African Americans were really better off in cities. The novelist Thomas Sancton remarked that "a tenement was a hundred delta cabins, plus tuberculosis."[23] These issues convinced those with the requisite resources to move out, as the assurance of white aggression was no match for the slow death of contagions.

Table 1. Expectations of Life at Birth (in Years), by Color and Sex, for Chicago

	WHITE		NONWHITE	
	Male	Female	Male	Female
1930	57.8	61.7	42.5	46.7
1940	62.6	67.2	51	56.3
1950	64.7	70.8	58.2	63.5

Source: Table adapted from information in Otis Dudley Duncan and Beverly Duncan, *The Negro Population of Chicago: A Study of Residential Succession* (Chicago: University of Chicago Press, 1957), 85.

CAUGHT IN THE WEB OF VICE

In 1918, the writer Langston Hughes came to Chicago for the first time and walked "the Stroll" along State Street between Twenty-Sixth and Thirty-Ninth Streets. "South State Street," Hughes recalled, was "a teeming Negro Street with crowded theaters, restaurants, and cabarets. And excitement from noon to noon. Midnight was like day. The street was full of workers and gamblers, prostitutes and pimps, church folks and sinners."[24] Although Hughes's impression reflected the thrill of the big city, for the African Americans struggling for respectability and a proper place to raise their children, this atmosphere was far from ideal. The desire to make "respectable" spaces on the South Side was not merely a superficial struggle to define class distinctions, it was an imperative driven by notions of proper surroundings.

In the late nineteenth and early twentieth centuries, Chicago elected officials, law enforcement, and scores of citizens deemed vice a "necessary evil" that could be controlled and regulated. The authorities allowed brothels and gambling dens to operate in the South Side Levee district bounded by Eighteenth and Twenty-Second Streets, Federal and State. Moral reformers questioned the strategy of abiding vice districts, and in reaction to mounting pressure, officials effectively closed the Levee in 1912.[25]

Gambling, prostitution, and drug dealing did not end with these actions, but rather seeped into certain districts, including the Black Belt, creating an atmosphere of open vice. Along State Street, men urged pedestrians to "Try your wrist today? Try your wrist?" Craps and poker enterprises flourished, while neighbors put up with day-and-night rowdiness.[26] As early as 1913, Sophonisba Breckinridge noted, "It is probably not too much to say that no colored family can long escape the presence of the disreputable or disorderly neighbors."[27] The situation was not exclusive to Chicago. Across the country black communities routinely abutted vice zones, serving as a glaring reminder of municipal racism. "I don't believe it would be an exaggeration to say that on nearly every other street in Negro neighborhoods there is at least one brothel or house of assignation maintained for the almost-exclusive patronage of white men," the journalist Roi Ottley found. "In many Negro communities there is no such thing as a *strictly residential area,* largely because of relaxed supervision and total indifference from absentee landlords."[28] Though the middle class complained the loudest, hardly any families wanted to live amid an adult amusement park.

The significant role of vice in the political economy of the ghetto translated into mixed reactions to and definitions of "crime" among residents. Since working in the rackets was often one of the few ways of making steady money, it attracted even the "respectable" and college educated. Ada "Bricktop" Smith, the famous jazz singer, recalled that her mother boarded only "nice working people" who were married, but was often disappointed to find that "even nice working people engaged in 'funny business.'"[29] Entrepreneurs profited from vice, for others it was steady labor, and some were thrilled by the scene. For a young Bricktop, buffet flats (converted apartments offering a full assortment of illegal services) were not a perilous nuisance, but rather exhilarating after-hours party spots rife with liquor, harmonization, and easy laughter.[30] While a black journalist viewed all-night "black and tan" saloons as evidence of the "white plague" of "white men in search of Negro women," Ben Hecht argued that interracial dancing "wiped out the color line with liquor, music and sex."[31] When it came to leisure, one man's menace was another's sign of progress.[32]

Yet, most black Chicagoans rejected an "anything goes" attitude toward vice. They railed against the ubiquity of municipally sanctioned amusements, and neighborhood clubs made sincere efforts to rid areas of unsavory nightspots, contending that vice should be "removed from the residential districts."[33] The *Chicago Whip* accepted that prostitution and gambling were unlikely to disappear anytime soon, but "we can only hope that it will be segregated and removed from residential sections where people make the pretense of decency."[34] Residents did not necessarily begrudge the men and women who made their money from organized crime, but did object when they operated in their neighborhoods.[35]

Prostitution garnered the most objections. It was already a problem in black areas by the early 1910s, as operators shielded their operations through deals with organized crime, politicians, and the police.[36] As migrants arrived, they discovered that men and women who sought the "gay life" visited the Black Belt.[37] In 1917, the *Chicago Tribune* observed that a dozen "disreputable" houses operated openly within a few hundred yards of the Twenty-Second Street police station.[38] By 1928 the *Chicago Defender* reported that there were 2,750 buffet flats and brothels in the majority-black Second, Third, and Fourth Wards that operated without interference, with some of them visited regularly by policemen.[39]

Black Chicagoans were aware that white power structures allowed vice to proliferate, forming what historian Kevin Mumford calls "another spectacle of sexual racism."[40] Organized crime figures drew the color line in the upper echelons of vice management, while raids by the Chicago police's "wrecking crew" focused on black-owned establishments and "black and tan" saloons. Some brothels in the Black Belt even enforced Jim Crow, infuriating African Americans by flaunting open vice and topping it off with discrimination.[41] The *Whip* complained that "white hoodlums and vile women" infested neighborhoods, while the *Defender* reported that 60 percent of brothels were controlled by whites who lived outside the district, and begrudged the cultural and economic imperialism of white pimps and customers. "They have come to the South Side with their vice and filth, and have taken the cash to other sections of the city to beautify them. When money leaves the district in this fashion it never returns."[42]

Despite organized efforts against "disreputable women" and their pimps, the battle often seemed unwinnable as protests made to landlords and law enforcement fell on deaf ears. Even when police buckled and made arrests, judges passed out small fines and prostitutes were back in a day or two, "plying their trade with brazen audacity," sometimes even in the same buildings with "respectable people."[43] Much to the chagrin of residents, the sex trade overwhelmed their communities. "Window tappers" solicited day and night, sounding "like hail beating on the pavement of a city street," while pimps in faux cigar stores asked, "Don't you want to meet some nice girls, white girls?" Ropers and runners implored potential clients to check out what they had to offer, while fixers guided groups of white men. Vice dens sprouted like mushrooms next to churches and schools. In the early 1930s practically every house between Forty-Sixth and Forth-Seventh Streets across Michigan Boulevard from the fashionable Rosenwald apartments harbored "working girls." To area residents these conditions were a menace, even as there was a general understanding that prostitution was a last resort for most women.[44]

These notions of propriety cut across class lines, as working-class and poor families often had stringent versions of proper behavior. Migrants regularly adjusted the city through a church-based understanding of respectability based in the often mislabeled "middle-class" traits of economy, restraint, and moderation. They did not passively accept middle-class uplift ideologies; rather, they arrived with their own ideals of conduct. Fretful parents realized that the "wide-open" ghetto introduced children to far more dangers and enticements than rural areas. A survey of poor and working-class blacks in 1937 indicated that one-half attended no public amusements, cabarets, or taverns. "I don't go to theaters, dance halls, ball games, and things like that," a domestic worker explained. "It just don't [sic] go with the rules of the church."[45] Sermons in mainline and storefront churches explicitly denounced prostitution and urged congregants to resist the temptations of the city. Pastor S. E. J. Watson of Pilgrim Baptist Church railed against "the old woman whose house is the way to hell." "There was nothing that was going on in Sodom that is not going on in Chicago," a spiritualist preacher sermonized. "If God don't know what's going on, let him put on clothes like anybody else, and walk down Calumet Street."[46] These protestations to prostitution and dissipation came from a variety of voices in the Black Belt. Churchgoers were dismayed that whites tarred them as criminals because they lived and worshiped in vice-ridden areas, and they responded by stressing their abstemious personal lives. If they caught a break, they usually sought to distance themselves from vice by moving.

Families trying to live the "upright life" made a major priority of leaving sordid settings. According to Drake and Cayton, "We can't raise children right around here" or "We're stuck here" was a constant complaint, and even stable families confronted daunting obstacles in their struggle to keep their children "straight."[47] A young Dempsey Travis witnessed women stopping men on streets near his family's apartment. At first he thought they were lost and asking for directions, but the men would repeatedly follow the "lost" women into alleys or hallways. After more incidents like this, Travis's father finally decided that his family deserved a "better environment" and moved.[48] Most families, though, lacked the means to get out, and even as the territory open to them gradually and violently expanded, prostitution and seedy nightspots followed with the approval of politicians and police who padded their incomes and funded their campaigns through graft. "Everywhere the self-respecting colored citizens, singly or in groups, have fled to new neighborhoods free of vice as a haven for their children and families," the *Chicago Bee* noted. "Fast on their heels vice has followed in their wake, a menace to society at large and colored groups in particular."[49] The well-to-do learned they could not defeat the forces that encouraged organized crime in their communities. In response, they tried to establish and maintain homogeneous, exclusive enclaves, even if it meant taking unpopular stands.

MAKING MIDDLE-CLASS RACE SPACE

Higher-status African Americans attempted to put some room between themselves and the lower classes even before the tumult of the Great Migration. Undoubtedly aspirations to make exclusive race spaces were due to a degree of social snobbery. As early as 1907 one aristocrat claimed that "an excess of democracy exists among Negroes."[50] Another resident stated that his family was "not satisfied with the neighborhood where the masses of Negroes lived" because they were "low and degraded."[51] Middle-class blacks commonly chose their mates, church affiliation, social activities, and peer groups based on the class of people they chose to mix with. An attorney who had worked his way up from the plantation asserted that class separation was natural, as "there must be some discrimination in order to get along in life." Socialites mingled at the Appomattox Club, the Civic Century, and the Tuskegee Club and formed fraternities and sororities that brought together the more "advanced" element of the "the Race."[52]

The middle class thought they should encircle themselves with neighbors of comparable morals, dispositions, and standards. "The real problem of the social life of the colored people in Chicago, as in all northern cities, lies in the fact of their segregation," prominent writer and activist Fannie Barrier Williams remarked in 1905. "The huddling together of good and bad, compelling the decent element of colored people to witness brazen displays of vice of all kinds in front of their homes and in the faces of their children, are trying conditions under which to remain socially clean and respectable."[53] In 1910, the forerunners of the National Urban League grumbled that segregation, high rents, and boarders meant that "respectable Negro neighborhoods find themselves unable so far to keep out persons of doubtful or immoral character."[54] A Southern-born doctor lamented that blacks were "constantly being exploited by real estate dealers," but his main gripe was not really racial exploitation but rather that this discrimination forced them "into a limited area where the upper classes must mingle with the lower" so that "the bad pollutes that which otherwise might be good."[55] The Black Belt in Chicago was surrounded by neighborhoods where different European ethnic and religious backgrounds coalesced around the principles of cosmopolitan, middle-class life. But because violence and restrictive covenants constrained living space, in black areas of the urban North all classes were crowded together.[56] As Frank Marshall Davis wrote,

> Across the street from the Ebenezer Baptist Church,
> women with cast-iron faces peddle love
> In the flat above William's Funeral Home
> six couples sway to the St. Louis Blues
> Two doors away from the South Side Bank
> three penny-brown men scorch their guts with four bit whiskey
> Dr. Jackson buys a Lincoln
> His neighbor buys second hand shoes
> —the artist who paints this town must
> use a checkered canvas.[57]

Though critics expressing nostalgia for the class blend of Jim Crow Chicago could point to the successful role models in this "checkered canvas," the role models themselves usually detested living in a seedy, overcrowded, and unhealthy area.

The upwardly mobile often charged that if they could separate themselves from the poor, interracial connections could improve the racial climate, as long as they were between the sophisticated ranks. The *Broad Ax* argued that the "ardent hope" of white Chicagoans was that the lower classes would always be confined to the ghetto, while African Americans with "culture and refinement" moved into white neighborhoods.[58] A black Chicagoan lambasted white improvement associations for their unfair, un-American actions against aspiring homeowners, but volunteered that the "better class" of blacks "stand ready and willing to assist any individuals or association to rid our community of 'undesirable citizens' based not on color, but upon moral fitness."[59] As pioneers routinely discovered, though, these visions of class-based racial harmony underestimated the depths of white middle-class intolerance.

Given the extent of the housing crisis, black efforts to maintain exclusive spaces entangled them in controversy. A black enclave in the Far South Side neighborhood of Morgan Park formed in the 1910s when a group of domestic and railroad workers built homes on cheap, low land badly in need of drainage. The district had a "boom-town" feel, as substantial brick and stucco homes sat next to those built in stages as finances permitted. By 1920, 73 percent of blacks in the area were homeowners. African Americans would occasionally venture out to the suburb on Sundays to look at the large residences interspersed with vacant prairie land and envision the day when they could erect their own dream house. One homeowner noted that while local dwellings seemed ragged, "they are comfortable, full of hope, and not loaded with debts. There are home-loving families in all of them." The Morgan Park Improvement Association, with a membership that included several black municipal employees, lobbied successfully to secure drainage enhancements, street paving, street lights, and sewers.[60] African Americans were 12 percent of the population of Morgan Park by 1920, and they channeled their economic and organizational strength into creating a vibrant community.[61]

Residents carved out a fragile racial truce in the area by agreeing that African Americans would not live east of Vincennes Avenue. Many of the district's native-born affluent whites relied on black domestic laborers, and the races maintained generally friendly relations. Children of all races, including a smattering of local "foreigners," attended integrated public schools, and there was no color line in area public accommodations.[62]

These "friendly attitudes" were put to the test in 1917, however, when John Resakes, a Greek real estate agent, and black landlord Eugene Mann solicited black renters for their twenty-flat building in Morgan Park after claiming that they had failed to secure white tenants. The audacious Mann was unshaven, fast-talking, and unafraid to boldly challenge Jim Crow norms. He and his partner encountered immediate antagonism from local whites, and Resakes asked for police protection for himself and the building to stave off "bombs, insults, and conspiracy." Many black locals, perhaps in an effort to maintain class standards and preserve the tenuous racial peace, agreed with the protest, and their improvement association and Baptist church went on record to support the efforts to defeat what the *Chicago Tribune* dubbed a "Negro invasion." A superior court injunction ultimately blocked the move-in, preventing Resakes from renting until he made certain improvements.[63]

In seeking the stabilization of their district, the black residents of Morgan Park walked a fine line between class and race interests. The *Chicago Defender* lambasted Morgan Park for preventing desperate members of the race the "opportunity to move into half-way decent quarters." The paper labeled Bessie

Ray, chair of the black improvement association, as a "traitor" and contended that "scalawags who are willing to bow to the bidding" of whites should "be tarred and feathered, whether members of the church or not." According to the *Defender* account, some African American residents of Morgan Park were also disturbed at the accommodation to segregation and stymied opportunities for housing, calling Ray a "white folk's nigger."[64] Critics scrutinized black middle-class exclusivity, a treatment that whites rarely encountered.

The delicate but amicable racial armistice in Morgan Park was rather unique in Chicago; the desire for an incipient middle class to spatially separate itself from the humbler elements of the race was not. The incessant search for "a better neighborhood" created spatial patterns within the Black Belt along class lines like those of the city as a whole. Higher-income residents generally migrated to the south end of the district. The north end became a low-income area and the point of disembarkation for Southern migrants.[65] In the 1910s and 1920s black homeowners formed improvement associations, a trend urged by the National Committee on Negro Housing, a group appointed by President Herbert Hoover as part of a larger conference on home building and ownership. The committee recommended an "aggressive campaign" to form improvement associations "among the more intelligent Negro" to work against "the intrusion of immoral persons" and the "intrusion of immoral conditions."[66] Against all odds, the well-to-do tried desperately to carve out high-status spaces, fighting both against white intransigence and the poor and working-class black Chicagoans who were also in a frantic search for improved housing.[67] A professional man, who with a physician, lawyer, and musician had been the first to enter a select area near Thirty-Seventh Street in the 1920s, felt he was forced to move after his neighborhood "rapidly degenerated" with the sound of gunfire and "the worst kind of cursing." He moved farther south, where it was "beautiful" with "well kept" lawns, but soon after the "same class of Negroes who ran us away from 37th Street" came creeping along "slowly like a disease."[68] The middle class continued their incursions into forbidden areas, but less well-off African Americans usually followed. Homeowners considered this situation detrimental to property values, community morals, and harmonious race relations, and they often directed their ire at the lower classes.

Black Chicagoans demarcated their class position through aesthetics and argued that the poor did not share these values. The middle class considered the Michigan Boulevard Garden Apartments, built by philanthropist Julius Rosenwald in 1928, as a paradise because of their modern interiors as well as their inner gardens, "landscaped with grass, trees, flowers, and shrubbery,

which is visible from practically every apartment."[69] Homeowners argued
that their lawns and gardens signified "pride and attention," while areas with
"unkempt" yards "full of rubbish" indicated that the neighborhood was a slum.
One letter writer to *Half-Century Magazine* identified herself as a resident of
"one of the better residence sections" of Chicago because her "neighbors are the
kind who keep their lawns trim and tidy, their windows clean and send their
children to school looking neat and clean." But other families in the area were
"trouble makers" because they presented themselves and their premises in an
untidy manner.[70] Instead of middle-class districts, Black Chicago tended to con-
tain middle-class islands, a building or block interspersed among overcrowding
and deterioration. Referred to as "oases in the slums" by the press, block groups
sometimes bought communal tools for garden and lawn work or hired a gar-
dener to landscape vacant lots.[71] The *Defender* and Chicago Urban League also
encouraged stabilization by running contests rewarding the "neatest lawn" and
sponsoring "block beautiful" programs.[72] The *Defender* urged readers to counter
white improvement associations' "dirty propaganda" by keeping homes clean
on the inside and out to "disprove such rot."[73] According to the middle class,
well-kept lawns, ornate landscaping, and home improvements signified success,
demonstrated urban adjustment and sophistication, and distinguished them
from the masses.

The goal of class separation was continually tested by waves of migrants and
the color line that boxed black Chicagoans into cloistered areas. The segregated
market created a grave housing shortage, a problem that city authorities and
private builders showed no interest in rectifying. Financial institutions "red-
lined" black zones, making new construction difficult, so families packed into
subdivided "kitchenette" buildings while weed-filled lots sat empty across the
street.[74] In the eyes of the successful, the housing shortage was criminal, but
there was something particularly odious about denying homes to those who
could afford them in places befitting their stature.

MAKING RACE SPACE: BLACK PIONEERS

For upwardly mobile families, homeownership was an "obsession." The *Defender*
remarked, "We were denied in years gone by the privilege of owning the roof
over our heads. . . . Now we grasp the first opportunity to invest our earnings
in property."[75] Property ownership signified status and thriftiness and brought

security, stability, and community approval. As residential districts became increasingly crowded, African Americans battled ferocious resistance and pushed out into middle-class areas. There, according to observers, they were able to sustain "a higher standard of living and a more vital community feeling." The spacious homes also provided privacy, "one of the rarest of the good things of life" in a congested district.[76]

Considering the time, expense, and extreme measures taken by whites toward the goal of complete containment of the black population, the methods employed to keep them hemmed in were not very effective in the long run. Chicago's African Americans were sometimes accused of submitting to "voluntary segregation" and of lacking "the pioneering spirit," yet they put persistent pressure on the walls of segregation.[77] The strikingly repetitive barrage of violence, harassment, and restrictions hurled at pioneers reads as a litany of misery, but it also reveals the dogged expansion of living space. Their stiff-necked response to this aggravation was a stark contrast to the skittish reactions of whites when blacks entered "their" neighborhoods.

Even before the fevered violence of the late 1910s and early 1920s, African Americans knew that moves into new areas would be contested.[78] As J. Saunders Redding recalled, the process was so draining and convoluted by subterfuge and conspiracy that "moving was almost like stealing."[79] Lending institutions usually refused to finance home purchases, shutting African Americans out of the mortgage market. The *Chicago Defender* reported that one downtown bank even sent out postcards stating "No Nigger Loans" in large type.[80] Real estate agents typically rebuffed them, and those that broke this code were frequently the targets of violence, intimidation, and boycotts.[81] Blacks often paid a premium for the privilege of owning a home, yet the racism prospective buyers encountered was just the beginning of their troubles.

The entrance of black newcomers into white neighborhoods followed a familiar pattern throughout the first half of the twentieth century. An affluent family utilized a white intermediary to purchase a home. Neighbors almost immediately panicked, with some putting their homes up for sale and others organizing to drive the newcomers out. Pioneers were virtually assured of threats and repeated episodes of violence against their property. In some instances, the assailants unmistakably intended to kill, and it is a wonder that more deaths did not occur.[82] The black banker R. W. Woodfolk owned a flat with one white and four black families as tenants. On February 1, 1920, a man with keys locked the tenants in their apartments to prevent escape and planted an explosive in the hallway. The blast was so large it shattered the windows of adjacent buildings, but miraculously no residents were killed.[83]

No arrests were made, as the authorities were usually uninterested in apprehending the perpetrators of racial violence. The indifference from law enforcement was tantamount to condoning violent acts, and in most cases the police were in accord with white assailants.[84] "For what good is a home," the activist Irene McCoy Gaines lamented, "if a mob, without fear of punishment, may come in the darkness of the night and bomb, burn or otherwise terrorize the owners of that home?"[85] Pioneers were usually surrounded by unfriendly neighbors and had to rely on their own methods of defense.

Despite these obstacles, pioneers sneered at restrictive efforts, moving steadily into formerly white areas and making a physical declaration of their social ascension and rights. From July 1917 to July 1919 there were twenty-four bombings aimed at black homeowners and black and white real estate men, yet the *Chicago Tribune* reported that "colored families refuse to retreat northward." Two years later real estate records showed that bombings had "little effect on property buyers" as the well-off continued to purchase homes. Politician and realtor Oscar DePriest, whose own property had been bombed, stated, "Negroes are going to move anywhere they can pay rent and if the white people don't like it, we'll run them into the damn lake."[86] Alderman L. B. Anderson reminded Chicagoans that Africans Americans were among the first residents of the city and were there to stay. "The Negro, if he is financially able to live in a modern apartment building," Anderson stated, "has just the same right under the Constitution to enjoy the comforts of such an abode as the white man."[87] In the face of the rallying cry of "They Shall Not Pass," the social worker Mary McDowell noted that black men and women persistently moved southward, with territorial gains standing "as a monument to the courage and diplomacy of the race that will not allow anything to stand in the way of their 'climbing higher—higher.'"[88] When whites in suburban Evanston expressed fears that blacks would "overrun" the city, a letter writer to the *Tribune* declared that "black people have as much right to overrun Evanston as Poles, Slavs, Jews, Greeks, Irish, New Englanders, westerners, southerners, white people, and any other people who live in this nation and who have their homes wherever they desire."[89] African Americans asserted the freedom to live where they pleased as a fundamental civil right, and studies established that the bombing campaigns were "futile," for they "will neither intimidate any considerable number of them nor stop their moving into a given district." Violence only succeeded in exacerbating racial antagonisms.[90]

Though most pioneers relocated for socioeconomic and family-based reasons, they also knew that each move into a new neighborhood struck a blow for the race. For African Americans, a minister noted, racially restrictive covenants were like "red rags." They were eager to break them, because "such things are un-American and un-Christian."[91] Upwardly mobile African Americans spearheaded the battle to defeat them in Chicago and across the nation, viewing their advancement as not only a matter of improving living conditions, but as fundamental to racial progress.[92] The motto of Chicago's Protective Circle, a group organized to protest bombings and the indifference of city officials, was "No backward step. Anywhere, providing it be forward."[93] Jane Jones's fictional pioneer McKenzie Wilson received threatening letters and offers to sell his home, even at a profit. Despite sleepless nights, Wilson did not give in, "lest the white people triumphantly declare they had scared him out and then they would treat the colored people even worse than they ever had."[94] Leaders such as W. E. B. Du Bois and Oscar DePriest sang the praises of those who refused to be intimidated and scolded those who folded.[95] For pioneers, a housing upgrade was not only deserved but helped break the ghetto logjam.

Pioneers were fully aware that whites would challenge every move into disputed territory. This was more than a "gut feeling," as African Americans heard about hostilities through peer networks and media accounts. Move-ins brought out the worst in the existing population, and the threat of carnage hung dauntingly. One family that bought in a white area recalled driving home every night expecting to see a heap of smoldering ashes where their house stood.[96] Extremely stressful moves evoked military connotations, as whites used terms like "invasion" to describe the process of integration, and blacks adopted terminology such as "pincer movement" and "advanced landings of paratroopers."[97] In Rudolph Fisher's fictionalized account of a move-in, an observer calls home buying "war—conquest of territory." The protagonist, a lawyer, who is "downright rabid" on racial matters, wants to enjoy his house "purely as an individual," but "just the same I'm entering it as a Negro." Embittered, he admits that his "chief joy in life is making [whites] uncomfortable."[98] Regardless of the amount of prestige or education achieved by members of the black middle class, they realized that their status would not protect them from violence or ensure any assistance from city officials.

In response, African Americans expressed a strong conviction in the necessity of aggressive self-defense. When whites threatened the life or property of African American families, the community consistently demonstrated that it would rise to protect them. The Washington, DC, East St. Louis, and Chicago race riots in the late 1910s were to a large degree triggered by antagonism over space, and African Americans viscerally proved that they would meet violence with violence. Their resolve demonstrated the collective fortitude of a people who had revolted against Jim Crow by moving north and now felt an increasing racial consciousness.[99] Veterans from World War I returned with confidence, knowledge of the gun, and a willingness to use it.[100] "It is the duty of every man here to provide himself with guns and ammunition," a Chicagoan declared after the 1919 race riot. "I, myself, have at least one gun and at least enough ammunition to make it useful."[101] These men positioned themselves as the antithesis of the "black pussyfoot" who had succumbed to white terror. Blacks recognized events like the Chicago race riot as tragedies, but also celebrated the exhibition of racial resilience.[102]

Armed self-defense was not the only method African Americans used to secure living space in Chicago, but it was probably the most effective. Peaceful attempts to appeal to city officials were rebuffed, whites ignored published broadsides counseling them not to join protective organizations or to participate in violence, and negotiations with the Chicago Real Estate Board and improvement associations went nowhere or were seen as accommodationist by other black Chicagoans.[103] For those willing to push boundaries, weapons became a necessity. As one Great War veteran stated, "I can shoot as good as the next one, and nobody better start anything. I ain't looking for trouble, but if it comes my way I ain't dodging."[104] This philosophy regularly guided pioneers. The Ossian Sweet case in Detroit was the most famous instance of armed self-defense, mainly because Sweet and his comrades hit their targets, but countless African Americans were armed and willing to use force to protect their families and property.[105] On the eve of the Great War, the Albert Dunham family built a home in suburban Glen Ellyn. Neighbors soon realized that Albert was not a dark-skinned servant of his light-skinned wife and attempted to expel the Dunhams through zoning laws. When this failed, a homemade explosive shattered newly installed downstairs windows. A determined Albert exited the early morning train from Chicago with a double-barreled shotgun. As locals watched warily, he performed an extended vigil with his gun every night until the last coat of paint was applied.[106] Similarly, after whites bombed his home in 1920, Crede Hubbard stated that he was arming himself with "anything I want from a Mauser to a machine gun," and if a suspicious intruder came his way, he would "crack down on him and ask him what he was there for afterwards."[107] While her husband, Carl, was fighting restrictive covenants in the courtroom in the late 1930s, Nannie Hansberry patrolled their house in Washington Park with a loaded German Luger, steadfastly safeguarding her four children.[108] For African Americans, firearms were often the logical response to aggression.

Frequent antagonistic experiences with working-class, white ethnics led many African Americans to peg them as violence-prone and pathological; sometimes it seemed their only joys came from keeping blacks one rung beneath them on the ladder.[109] Drake and Cayton noted that a common lament was that "foreigners learn how to cuss, count and say 'nigger' as soon as they get here," and blacks were particularly galled that poor immigrants speaking broken English could boast "no niggers live in this section."[110] Despite their own problems in America, or perhaps because of them, white ethnics proved to be poor allies in the fight against racial subjugation.

What disappointed pioneers more was the reception they received from the so-called "better class" of whites. Blacks typically viewed racism as a product of ignorance and hoped that higher-class people could see past race and concentrate on traits like character and achievement. "There's less friction in communities where the people are educated," a letter writer to *Half-Century Magazine* opined in 1920, "and most of the trouble occurs between the uneducated element of both races."[111] This conventional insistence that a more open-minded element existed was reinforced by occasional positive interactions with middle-class whites. Black men and women experienced plenty of racism, but some also had encouraging exchanges with whites: a friendly face at work, a business mentor, and a helpful teacher were not uncommon. They hoped that more of these interactions between high-status people would be "ennobling" and a chance for the white man "to test his vaunted democracy."[112]

As Frederick Jefferson and his family discovered in Oak Park, however, when it came to living alongside the white middle class as neighbors, receptions were often just as harsh as those in white-ethnic neighborhoods, with the only difference being that the affluent were able to hire out their dirty work. The Hyde Park–Kenwood Property Owners' Association notoriously held the eastern line of the Black Belt at Cottage Grove Avenue by employing gangsters. When the Crede Hubbard family bought a home in Kenwood in 1920, the association repeatedly asked him to sell. When the association could not meet Hubbard's inflated price, the members used their professional connections and attempted to enlist Hubbard's boss, the chief clerk of the Northwestern Railroad, to convince Hubbard to reconsider. The chief clerk refused to cooperate, and having exhausted these "businesslike" attempts, the association hired bombers to hit the house while Hubbard's sons slept.[113] Indeed, throughout the first half of the twentieth century, some of the most vicious racist propaganda emanated from middle-class residents.[114] Black newspapers lashed out at the segregationists, charging that they showed a "lack of civilization" and were not "bona fide Americans," but "low bred, shanty Irish" and "kikes."[115] Yet the truth was that educated, high-status whites regularly perpetrated hard-core racism. Though racial housing riots in working-class areas dominated the headlines, the *Defender* remarked that "respectable property owners, middle-class businessmen and great numbers of white 'liberals'" were solidly behind restrictive covenants, and these "phoney [*sic*] liberals and apologetic 'friends of the Negro'" were doing much to exacerbate the housing crisis.[116]

Where newcomers did not face violent resistance, they regularly discovered that whites were still averse to residing alongside them. The African Americans who moved into Lawndale on the city's West Side in the late 1940s, for instance, were the typical middle-class newcomers: doctors, lawyers, schoolteachers, government workers, and businesspeople. Many became property owners for the first time and were relieved at the cordial greetings they received from their mainly Jewish neighbors. There were no threats, no bombings or brick-tossing, and no menacing racial episodes. There was even a short-lived interracial attempt to maintain standards and create an amicable community. However, within months For Sale signs materialized. The exodus moved at such a hurried tempo that vacant apartments existed despite the postwar housing shortage. As Enoch Waters recalled, the Jews "fled as if pursued by Nazis." Newcomers were "plainly disgusted with the Jews, whom they felt had clearly demonstrated racial prejudice in fleeing."[117] The lack of aggression was small consolation when replaced by their rejection via wholesale flight. Pioneers achieved expanded living space for themselves and for the race, but white obstinacy denied the concurrent goal of racial integration.

OAK PARK REDUX

In 1950 the eminent chemist Percy Julian and his wife, Anna, also a PhD, bought an expansive home in Frederick Jefferson's old hometown of Oak Park. Percy Julian had attained degrees from Harvard and the University of Vienna, was the chief of soybean research for Chicago's Glidden Corporation, and had made world-renowned chemical innovations. The *Chicago Sun-Times* named

Dr. Julian its "Chicagoan of the Year" in 1949, and the exclusive suburb, which advertised itself as the "middle-class capital of the world," seemed to be the perfect fit for Julian and his family.[118]

Nationally, black economic and social conditions changed for the better in the 1940s. The March on Washington Movement and the Congress of Racial Equality awakened the civil rights movement in Chicago and across the country, as moderates became actively engaged in securing jobs and then full equality and democracy for African Americans nationally and "dependent peoples" globally.[119] Blacks in the Chicagoland area made substantial strides especially after pressure resulted in President Franklin Roosevelt signing the Fair Employment Act prohibiting racial discrimination in the defense industry. Unemployment plummeted, while earnings rose significantly, giving more home seekers the ability to search for improved housing.[120]

After the war a series of actions suggested momentum in civil rights. In the spring of 1947 Jack Roosevelt Robinson broke Major League Baseball's color barrier. Liberals, radicals, and civil rights activists compelled the federal government to rethink its traditionally lax enforcement of equal protection under the law and to assert its prerogative on the rights of African Americans. A year later in the landmark *Shelley v. Kraemer* case, the Supreme Court ruled that under the Fourteenth Amendment the government could not legally enforce racially restrictive covenants. Two months after that President Harry Truman abolished racial discrimination in federal employment and integrated the armed services.

Though blacks made advancements in their socioeconomic position and in securing civil rights in the 1940s, the housing situation got even worse in urban America, leading to pitched racial conflicts across the country.[121] In Chicago, 60,000 new migrants arrived, and the Mayor's Commission on Human Relations calculated that the Black Belt was overcrowded by 75,000 to 100,000 people. In response, African Americans renewed their push out of their cramped confines.[122] Violence resulted, and the Chicago Council Against Racial and Religious Discrimination noted that while a mass lynching in Georgia was in the headlines in August 1946, there was a "lynch spirit in our own midst" with 59 separate attacks on homes in the previous twenty-seven months, including 29 arson bombings, 22 stonings, 3 shootings, 3 house wreckings, and 2 stink bombs.[123] Major mob disturbances occurred at temporary housing set up for veterans and their families near Midway Airport in 1946, at public housing in Fernwood Park the following year, and in residential areas of Park Manor and Englewood in 1949.[124] Arnold Hirsch astutely labels this an era of "hidden violence" because of the mainstream media's intentional disregard for covering the events, but the intimidating incidents were not hidden from African Americans, who were well aware of what was likely to greet them when they crossed the invisible color line.

It was in this context that the Julian family bought their home in Oak Park. Though working-class whites fueled the postwar housing riots, the Julians' purchase in the fashionable town also caused a furor, and the family received anonymous threatening phone calls and other obstacles thrown in their way, including a city commissioner's refusal to turn on their water. On Thanksgiving eve, after the landscapers and renovators had gone for the day, a dark sedan pulled up to the Julians' fifteen-room house. Two men got out, broke into the home, and soaked the walls with kerosene. After failing to light the fuse, they tossed a flaming kerosene torch through a window and drove away. The crashing window alarmed the neighbors, and the fire department arrived before the gasoline ignited.[125] Nine months later assailants hurled a bomb at the Julians' home, which fortunately landed short and exploded in the yard. Though the assaults abated, the family continued to be the object of ominous threats for years.[126] Thirty-six years after white neighbors targeted Frederick Jefferson and his family for a forced eviction, Oak Park residents again made clear that they would not stand for black neighbors.

The assaults only strengthened the Julians' resolve. "We refuse to be intimidated," Dr. Anna Julian said defiantly. The move would be delayed due to the vandalism, "but we are going through with it. We are not going to be intimidated by hoodlums."[127] The Julian family hired private, round-the-clock armed security to patrol the property, an expense that ultimately cost upward of $10,000, and Percy himself brandished a shotgun and served as lookout with his son. For the Julians and for other pioneers who had battled racism at every step of their climb, the sting of rejection was nothing new. "We've lived through these things all our lives," Percy stated. "As far as the hurt to the spirit goes, we've become accustomed to that."[128] The Julians' search for housing in Chicago had already been distressing, as angry crowds gathered when he first tried to rent an apartment on the North Side, and the Glidden Corporation had to surreptitiously buy the family a home in Maywood to prevent the Julians from being turned down because of their race.[129] As the threats persisted in Oak Park, Julian articulated the republican mantra that emboldened pioneers. "We're American citizens and we're entitled to this. I'm on the lookout and will not stand for anyone taking my property. We'll die before they do it."[130]

Although a great deal had changed for African Americans in the first half of the twentieth century, in the field of housing the struggles largely remained the same. The upwardly mobile continued their quest to find whites who would see past race, yet the similarities between the violence directed at the Jeffersons and the Julians showed that their options were tightly limited and undeniably risky. Oak Park was supposed to be a suburb with "solid and respectable" residents; the so-called "better class" who would welcome the Julians. Though a vocal minority was infuriated by the attacks on the Julians' home and took steps to demonstrate their commitment to peaceful integration, the majority maintained a deafening silence or voiced their disapproval of the Julians' presence.[131] No one was ever charged in connection with the crimes, prompting even the conservative *Chicago Tribune* to question if the police force really wanted to make any arrests.[132]

The violence against the Julian family was overshadowed by the race riots in the neighboring working-class suburb of Cicero, where a family's move-in to an apartment building precipitated three nights of mayhem that required the Illinois National Guard to quell the disturbances. This attack was easier for the media—black and white—to comprehend. They expected white working-class ethnics to resort to violence to maintain their communities.[133] They found it more difficult to square the violence in Oak Park and the exclusion of Dr. Julian from the upper-crust Union League Club just a month after his home was bombed. Percy could not conceal his own disappointment at this latest snub from the "better element." "It appears to me that organizations like the Union League Club are as directly responsible as any other agency for such un-American incidents as the bombing of my home in Oak Park and the Cicero riots," Julian stated. "When individuals in high places behave as the Union League Club behaves ordinary citizens follow suit."[134] For black Chicagoans, the search for enlightened whites continued.

THE PRICE OF PIONEERING

Class distinctions within the black community created tensions, though usually not conflict in the classical Marxist sense. Most black employees worked for white-dominated firms, not the small black business class. As Langston Hughes pointed out, most of the "big Negroes" were not high enough to keep anybody down, much less the "little Negroes."[135] Blacks often faced similar limits on opportunities for economic and physical mobility, but not in the same degrees. Friction also frequently occurred between those who judged themselves "respectable" and those deemed unable or unwilling to live up to these ideals. There was a degree of class separation within the Black Belt, and this phenomenon became more apparent as the middle class expanded its domain. When African Americans in Northern cities advanced, they usually upgraded their settings and separated themselves from the substandard ghetto conditions.

Although critics occasionally chastised the middle class for leaving the ghetto and thereby abdicating leadership positions, the situation was much more complex. Pioneers never really were too far away spatially or psychically from the masses, and they often shared schools, parks, commercial areas, public spaces, and kin networks with African Americans from a variety of backgrounds. The Julians were censured in some corners for moving out and scrutinized by friends who questioned why they would endure such treatment "just for the right to live among whites." Yet they stayed connected to black civic institutions and assumed leadership roles.[136] Pioneers often argued that they were fulfilling their respective racial roles by making more space for all and that there was no variance between private ambition and racial benefits. Every gain in territory meant more breathing room for everybody.

The steady expansion of Chicago's ghetto was tangible evidence that African Americans never acceded to segregation. As James Gregory notes, these urban pioneers are often ignored by scholars, or their brave actions are explained away as the natural outcomes of rising economic fortunes, population growth, and pressures on the existing housing stock.[137] Yet for the men and women who took the step of moving out, the process was filled with hope, anxiety, and dread. Housing in urban areas passed from white to black as the ghetto expanded, but usually only after emboldened African Americans broke through the lines of segregation. In Chicago, blacks went from being a significant presence in just 8 percent of the city's census tracts in 1920 to 22 percent by 1950, and given the impediments, this space was hard-earned.[138]

Most immediately, though, the upwardly mobile acted in the best interests of their families, something nearly all African Americans sought to do. If they moved up socioeconomically, a physical relocation usually followed. Blacks continued to strive for their piece of the American Dream, and with the onset of liberalism in the postwar United States, optimists trusted that the time had come for the white and black middle classes to integrate. However, as the next chapter shows, the persistence of racism and discrimination largely dashed those hopes.

CHAPTER 3

CAN THE MIDDLE CLASS
SAVE CHICAGO?

"What the best and wisest parent wants for his own child, that must the community want for all its children. Any other ideal for our school is narrow and unlovely; acted upon, it destroys our democracy."

—John Dewey, *The School and Society*, 1899

In March of 1955, two African American newcomers to the Chatham neighborhood on the Far South Side of Chicago, Washington Burney and John Sloan, attended a community meeting at the local YMCA. More blacks had recently entered the area, but what Burney and Sloan saw did not surprise them: three hundred whites and no other black faces but themselves. Their presence added to what was already an edgy atmosphere, but the agenda proceeded in an orderly fashion. Finally, however, one impatient resident blurted out what many of the attendees really had on their minds. "Stop horsing around. How are we going to keep these colored people from moving into our neighborhood?" The question sucked the air out of the room. Reverend John Hayes, the chair of the neighborhood association, hastily adjourned.[1]

For a second meeting a month later to specifically deal with the influx of African Americans, Burney and Sloan recruited seventy-five other black neighbors to attend. Although whites held varied opinions on integration, many liberals recognized that resistance was doomed to end in failure; it had consistently led to violence and racial turnover in other South Side communities. At the assembly, a majority of the three hundred whites and seventy-five blacks came to a startling consensus: they would attempt to coexist in Chatham.[2]

However, by 1963, Chatham was a "black" community. "Within two months' time, the exodus started," recalled Washington Burney. "Once it started, it was just like a flood. You'd wake up and see a van in front of the house next door, and wonder what happened to the Olsens. They moved out in the middle of the night, and the Joneses moved in."[3] Whites made a steady retreat, leaving African Americans to try to maintain their communities and schools despite the drain of resources and political clout. Chatham exemplified the aspirations and ultimate failures of middle-class racial integration. Unlike most studies of neighborhood change, this chapter focuses on the perspectives of African American newcomers and the whites who tried to make integration work, examines the stumbling blocks, and then details how black residents sought to preserve community advantages, leading to conflict among African Americans over status, behaviors, and respectability.[4]

Many liberals were optimistic about integration along middle-class lines in the postwar era. Newly developing "suburbs in the city" such as Chatham and nearby Avalon Park held out the possibility of planting the seeds of a pluralistic, democratic society. African Americans moved southward in the 1950s, and Chicago newspaper headlines hailed interracial cooperation and implied that these urbanites had the necessary traits to create mixed areas.[5] After all, these were cosmopolitan places where European ethnics, once bitterly divided by racial and religious differences, had melded along lines of middle-class respectability. "Who are undesirables?" a local priest asked at a community assembly. "Not too many years ago the Irish were classified as undesirables.... The Poles have been called undesirables, so have the Italians, the Mexicans and the Jews. If the colored find themselves called undesirables, they can feel themselves in good company."[6] Weren't middle-class Chicagoans willing to recognize that African Americans were just the latest group to be welcomed into the melting pot?

Apparently not. "Integration" in Chatham, as in so many other Chicago communities, was short-lived. Despite liberal efforts, most of the white population left. The turnover in Chatham and nearby communities revealed entrenched racism in the postwar white middle class, as they effectively doomed black urban areas to the perils of hyper-segregation and disinvestment. White flight from desirable locales was not an innocuous act, but rather social violence against cities and their minority residents. The African American newcomers to Chatham

were almost always of equal or better class backgrounds than the existing inhab-
itants, but high status and levels of education could not attenuate the attitudes of
fleeing whites.[7] The reality of fear, suspicion, and loathing of African Americans
overwhelmed the efforts of integrationists. Racism was more visible through the
deplorable violent actions of working-class whites in Chicago, but middle-class
whites held the keys to saving the city. Overwhelmingly, they chose to leave.
Black home buyers simultaneously considered community stabilization as a way
to solidify their individual gains and advance civil rights. As whites fled, they
struggled to make the best of their opportunity in Chatham. Unlike whites, they
had no other options.

CONTACT HYPOTHESIS

Middle-class neighborhoods fit the "contact hypothesis" proposed by the influential social scientist Gordon W. Allport. Allport theorized that intergroup contact had dubious value for diminishing prejudice unless it was complemented
by an equal status between the accommodating participants and supported
by local institutions.[8] When addressing the problem of racial change in urban
areas, many Americans adhered to the notion that the middle classes were more
likely to accept integrated living than poor and working-class residents.[9] They
saw the white middle class as more self-assured, and its cultural standards compatible with the emerging black middle class. Surveys indicated that the better
educated, especially those with some college education, had higher "general
tolerance values" and were more protective of civil rights for all Americans.
Polling of Northern whites in the 1950s and 1960s also suggested that education
diminished racist attitudes, and whites were increasingly open to having blacks
from the same social class as neighbors.[10] Interracial activists placed their trust
in this equal-status contact. Groups sought higher-income families to be the
first in white neighborhoods, believing they would not "fit the stereotype" and
would be accepted.[11] As Thomas Sugrue notes, "Over the course of the 1950s,
civil rights in the North took on an increasingly therapeutic cast."[12] Confident
integrationists argued that if whites could just jettison personal prejudices and
intermingle with like-minded African Americans, racism would fade.

Middle-class blacks also expressed confidence in prospects for integration if
society fostered the right kind of contacts. The troubles in working-class areas
were intense because, as one black Chicagoan alleged, "many of the homeowners

in the area were first- and second-generation Europeans. People who tend to be clannish. They really don't understand about Negroes."[13] Arrivals may not have expected to be fully accepted in higher-status areas, but they thought they would be tolerated, unlike in blue-collar areas where, as one woman remarked, "If you just *walked* out there, they would get violent, or run you back home."[14] Drake and Cayton noted that "'getting to know one another' as a solvent of racial tensions" was a "mystical faith" in some quarters of the black community, but only if it involved "people of similar tastes and interests."[15]

Drake and Cayton also remarked that the onus for integration was on the white middle class, who "set the tone" for race relations.[16] By the 1950s, they appeared to be coming around to equal-status contact as a solution. Many hoped that whites and blacks of equal status would unite along middle-class lines, an acceptably "American" form of exclusion. "The middle class in America is keenly conscious of the threat of lower-class encroachments," the civil rights activist and housing expert Robert Weaver noted. "This has long been a national characteristic, perhaps an inevitable consequence of a socially mobile people who are status-conscious."[17] Nationally, the popular press ran repeated accounts of middle-class whites accepting upwardly mobile blacks as neighbors. The stories in the articles were basically the same: African Americans entered middle-class neighborhoods and the existing residents, after some trepidation, gradually came to the realization that they had much in common with the newcomers.[18] Commentators claimed the issues facing middle-class areas were not "race problems," but "class problems" that neighbors could solve together.[19]

The Chatham and Avalon Park areas appeared to have all the necessary ingredients for successful integration. "The intelligent introduction of Negroes and other minorities into white communities of similar economic and social background," neighborhood activist Thomas Gaudette declared, "is the only realistic hope of maintaining the basic social, cultural, and religious values of the communities."[20] Integrationists believed that the well-educated, self-assured denizens could coalesce in a leafy area featuring an appealing mix of stately brick bungalows, charming flats, and attractive apartments. They hoped that these people would break the trend of neighborhood change. "The newcomers in this neighborhood have the same aspirations and values as those who have lived here longer," a resident wrote in the community newsletter. "We can live peacefully together if we work together to maintain our neighborhood."[21] A local apartment complex association put this theory into action by declaring an open-occupancy policy in 1959. Proponents reasoned that this plan would "give Chicago and America an example of integrated housing in surroundings which have characteristics to make success possible."[22] Management announced that "applicants for vacancies in the village will be screened and selected with the objective of creating a high-grade racially integrated community. . . . We will not compromise our present high standards including the caliber of tenants as well as the quality and maintenance of service."[23] Planners directed these words mainly at whites, assuring them that nothing would change in their buildings except for the color of their neighbors. For most whites, though, this was no small adjustment.

Despite wishing for equal-status integration and the existence of a "better class" of whites, the African Americans who moved into middle-class neighbor-hoods in the 1950s and 1960s had few illusions about their reception. Battles over racialized space in Chicago had been constant, and whites had greeted blacks with violence at nearly every turn.[24] As one realtor noted, "Any colored person going into an area where there is a crystallized feeling, he is taking his life in his hands."[25] From 1956 to 1958 there were 256 reported incidents of racial violence in Chicago, including five deaths and thirty-eight cases of arson, mostly in areas of racial transition.[26] One African American man living in a border area admitted that "when I leave for work in the morning, I leave with the haunting dread that my own home and family may be the victims of vio-lence in my absence." He had full reason to fret, as incendiaries had bombed two black homes nearby.[27] Across the country, home seekers remarked on the emotional toll of finding a "good neighborhood." As a physician observed, "Any kind of move for a Negro family today is expensive in terms of dollars and ruin-ous in terms of mental happiness."[28] Yet they continued to brave the barriers, as expansion in the early 1950s was so fast and furious that families moved into a formerly all-white block every ten days.[29]

Pioneering African Americans had diverse motives and expectations. They were an accomplished group and believed that the American Dream extended to freedom of residence.[30] Among those moving to Chatham were Arthur Turnbull, the first African American to graduate from the University of Chicago's business school; Dr. Welton Taylor, a Tuskegee Airman and famed microbiologist; Reverend Robbin Skyles, the founder of Illinois' first black Lutheran church; and Ernie Banks, the Chicago Cubs' first African American player.[31] Most were less distinguished, but made up a cross-section of the middle class, such as small business owners, professionals, and many government workers.

Some newcomers were optimistic for a new era of race relations, stating that integration was a test case for the survival of American democracy. Welton Taylor, for example, frequently challenged segregation in the military. Afterward, his family integrated veterans' housing at the University of Illinois and joined with white allies to end discrimination in area restaurants and theaters.[32] He argued that Chatham should be a place "where neighborliness is a positive attribute, not just a cornball thing thought up by squares to be ridiculed by beatniks."[33]

Others were more guarded, explaining that they were not seeking integration as such, but safe places with spacious homes, transportation options, and esteemed schools. A study of pioneers showed that they usually had some professional interracial interactions, but their goals were not solely about improved race relations.[34] "We didn't move in to socialize with these people," a Chatham resident affirmed. "It was just that this was the home we wanted, but if they're friendly with us, we're friendly with them."[35] According to journalist Carl Rowan, many blacks were conflicted by the yearning to move wherever they pleased and be "just plain Americans," yet still felt they should display "racial pride." They wondered if their move to a new neighborhood represented another step toward equality or signified a desire to "be white." Most heard whispers that they were deserting the race. Some responded angrily. "I don't want to be a white man," a pioneer responded. "I just want to live like one."[36]

Not surprisingly, blacks often professed matter-of-fact reasons for integration. With no whites around, one homeowner in a changing area noted, "The police will begin to think of our neighborhood as a Negro district, real estate brokers will think so, the teachers and trash men. And gradually the experienced teachers will ask for transfers. The policemen will appear more rarely. The broken street lamp will go unrepaired. The gutters will be unswept."[37] In Chicago, a mixed neighborhood had benefits that went beyond lofty idealism.

Stabilization was essential to the black middle class because they had few other options. The legal victories against racially restrictive covenants that culminated with the Supreme Court's decision in *Shelley v. Kraemer* in 1948 failed to create a culture of open occupancy in the metro area. Ten years later, the *Defender* observed, "The technique of excluding Negroes from desirable residential dwellings has lingered on, so far unaffected and unopposed. It is a conspiracy entered into by real estate holdings with a view to defeating clandestinely the broad processes of unrestricted occupancy."[38] A journalist estimated that from 1945 to 1962, only nine families moved into white-only suburban areas. That figure rose gradually during the 1960s, but blacks still encountered stubborn impediments. In addition, not until 1966 did a North Side Chicago neighborhood welcome African Americans, when one hundred religious and community groups declared that Rogers Park was open to all.[39] While whites could flee to rapidly multiplying suburban developments, blacks faced the "Chicago Wall." "The suburbs are just as much a closed society as the South," an American Friends Service Committee official remarked. "Chicago's system of separation of the races differs from Mississippi's only in degree."[40]

Though there were no major riots in middle-class areas, African American newcomers lived in fear of racially motivated assaults. True to form, vigilantes in Chatham perpetrated sporadic acts of violence and harassment and circulated a weekly broadsheet maintaining that "white people must control their communities" and voicing support for Southern segregationists such as Mississippi senator James Eastland.[41] The gospel singer Mahalia Jackson noted that "even though it's not anywhere near as bad as the South, my second home, Chicago, gave me a bad time, too, when I set out to buy a home." Jackson owned a "nice apartment," but "dreamed of having a house all to myself, a little place with trees and grass and a garden."[42] In 1955, she drove into outlying districts inquiring about houses for sale, later admitting that the attention she received from white fans "had sort of confused" her, as she supposed that their respect for her talents might translate into a desire to have her as a neighbor. But after repeated rebuffs, she turned to a real estate agent, who found her a home in the heart of Chatham that a surgeon was "proud" to sell to Mahalia Jackson.[43]

Unfortunately for Jackson, many other whites were not so "proud" to have her as a neighbor. "You'd have thought the atomic bomb was coming instead of me," she recalled. Neighbors held emergency meetings and tried to block her purchase. Her phone rang at all hours of the night, and one caller warned, "You move into that house and we'll blow it up with dynamite. You're going to need more than your gospel songs and prayers to save you." Jackson claimed she had not set out on an integration crusade; she just wanted "a quiet, pretty home to live in," and after praying for God's guidance, she bought the home.[44]

In 1956, the year Jackson moved into Chatham, a wave of racially motivated vandalism swept the neighborhood. Terrorists firebombed one home and damaged another. They shot out Jackson's windows. In response, police were posted outside her home for nearly a year.[45] While some neighbors came to welcome her, as Jackson looked out her picture window she could see For Sale signs popping up on lawns "like daisies," a lucid indication that neighbors were leaving because of her skin color.[46] Sadistic incidents and threats continued, and in 1959 the *Defender* lumped the "open violence" in Chatham–Avalon Park with the nightly riots in working-class areas.[47]

Considering the violent incidents in the area, it was telling that so many African American newcomers classified their experience as relatively peaceful.[48] The integration of middle-class areas took place in a hostile racial climate, but there were no riots or mob actions like those seen in working-class neighborhoods. Black Chathamites experienced enmity as they settled, but they also found hospitable neighbors who wanted to make integration work.

UNITY THROUGH CONFLICT

Though pioneers encountered resistance, some whites indicated they were ready for interracial living. Many had fled one or more times already and were tired of the process. They warily observed the hostile transformations in the line of expansion and wanted to avoid that chaos.[49] Local institutions tried to foster peaceful integration. The Chatham YMCA already included Jews on the board of directors and welcomed blacks as members and staff when the entered the area. In 1960 the Chatham Lions Club became one of the first integrated chapters in the nation. The Chatham Chamber of Commerce coordinated efforts with the Cosmopolitan Chamber of Commerce, which had changed its name from the Chicago Negro Chamber of Commerce in the 1950s to demonstrate its integrationist orientation.[50]

Many Chicago liberals believed integration was an outward expression of their respective religious faiths. Across the Southeast Side, an impressive effort was made among clergymen as they broadcasted the message of Judeo-Christian welcome from nearly every pulpit.[51] Liberal ministers took on the task of integration rather than disintegration in the mid-1950s despite heavy "pressure" and "ridicule" from dissenting members of congregations.[52] St. Joachim's parish in Chatham insisted that parishioners welcome African Americans as equals and enrolled black students in its school by the mid-1950s.[53] A group of local Catholic lay activists pledged to "help each other to grow in the love of God and our fellowmen through our jobs and through our interest in good homes and sound urban planning."[54] Chatham–Avalon Park Community Council president Thomas Gaudette, who was motivated as much by an uncompromising faith in Catholic universalism as in neighborhood stabilization, often devoted thirty hours a week in his spare time to further harmony among neighbors.[55] Protestant ministers believed it was a theological duty to stay in the city and that "it is not enough to be against segregation. Both the mandate of the Judeo-Christian tradition and realistic attack on the problems of metropolitan life require movement toward integrated communities."[56] Jewish residents quoted from the books of Leviticus and Malachi, reminding their neighbors that there was a single standard for the stranger as well as the native.[57]

Most white residents needed no religious justification for staying, as much of the development on the Far South Side was nearly brand-new. Developers drained a swampy area and built homes, apartments, and shopping centers after the war, and locals made large investments in new recreation facilities and churches.[58] The 1954 unveiling of a $300,000 Young Men's Jewish Youth Center in nearby South Shore certainly gave no indication of dissatisfaction with the surroundings or a sense that white flight was imminent.[59] As a letter sent out by Chatham clergy in 1954 asserted, "It is of very doubtful value to try to exchange a community of good homes, schools, churches, stores, and transportation for an area where these things are lacking, simply because a person of a different skin color moves into your block, wanting, the chances are, to be a good citizen in the community."[60] Many Chicago whites thought that black newcomers would lower home values, but that was not a foremost concern from local homeowners. Realtors boasted that Chatham would maintain favorable or better housing prices than comparable city communities, as it contained all the amenities residents sought, including high-performing schools. Peter Rossi, a professor at the University of Chicago and resident of the Marynook subdivision in Chatham, called these new areas "semi-suburbs," which included alluring features such as detached houses and wide, low-traffic streets lined with trees.[61] Many residents had put down roots and took pride in their surroundings.[62] Unlike other Chicago neighborhoods suffering from decline and overcrowding, residents in Chatham and nearby middle-class communities expressed contentment.

The intolerant sought to strengthen the invisible racial walls around their communities, but liberals also prepared. In the early 1950s, for instance, they established the Chatham–Avalon Park Community Council (CAPCC), an association that broke with tradition by declaring that stable integration was both inevitable and welcomed.[63] Reverend John Hayes, the council president, observed that while most neighborhood organizations wanted to build an "iron curtain," the CAPCC encouraged whites to deal with newcomers calmly and rationally. He linked pioneering to colonial struggles in India, Egypt, and

Vietnam, as "people everywhere are demanding to join the human race."[64] Other
community associations in the area followed suit, although members roiled in
tumult regarding the meanings of integration. The West Avalon Community
Association, for example, split into a conservative faction that argued for quietly
easing in newcomers and an activist bloc that proposed getting involved through
demonstrations at local beaches and picketing discriminatory employers.[65] The
breach presaged future cracks in the liberal consensus, but these groups did
succeed in marginalizing reactionary segregationists.

The most dynamic white activist in the Chatham area was Thomas Gaudette.
Born in Massachusetts and raised in a large, socially progressive Catholic home,
Gaudette grew up imagining that church and the community "are the same
thing....I don't understand how you make a distinction." He flew forty missions
as a bomber pilot in World War II and was shot down over Prague. After the
war he helped his brother, a priest, with an integrated unionization drive at a
can factory in Mississippi and then went back home to attend Boston College.
There he married Kay Sullivan, graduated, and became a traffic manager with
the Admiral Corporation. Kay and Tom moved to Kay's childhood neighborhood of Chatham, and Tom appeared to be on his way to becoming an "organization man," or, as he put it, a "simple man" who "came home every night at 5:30
and had kids." The gutters were clean, and his grass was cut, but Tom and Kay
realized that their lives were "a fucking waste of time." After a predatory realtor
visited his house, Gaudette went to a neighborhood meeting and realized he
needed to get involved. Gaudette, spurred on by his wife, became president of
the CAPCC and mixed so easily with black neighbors that some dissenters at
his parish whispered that he "loved niggers." The insults only emboldened him,
though, because like many activists in the period, he sensed he was on the side
of justice. "I was righteous, and I was right," he recalled. "And I would say give a
moral person power and you've got yourself a problem, baby, because there is no
debate. The moral person is right. I know the feeling, ya feel good."[66]

Through his activism he became familiar with the rabble-rouser Saul Alinsky.
Alinsky's tactics convinced Gaudette that he could unite neighbors through
conflicts that would bring out common interests. Gaudette, a former amateur
boxer, reveled in this strategy, confronting friends and foes with subjects that
his polite neighbors considered taboo, especially the topic of race. He contended that discussions of "human relations" and "brotherhood" were "Hyde
Park liberal crap" as the community did not need "do-gooders," they needed
to fuse around tangible goals.[67] The CAPCC, led by Gaudette and spurred on

by an active membership, found the conflicts they were looking for in unifying campaigns over zoning, the closing of taverns, and a showdown with the Nation of Islam.

Much to the delight of Gaudette and other liberals, integration appeared to be working. Local institutions opened their doors, and blacks and whites interacted in block clubs, bowling leagues, and in the pews.[68] On the Edward Murrow television show, Mahalia Jackson, who had been pained by her neighbors' cold greeting, received an integrated delegation from the CAPCC.[69] Optimistic whites argued that it was beneficial to live in a mixed community and touted the advantages of city life.[70] *Fortune* magazine noted that more parents were staying in the city because they wanted their children "brought up in an environment closer to reality," exposed "to all kinds of people, colored and white, old and young, poor and rich."[71] One woman moved her family back from Park Forest, calling the suburb an "artificial community." "You can't teach your children democracy unless you're willing to live in an area that is democratic," she argued.[72] Whites were reassured when their new neighbors seemed similar to old neighbors.[73] Some blacks agreed. After a planned interracial home visit, one black Chathamite noted, "We were all so much alike it was sickening."[74] A *Chicago Tribune* headline proclaimed, "Chatham Integration Is Successful." Families had not panicked, and the area had made integration a "living experiment."[75] The CAPCC won awards for promoting brotherhood, and people flocked to see how the neighborhood had done it, while groups from New Jersey to Ohio invited Gaudette to speak.[76] "We are finding that Negroes have the same fears we do," one resident noted. "They don't want the neighborhood to decline any more than anyone else."[77] The rest of the city was looking at Chatham to see what happened when an esteemed community integrated. Would the area maintain its cachet? Or would it become just another run-down extension of the ghetto?[78]

Residents bonded to maintain the prestige of the area by preventing homes from being subdivided into apartments. In middle-class areas, the *Chicago Defender* noted, black homeowners were determined to "fight harder against possible 'blight' than any other group of citizens. . . . Primarily they will be on guard against the kind of 'kitchenetting' or overcrowding that has ruined every other neighborhood."[79] They invested heavily in improving their homes and had taken special interest in making sure their neighbors did not lower values.[80] Homeowners hoped that meticulousness would alleviate prejudice and help others move out of the ghetto peacefully. However, this also meant that the middle class felt they needed to keep their less respectable brethren out of their communities. One newcomer made his preference for neighbors clear when he told the *Daily News*, "As for me, I'd rather have a decent white family next to me than some Negro family fresh from the slums." Louis A. Fitzgerald, an African American CAPCC member, understood that the dual housing market imposed an artificial "color tax." "Many Negroes have to take exorbitant mortgages," Fitzgerald lamented. "Then they carve up their homes to get more income to meet payments." Nevertheless, Fitzgerald concentrated on stopping illegal conversions of single-family homes into apartments, as protecting property investments was a more immediate and more realistic goal than trying to tackle the gargantuan housing predicament faced by African Americans.[81]

Homeowners made joint petitions at city zoning hearings to preserve their community. In 1958, five hundred Chathamites packed city hall to contest multifamily housing. After their victory, one Chathamite after another made clear that they were determined to prevent blight. "As a mother and a teacher I will strive to do whatever I can to make this neighborhood a wholesome place in which to raise a child," a resident avowed. "Any attempts to change the character of the neighborhood I will fight militantly." And militant they were, repeatedly thwarting zoning changes throughout the next decade to fight what many called the "evil" of slums.[82]

In addition to zoning, locals made a "significant interracial effort" to shut down taverns. As shop owners relocated to the suburbs, pubs often filled the empty spaces. According to Chathamites, these establishments attracted the wrong kind of clientele. In response, the CAPCC took advantage of an obscure Chicago law that allowed individual precincts to vote dry.[83] Supporters assured voters that this was not a temperance movement (even Gaudette's Irish-Catholic father argued that this drive went "too far"), but there was a difference between social drinking and public nuisances. "Due to the fact that the social activities of the community are conducted either in the form of back yard barbecues or as basement recreation socials," a black resident claimed, "the patronage of the taverns operated in the area was transient."[84] Locals thought the pubs invited an unwanted, boisterous style of revelry. An African American leader called this the "Cousin Willie" problem. A migrant suddenly flush with cash spent too much time in South Side bars, "and he's a good bet to get himself in trouble. In fact, he gets us all in trouble."[85] On this point, middle-class Chathamites were in agreement. From the outside, observers marveled at the integrated activism on the Southeast Side. These victories, however, masked festering problems.

CLASS AND THE SCHOOL PROBLEM

Though blacks and whites were able to come together over neighborhood status concerns, the local public schools proved to be their undoing. For the middle class, schools were usually the decisive factor when choosing where to live. Having achieved their own upward mobility, parents sought to pave the way for their children to maintain their class position, or better yet, to rise to the next level.[86] Although the postwar years were a boom time for the white middle class, they had persistent anxiety about losing their status or their children moving downward. Since education would determine a great deal of their children's future, it was no longer a fixed asset, but rather something to be graded and critiqued. If the local school came up short, changes needed to be made.

The Chicago Public Schools (CPS) experienced ups and downs in their effectiveness in the first half of the twentieth century, struggling episodically with overcapacity, corruption, and funding shortfalls. By the 1950s, though, they were in what historian John Rury calls the "golden age" of their existence, "a time of prosperity and growing confidence in the schools." Under Superintendent Benjamin Willis, class sizes dropped by 20 percent despite enrollment swelling by 10,000 students each year. Augmented teacher salaries, introduction of new curriculum, and enhanced summer and after-school programs signaled innovation. Early in his tenure, many black Chicagoans were impressed by Willis and urged him to do more to close the racial gap.[87]

However, prosperity veiled growing troubles. The changing socioeconomic composition of the city, de facto segregation, middle-class flight, and the deterioration of the inner city contributed to the growing crisis. In the 1950s, the black population in Chicago increased by 321,000, while the white population dropped by 399,000.[88] In addition, the baby boom and Southern newcomers put tremendous stress on facilities and staffs. Migrants were often handicapped by Southern education and poverty, and they entered overflowing buildings. The number of students in Chicago public schools rose 180,000 from 1953 to 1966, even though the population of the city fell 70,000 in that period.[89] Few middle-class whites were willing to remain in neighborhoods, no matter how aesthetically pleasing, if they felt that the schools could no longer assure their children's futures, especially when the suburban alternative beckoned. According to Dr. Robert Havighurst's 1964 study of the CPS, "Chicago's chief problem is this: how to keep and attract middle-income people to the central city and how to maintain a substantial white majority in the central city."[90]

While whites still lived on the South Side, many African Americans contended that integrated classrooms were desirable from the standpoint of race relations and would not be neglected by the power structure.[91] Even though they had experienced the racist limitations of the United States firsthand, parents were deeply invested in their children's futures. "No matter how bitter or disillusioned people were with their lot and/or the system, when their children were born they dragged out and polished up the old Up-the-Ladder-Dream," Southsider Melvin Van Peebles recalled. "They were dead positive that life would be kinder to their children."[92] They braced their children for harassment, arguing that it was worth it when compared to enduring a second-rate schooling and that "education of association" could eventually lessen race prejudice.[93] Classrooms, black activists suggested, should be laboratories of democracy and tolerance.

For most white students and parents, though, integration was not the harbinger of a better future, but a signal of deterioration. Racial, ethnic, and religious animosities simmered among youths across the city, often spilling over into attacks during prep sporting events. The hostility became so heated in 1954 that the police commissioner half jokingly suggested the city should "abolish basketball."[94] Many whites firmly opposed integration in the late 1950s as small riots broke out at high schools across the city.[95] At Hirsch High in Chatham, even the juvenile delinquents said they were leaving. "We may try South Shore [High School]," one explained. "No colored over there. We had fifty of 'em [at Hirsch] last winter. We may have a hundred next year."[96] Whites held a near-consensus stance that schools with black students were "bad"; even the "toughs" wanted out of them. Across the country, they left in anticipation of desegregation. "Urban became synonymous with poor public education," historian Jack Schneider notes, "and that perception, when acted upon, became a reality."[97]

The school problem inspired an integrated summit in June 1960 sponsored by the Marynook Homeowners Association (MHA) and the CAPCC. Locals sensed that the packed elementary schools on double shift were the prime threat to durable mixed communities, and they alleged that Hirsch High School was undergoing the "typical ghetto pattern" of transformation from better than average into a "disciplinary barracks." Black and white parents complained that Hirsch was not serving their college-bound progeny, as it had been "flooded with poorly prepared youngsters" from working-class areas north of Chatham.[98] To remedy this, the MHA and CAPCC collaborated on the "Marynook Plan," an audacious attempt at interracial cooperation along middle-class lines. The plan proposed a "Regional High School District" and envisioned the five high schools on the Southeast Side of Chicago as "educationally specialized": two college-prep schools, enhancement of the Chicago Vocational school, a commercial school for business students, and a career-orientation school for "at-risk" students, all with loose transfer rules for students who changed their "life goals."[99] The plan garnered local support and inspired a lawsuit to force Superintendent Willis to accept open enrollment.[100] Educational experts touted the strategy to stabilize the racial balance and stem middle-class flight.[101]

While the authors of the Marynook Plan did express concern over the problem of "at-risk" and "unemployable" pupils, the main thrust of the plan was stabilization along class lines. As the political scientist Norton Long noted, the child-centered middle class felt increased pressure to "keep up with the Joneses in the education of their children" and worried that their children could be dragged down by lower-class peers. "No one who has seen educated Negroes desperately striving to protect their children and their civilized values from the patterns of the plantation South need cringe at the charge of being a segregationist," Long argued. "What badly needs facing is the *kinds* of segregation that are justifiable."[102] According to reform-minded middle-class Americans, racial segregation was wrong because it ignored the individuality of black children. But *class segregation* could insulate the middle classes from the negative influences of the poor and maladjusted.

The Marynook Plan not only addressed the problem of Chicago's inability to maintain integrated communities, but also charged that the CPS were not adequately serving the needs of college-bound, "gifted" children.[103] Parents consistently tabbed Hirsch High as the primary hurdle to maintaining integration, and by 1962 only twenty-six whites remained.[104] Supporters expressed confidence that the Board of Education would listen to their demands, because they were "not that stupid" to ignore middle-class parents in an area in the national spotlight.[105] The Marynook Plan divided children along class lines, ensuring that elite high schools would not be encumbered by vocational-track and problem students. When middle-class parents urged that their children needed a broader curriculum, they meant Latin, not metal shop.

The Chicago Board of Education repeatedly rejected schemes like the Marynook Plan before finally agreeing to a controversial and short-lived "clustering plan" in 1964. Willis, like many educators in this period, remained committed to the neighborhood school, arguing that it "emphasizes the role of the school in community life." He reasoned that attempts to change these borders for class or race reasons were political and not among the goals of public education. "I'm an educator, not a social worker," Willis argued. "I don't go around counting Negroes, Indians, Hindus or any other group." Blacks and whites generally viewed neighborhood schools in drastically different ways. As one expert deduced, "Neighborhood schools symbolize, above all else, the effort of America's vast middle class to transmit shared values and aspirations to its children." But for urban blacks, these same arrangements meant arrested mobility and "a slow suffocation in the darkness of the ghetto."[106] An official report from the Board of Education agreed, arguing that the neighborhood school "operates now to retard the acculturation and integration of the in-migrant Negro in Chicago and in the metropolitan United States as a whole."[107] The integrated team that formulated the Marynook Plan thought they had a solution to please everyone and were disappointed that Willis seemed to ignore community desires because of his devotion to the neighborhood school.[108]

Additionally, many Chicagoans suspected that Willis, the Board of Education, and Mayor Richard J. Daley had "political" reasons for confining black students in ghetto schools, judging segregation as the only way to keep whites in the city. As the *Daily News* noted, city officials were "well aware that many thousands of white families, justifiably or not, already have fled the city rather than send their children to school with Negroes."[109] These suspicions were confirmed in a school board report demonstrating that 85 percent of Chicago students attended segregated schools. Despite Willis's massive building efforts, 40 percent of black schools had more than thirty-five students per classroom, while white facilities had space for seventeen thousand pupils.[110]

Willis became a lightning rod for Chicago's education tribulations. His stubborn insistence that the system was not segregated made him the focus of near-constant protests. Chathamites blamed him for hastening the departure of the middle class and shattering racially mixed areas yearning for stability. According to one CPS board member, "Ben Willis virtually sank the Chicago public schools."[111] If so, Willis had plenty of help. Until 1963, when he temporarily resigned and disappeared for a short period, his policies were consistently supported by city administration, the business community, the press, the board's only African American member, and most whites.[112] The problems were much deeper and systemic than the decisions of the superintendent. One expert concluded that Willis was reluctant to change policies, but he was also pressured to maintain separate schools by "a vociferous minority group which is blatantly anti-Negro and constitutes the local version of the 'white backlash.'"[113]

Black Chathamites, realizing that their hopes for integration were fading, opened a two-front battle by spearheading the civil rights activism against Willis. The school protests grew from a murmur to a shout by the mid-1960s, as tactics grew more confrontational and participation exploded. Integration nudged forward in Southern cities, but progress in Chicago was scant. In 1961, for example, the *Sun-Times* reported that integration was "peaceful" in Dallas, but pictures showed schools in Chicago denying enrollment to black students.[114] CAPCC took an early lead, joining the Congress of Racial Equality, the Student Nonviolent Coordinating Committee, and local civil rights groups in demanding educational equity. In 1961, while the CAPCC collaborated on the Marynook Plan, the group also hired attorney Paul Zuber, fresh off a victory to desegregate the schools in New Rochelle, New York, to launch a suit against the Chicago Board of Education.[115]

While Chatham parents instigated the legalistic phase, they also began a direct-action component at Burnside Elementary as fed-up mothers initiated a sit-in in January 1962. Burnside had been overloaded for five years; it had approximately 1,600 pupils at a facility built in 1898 to handle 865. Nearby Perry remained all-white and used eleven rooms for the blind and deaf, an allocation of space that parents referred to as a "ruse for filling the school and fending off the transfer of Negroes."[116] Supporters rallied behind the protests, participating in picketing and other demonstrations at the building until police arrested them for trespassing. But the arrests only emboldened the activists, as Judge Joseph J. Butler dismissed the charges and approved of sit-ins as "courageous" and a "good mode of expressing opinions," while calling for the Board of Education to speak to the dissidents. The problem was deeper than trespassing, Butler added. If the school board is promoting segregation, "the people have a right—almost a duty—to fight."[117]

Activists mounted a full-scale campaign. "The battle line must be drawn somewhere in the struggle to democratize the Chicago schools," the *Chicago Defender* declared. "Burnside is just as good a place to start the fight."[118] In April, a coalition of neighborhood groups from working- and middle-class areas came together with the Urban League and NAACP to form the Coordinating

Council of Community Organizations (CCCO) as a "common front" on civil rights issues.[119] The CCCO launched a variety of tactics to integrate classrooms, including litigation, picketing, and independent investigations of empty classrooms in white locales, while pressuring Superintendent Willis and the Board of Education to implement transfer plans. The activities culminated in a one-day boycott on October 23, 1963, when 224,770 children, nearly half of CPS students, stayed home.[120]

Contrary to the criticism launched against the black middle class, their actions in the schooling fray showed that they were willing participants in civil-rights activities, including participating in direct actions and forming broad coalitions. One community newspaper observed that "Negro businessmen, professionals, day laborers, housewives, high school kids, and ADC mothers" were taking part in the "extraordinary measures" to improve education. Though the Burnside actions were started by middle-class parents, they were soon lending their organizational power and expertise to protests across the South Side.[121] Indeed, contrary to the stereotype of the self-satisfied, detached Black Babbitt, a study of Chatham African Americans published in 1971 revealed that 75 percent of white-collar blacks were active in the civil rights movement, and 40 percent had participated in direct action.[122] The race and class dynamics that played out locally put middle-class African Americans in complex situations that often left them conflicted over balancing neighborhood concerns and wider goals. Instead of withdrawing, they sought a balance that brought contradictions but also progress.

PANIC AND FLIGHT

The headline-grabbing success of integrated activism in Chatham obscured the steady white retreat. On a national level, white flight was a complex phenomenon. As historian Amanda Seligman demonstrates, those exiting often had "multiple sources of discontent with the postwar urban environment" that went beyond racial integration.[123] However, whites in middle-class neighborhoods on the South Side rarely expressed dissatisfaction with the city in words and actions. Leave they did, though, sometimes taking a large financial loss on their homes. When "blockbusters" descended on changing middle-class areas in the 1950s, they found fertile ground for business as edgy homeowners fell for the scare tactics of real estate agents.

The nationwide practice of blockbusting almost always accompanied the entry of African Americans into formerly all-white areas, and turnover followed a familiar cycle. Real estate agents—black and white—made vast profits by fomenting panic and buying low from skittish homeowners and then selling at inflated prices to eager African Americans. The agents also solicited black homeowners, seeking to buy their single-family homes and subdivide them.[124] Some ethically challenged realtors used dirty tricks to spread fear, including late-night phone calls, placing deceptive Sold signs in yards, and staging a phony gang fight to scare neighbors, involving cries of "Don't shoot!"[125] Blockbusters in Chatham included the respectable and the shady, the professional and the amateur. There was money to be made, and some had a nose for it. Julian Black, a former comanager of Joe Louis and a policy-wheel baron, handled home sales, as did reputable downtown bankers who waited for the speculators to "break" a block before descending like vultures. While residents commonly likened blockbusters to snakes, some black newcomers admitted that they were necessary. "White home owners' groups won't allow sales to Negroes," a realtor active in the area stated. "There also are mortgage conditions for Negroes. This usually makes it necessary for a speculator to go in first."[126] The *Chicago Daily News* reported that the "panic peddlers" took a vicious toll on attempts at integration. "Any chance to create an interracial neighborhood is undermined and the so-called Negro 'ghetto' merely is extended. And more whites make the costly flight to the suburbs."[127]

The blockbusters' constant badgering and scare tactics enraged residents, especially integrationists. "Any man who would use misunderstandings between races as a means to make a buck should be horse-whipped," Gaudette wrote to a Jewish group. "He does more harm than all the Communists in the country today and the trouble is he might be one of our neighbors."[128] In 1960 twenty interracial activists in Chatham engaged in civil disobedience, uprooting about a dozen For Sale signs that they claimed had been put up by blockbusters. The crowd started a bonfire in an empty lot and waved placards reading "Realty Goons Get Out," "Jail Blockbusters," and "Panic Peddlers Are Un-American" before police dispersed them.[129] The protests made a brave stand against neighborhood change but could not address the deeper reasons for turnover.

While some residents panicked and fled, others drifted away quietly, even shamefully. Many middle-class whites were eager to maintain the veneer of liberalism and claimed they were not leaving the city for "racial" reasons. Instead, they stressed socially approved motives, with the most frequent response that it was "better for the children."[130] Liberals cited education as the major reason, as Daley and Willis may have been correct in their assessment that the only way to keep whites in the city was to keep black students out of their schools. Across the country, whites often assumed that integration would press standards downward.[131] In their minds, this was due either to environmental factors, as black children had "deprived educational backgrounds," or hereditary causes, as blacks lacked the "potential for achievement." According to *Time* magazine, black and Latino migrant children were "different" than the European immigrants of yesteryear. Already having achieved American citizenship, "they are shorn of the drive that spurred their predecessors, weirdly cut off from the middle-class culture that teachers abide by." Few white parents thought there was anything left to do but move.[132] As a Marynook resident recalled, "It takes more than attitude" to realize integration, and locals generally agreed that the area high schools were "catastrophic." His family joined the "migration" to suburban Flossmoor.[133] A Chicago school board report admitted that integration was in danger of becoming a "theoretical matter," because it "cannot be achieved without white students."[134] Over time, this prediction was largely borne out.

It wasn't just the educational standards that bothered whites, as most parents also strongly objected to interracial dating. Once sex differences became apparent in the junior high years, white families either left or sent their children to schools in different neighborhoods. A survey of white women on the South Side in the early 1950s revealed that even those who were completely democratic in terms of housing for African Americans still objected to mixed junior high schools, indicating that integration would be fleeting. One middle-class woman claimed to have "no prejudice against Negroes," yet still acknowledged "I don't care for intermarriage. I think the mother has a right to be anxious if her daughter is with Negro boys."[135] Interracial sex, for many parents, was beyond the pale. For many white families, the threat inherent in the sexually charged realities of adolescent life trumped any neighborhood attachment. In 1959, the *Daily News* reported that parents often admitted they would stay in Chatham if they "could send [their] kids to a white school." Even if the Chicago Board of Education would have accepted the Marynook Plan and divided borders along lines of class and ability, it is doubtful that this would have stemmed the tide of flight.[136]

White boundaries not only provided a rationale for leaving the city, they also reinforced gender norms. Men bolstered their masculinity through the "preservation" of white womanhood and seized an opportune justification for their otherwise "unmanly" exit. "No husband and no family man can long withstand the fears of his womenfolks," a frustrated white liberal noted. "He simply packs up his family and moves." One of the first to sell in Chatham reported that he was leaving because the sight of African Americans on his street had his sister "so worked up it was horrible."[137] By containing supposed black aggressiveness and saving wives and daughters, white families restructured flight as a safely masculine gesture rather than as a panicked retreat.[138]

In a sense, middle-class whites failed to embody the "contact hypothesis" in part because its tenets were fundamentally true.[139] Many had rebelled against their own parents' warnings not to marry outside of their own ethnicity or faith. In some respects, the conscious fixation on miscegenation revealed the collective belief in the inexorable certainty of "race mixing."[140] If they had any doubts, they were quickly erased by the cross-racial relationships that sprouted in church youth groups and in schools. Middle-class, educated people could express positive feelings on the "rights of Negroes," but sex across the color line was usually feared and despised. Intermarriage of their offspring would result in a status calamity, negating race privilege.[141] A 1958 Gallup poll found that 96 percent of whites disapproved of marriage between blacks and whites. As David Hollinger notes, hard-core segregationists charged that civil rights agitation was just an elaborate plot to encourage miscegenation. Integrationists could not dismiss the allegations because a significant number of Northerners shared these suspicions.[142] A Chicago realtor contended that parents "worry about their children merging with them [blacks] in school. They worry about marriage. In discussing with white people, *invariably* you find the problem about the children." Another estimated that 90 percent of whites left the city because of mixing in classrooms. "That's one of the most basic things in the whole business," he stated. "They don't want their children to mingle."[143]

When the school board rejected redistricting plans, liberal whites in Chatham developed a validation for flight that diminished the importance of race and stressed class and the continuance of generational social mobility. As a writer in the *Atlantic Monthly* observed, when Negroes moved next door to and into the same classrooms as whites, they were no longer an "abstraction," but a "concrete reality," posing a dilemma to liberals who supported equal rights. Middle-class whites alleged that they had not failed Chicago; rather, the city, especially the public schools, had failed them. Some moved out surreptitiously to avoid the awkward conversation with neighbors. Others insisted that they wanted to stay but could not expose their children to substandard education. One resident of Marynook claimed that the community had fought long and

hard for integration, "but the schools have been our worst enemy."[144] Verna Dee
Goren, who stayed in the area, was "infuriated" by these excuses, noting that
the local schools were excellent and the African Americans moving in were
obviously upwardly mobile. "Whites used education as an excuse," her husband,
Mike, recalled. "Everyone thought their kid belonged in Harvard."[145]

The racial advantages of whiteness were also crystal clear in this scenario.
When the effort to realign the schools failed, whites had the convenient "escape
hatch" of the suburbs, most of which were effectively closed to racial minorities.[146]
Government incentives and urban/suburban disparities basically bribed them
to leave cities.[147] In the mid- to late-1960s, for instance, Chicago spent $614 per
year to educate each high school student, while neighboring Evanston spent
$1,096. Whites left, further shrinking the city's tax base.[148] The cookie-cutter
postwar developments guaranteed a baseline level of class stability and self-gov-
ernance. There white Americans could actively influence their districts without having to deal with the class and race diversity. A major mission of public
education in a democracy was to give children from all backgrounds a chance
to achieve social mobility. However, with the explosion of suburban fiefdoms
in the second half of the twentieth century, the white middle class announced
to the country that fulfilling this mission was not their problem. An exhausted
Gaudette looked back and realized that his tasks were Sisyphean unless the
entire metropolitan area was part of the solution. "We are forced to confront
these issues, whether it's racial, whether it's education, whether it's violence .
. . as a city." Unfortunately, the middle-class whites best equipped to deal with
these issues turned their backs and moved out. The suburbs, Gaudette wearily
admitted, were Chicago's "obvious problem."[149]

Where whites obfuscated, blacks saw racism. Newcomers, the clear majority
of whom were accomplished citizens, regarded this abandonment "as a strongly
implied slur on Negroes." For Mahalia Jackson, the rejection by her Chatham
neighbors was "like being put out of a family."[150] The black journalist Hoyt
Fuller maintained that flight revealed the hypocrisy of Northern white liberals. "It was one thing to strike a liberal pose in favor of Negro rights so long
as what was involved only amounted to a question of unsegregated seating on
a Southern bus, or free use of a public park, or even unrestricted service at a
sandwich counter," Fuller wrote. "But it is quite another matter when this lib-
erality is put to the acid test in terms of jobs, schools, and housing, areas where
some adjustment and possible inconvenience on the 'liberal's' part is required to
make Negro equality an unqualified reality."[151] The immediate panic of flappable

residents and the outwardly racist did not surprise most newcomers as they had seen it all happen before. What really stung, though, is when whites left even after African Americans had proven their worth. "At first I couldn't understand why people were moving out so suddenly," a pioneer recalled. "It was like having a tooth pulled for no reason. And then I couldn't understand why people *kept* leaving, why the individuals who didn't leave right way couldn't see that those of us moving in were at the same economic level—that we had similar values."[152] The relocation process was already exhausting because of the tension and fear involved, and it became even more wearing as black residents realized that their neighbors chose not to see them as individuals.

AFTER WHITE FLIGHT

African Americans were chagrined, but they had no time for vexations as they set out to make the best of their new surroundings. They had the sense that they were a part of a rising middle class and wanted to ensure that Chatham remained "quiet and dignified." As soon as whites moved out, black residents began to wonder: Who is going to move next door?[153] Flight had not "left" communities open to blacks; rather pioneers had claimed these spaces through initiative and ambition and were not about to let their neighborhoods slide.[154] One study of Chicago in the 1960s demonstrated that Africans Americans were not entering new areas at random, but rather were actively seeking "family-oriented, middle-class communities," demonstrating the "power and predominance of a new black middle class."[155] Where whites and demographers saw an "expanding ghetto," African Americans spotted opportunity. In 1962–1963, black Chathamites invested nearly $9 million in new home construction, one of the largest amounts in any city area.[156] These "gilded ghettos," as St. Clair Drake called them, were "indistinguishable from any other middle-class neighborhoods except by the color of the residents' skin."[157]

Black areas in cities across the North continued to be segmented by class, but compared to middle-class whites, middle-class blacks still lived near the poor and working class. This fostered more interactions, but the black middle class also witnessed bleak cases of decay in adjacent areas. Single-family homes rarely retained their integrity, as owners maximized revenue by converting them to kitchenettes. Districts such as Woodlawn and Kenwood, beset by congestion and absentee landlords, declined as buildings began to take on the appearance of "old war ruins."[158] These nearby examples of decline made the black middle class even more attentive to stabilization. Home upkeep became a second religion, and nonconformists faced the ire of neighbors.[159] Welton Taylor, who succeeded Gaudette as the president of the CAPCC, differentiated between "neighborhood" concerns and the black middle class's leadership role. He argued they needed a "willingness to accept responsibility for problems that affect the community." However, "a neighborhood is primarily for the people who live in it. We can't run it for transients who have no stake in the community beyond the bottles they leave on the lawns on Sunday morning. If that's snobbery, then I'm a snob."[160] Lewis Caldwell, a former social worker and future state representative, also blamed bad behaviors for disorder. He argued that whites in Chatham and Marynook had good reasons for leaving, because too many African Americans tolerated street crime, failed to engage in civic activities, and valued Cadillacs over fixing broken windowpanes. The civil rights movement was making headway, but Caldwell wondered, "Will Negroes be ready for first-class citizenship which carries with it first-class responsibility?"[161] Many well-to-do blacks felt they needed to set a good example for other members of the race but were impatient with those who refused to follow along.

Unlike the white middle class, prosperous blacks acknowledged their racial uplift duties. However, they also felt the squeeze of the expanding ghetto and unresponsive white elites. In their minds, the "neighborhood" consisted of fellow homeowners and tenants, exposing the limits of a larger "black community." Some felt torn over this divide. An accountant living in Chatham likened joining the middle class to "getting into your backyard, landscaping it, and putting a fence around it." He was glad to be out of the slums but acknowledged that blighted areas were only two miles away, tying black fortunes together. "We are not going to move appreciably now until the whole group moves."[162] Many middle-class blacks struggled with balancing demanding personal advances with the immense work of broad-based civil rights gains.

Despite concerns for racial solidarity, middle-class African Americans often channeled their energies into stabilization. In Chatham, fast becoming "the only ghetto with a two-year waiting list to get in," black residents sustained the regulation of taverns, acts that were first undertaken by integrationists. The *Bulletin*, a local newspaper, noted that despite the racial turnover in Chatham, the agenda of the CAPCC was unchanged, as the organization sponsored another local-option referendum to close more saloons. "The stage and setting are the same; the actors are different; the outcome cannot yet be predicted."[163] Although white-owned businesses ran ads in the local papers proclaiming, "We are here to stay," the main business arteries soon became "ghost towns" as businesses joined in the suburban exodus. In black minds, shady real estate operators, seedy taverns, and disreputable churches took an excessive amount of this empty retail space.[164] According to one African American, too many were getting into the "barbecue shops, the beauty shops and the chicken shacks, and the people in the middle-class community just don't want this type of business."[165]

Class-based concerns drove the tavern-closing movement, but it was also a reaction to segregated vice that had long beleaguered black Chicagoans. Activists had engaged in long-running battles to regulate unruly taverns.[166] Chathamites claimed they were not opposed to social drinking, but that bars had consistently been a "menace" by staying open at all hours, serving minors, tolerating gambling, and most exasperatingly, serving as fronts for prostitution.[167] Bars in Chicago often fell under the outright or shadow direction of gangsters and served as vice depots, with the police taking regular payoffs. The Chicago Crime Commission reported that even "mom and pop" pubs were being muscled by "the hoodlum element." Chathamites need only look a dozen blocks north, where "Sin Corner" operated unmolested at Sixty-Third and Cottage Grove, for evidence of the dangers of organized crime under police protection.[168] "Ours is a good and stable neighborhood," a minister reported after the West Avalon Community Association closed a nightclub. "One way we intend to keep it that way is to keep riff-raff bars away from here."[169] Black civic leader A. L. Foster, who opposed closing the bars, admitted that the "direct action" of "irate citizens" was not unexpected when owners allowed "prostitutes, sex diviates [sic] and plain hoodlums to make their places their headquarters."[170] Though the local option seemed drastic, experience taught residents that they needed to take aggressive action.

Taverns provided the wrong kind of secular entertainment, but the black middle class also wanted proper sacred institutions. They often associated storefront churches with encroaching blight. Many critics considered them "eyesores" and "undignified" and maintained they precluded the "high type" of businesses while attracting "undesirables."[171] Self-made revivalist preachers seemed to outnumber congregations, and critics linked them to sexual shenanigans and immorality.[172] Driving out "ghetto churches" became a customary part of preserving community standards. An African American president of a South Side neighborhood council listed the closing of three storefront churches alongside such ordinary actions as mosquito abatement, lobbying for traffic signals, and the creation of a community playground as the group's achievements in 1963.[173] Gaudette said he was unaware of the level of animosity from the black middle class toward the poor until the storefront church campaign. They told him, "This is what we ran away from: the storefronts, the loud music, the taverns, the prostitutes." They had no intention of letting Chatham fall into the same pattern.[174]

Storefront churches were not the only religious institution targeted by Chathamites. In 1960, they made clear that they wanted no part of the Nation of Islam. The Nation's plan to build a religious and commercial center in the heart of Chatham not only frightened the remaining whites, but also aroused the fury of blacks who deemed the sect a serious threat to maintaining a stable, middle-class community. The Nation of Islam acquired a parcel of land in 1960, between Eighty-Fifth and Eighty-Sixth Streets, through the plotting of Alderman Thomas Keane, Mayor Daley's number two man.[175] Keane and his associates profited handsomely from city property that ended up in the hands of the Nation of Islam, which planned to build a temple, school, hospital, and shopping center (in 1974, a jury convicted Keane of using his position to buy tax-delinquent property and sell it at inflated prices).[176]

As word of the planned $20 million complex spread, residents organized vigorous opposition. Gaudette had never heard of the Nation of Islam, but area blacks called him to a gathering and told him, "We can't let them in!" They demanded that the CAPCC take action, and the group's leaders decided that the land was earmarked for a long-desired park. In truth, locals had previously rejected park plans because of fears of encouraging juvenile delinquency. Now, with the Nation of Islam devising a major development, Chathamites suddenly deemed a park a necessity.[177] The dispute flared into what the *Chicago Tribune* called "one of the bitterest neighborhood fights ever brought before the park board."[178] Gaudette fanned the flames. In testimony to park commissioners, Gaudette lost his "Irish temper" and referred to the Nation as an "extremist religious sect" and "zombies facing east." Other residents also associated the "verbal militancy" of the movement with violence. When bow-tied members came to park district meetings, the CAPCC recruited police living in the area to stare them down.[179]

Chathamites shunned the sect's goal of racial separation and its appeal among the poor and ex-convicts, and residents bombarded City Hall and the park district with complaints. After receiving an unsatisfactory response, every area neighborhood group coordinated to keep the Nation out.[180] The Nation of

Islam and its high-profile lawyers accused residents of racism. Attorney George Leighton, who had served as vice president of CAPCC, resigned from the group, stating, "This project is now being used to deprive people of the land because of their race and religion." He compared the CAPCC's tactics to those of the White Citizens' Councils in the Deep South. A Nation of Islam spokesman asserted that the reason the CAPCC "is siding with influential whites against us is that they hate Muhammad for teaching Negroes to wake up and start doing constructive things for themselves and their race."[181] Curiously, neither side mentioned the class conflict at the heart of the matter. Racial discord gripped the nation during this period, and Chicagoans were unable to make sense of the situation without using racial language. For instance, the *New Crusader*, a radical black newspaper, alleged that Chatham quashed the Nation's plan because Gaudette was a segregationist and that Taylor advocated "a program of racial self–Jim Crow."[182] Proponents of the park plan shot back, claiming this was simply a case of objecting to what they considered unsuitable land use. Chatham was now 90 percent black, they pointed out; race could not be the main concern.[183]

For middle-class Chathamites, the Nation of Islam was an unwelcome neighbor. The notoriety of the group and their expansive plans for the parcel probably heightened opposition, but locals had firm ideas about the class makeup of their community, and the Nation's working-class membership and radical ideology were not part of their vision. At a park district hearing, Taylor reminded commissioners that the community was changing, but 99 percent of residents supported a park rather than the Nation of Islam. The protest succeeded, as the park district annulled the sale and built a park on the plot, naming it after Nat King Cole.[184] Chathamites won, but they opened themselves up to bitter condemnations, which only continued as they stymied the construction of multifamily projects.

FLEXING POWER

The black population in the city grew by nearly one million people from 1940 to 1970, and African Americans continued to face a shortage of passable housing. Government authorities frequently dealt with this problem by constructing high-rises, and the black middle class made clear that they objected to subsidized developments in their vicinity.[185] Across the nation, urban politicians walked the tightrope of balancing needs for shelter against the objections of black homeowners, exposing racial fissures in the civil rights era.[186] Blacks were at a severe disadvantage in the placement of public housing. City council resolutions and Illinois state laws passed in the 1940s gave aldermen veto power over sites proposed by the Chicago Housing Authority (CHA), and white aldermen in outlying areas nixed sites in their wards because they believed public housing would bring in "negroes" and other "undesirable people." Thus, despite most of these wards having the only vacant land readily available, most projects were constructed in "blighted" districts requiring massive "urban renewal" that displaced African Americans, including many homeowners.[187] This resulted in highly visible, racialized, concentrated poverty, as the CHA warehoused the poor in austere projects. From 1955 to 1968, the CHA built or was in the process of constructing 10,256 family apartments. Of these, 10,193, or more than 99 percent, were located in black districts.[188]

Though battles over public housing existed within a discriminatory market, African American resistance to it should not be discounted as merely a side effect of racism. From the proposal of the first public housing project in the late 1930s through the 1960s, a segment of African American homeowners protested the government constructing them adjacent to their properties. These residents frequently maintained that they were responsible citizens, property investors, and taxpayers, thus distinguishing themselves from public housing recipients. The dual market squeezed middle-income blacks, and slum clearance did not serve their interests. They were also aware that segregationists safeguarded acres of vacant land in the city's outskirts and suburbs.[189] The poor bore the brunt of the shortage, but urban renewal and public housing also imperiled middle-class gains.

Black homeowners resisted public housing projects repeatedly after 1940, stirring controversy. In the 1950s and again in 1967, for example, the CHA proposed units for the Far South Side neighborhood of Morgan Park. In these instances, black residents joined white neighbors in opposition.[190] Civic leaders claimed that local schools were already jammed to capacity, and public housing would upset the fragile "racial balance" at Morgan Park High School. Wilson Frost, the black alderman of the Twenty-First Ward in 1967 and former CAPCC attorney, had lived in public housing himself in the early 1950s. Yet he also opposed the development, stating that while he was not against public housing per se, he did think it unsuitable for his ward.[191]

Black neighborhood groups attracted heavy criticism for their exclusionary contrivances, sometimes from within their own ranks. One community leader stated he could not justify his fight for the underprivileged throughout the city while endorsing a policy that "says that housing for the poor is off limits in my own community," while a letter writer to the *Defender* challenged anti–public housing forces to "see how some people [in the slums] are living. Before I would live like that I would go back South."[192] E. Franklin Frazier argued that some members of the black bourgeoisie were opposing low-cost public housing so that they could continue to exploit the scarcity as slumlords. "While their wives, who wear mink coats, 'drip with diamonds' and are written up in the 'society' columns of Negro newspapers, ride in Cadillacs," Frazier snapped, "their Negro tenants sleep on the dirt floors of hovels unfit for human habitation."[193] Among the city's worst slumlord offenders, according to investigations, were policy king Dan Gaines, who owned the "worst kept apartment building in Chicago," and the prominent Hansberry family, who reportedly preferred to pay small fines rather than fix their units.[194]

In Chatham, the CAPCC made its opposition to multifamily housing an organizational tactic and a point of pride.[195] In 1968, Milton Lamb of the CAPCC went on the black affairs television show *Our People* and boasted that his group, which had ten thousand members, had defeated the proposed construction of two seventeen-story high-rises in the area. "That's black power," host Jim Tilmon commented. "It's certainly a real pleasure to see someone is really making this black power work successfully." The host also asked Lamb, a loan officer for the black-owned Independence Bank, to respond to allegations by radicals that the middle class cared little for the black masses. "We don't mind being middle class so long as we don't lose our identity with those who are less fortunate," Lamb replied. "We do everything we can to try to instill in the minds and the attitudes of people who do not fit into this middle-class category the notion that they too can accomplish and they can have the same things we have for the most part."[196] The exchange reflected the diversity of thought in the late 1960s on how to strengthen political muscle. While prominent groups such as the Black Panthers offered a social democratic vision of community uplift, the CAPCC argued that their increasing clout constituted progress as role models, even if it kept the less affluent out. Racial pride and class exclusion mixed uneasily on the episode, as Lamb appeared along with state senator Richard Newhouse, who bashed the police department's "stop and frisk" policies, and the author James Baldwin, who proposed black police for black communities. Though class conflict simmered in Chatham, the show presented Lamb as another example of African American political and economic potency. While many blacks in Northern cities needed living space, the middle class simultaneously resented authorities unfairly steering projects to their communities.[197]

Racial subordination created distinct complications for the African American middle class, and they felt they had to defy forces threatening their neighborhoods. Community stabilization sent a clear signal to whites that solutions to the racial problem were not going to be purchased on the cheap by leaning on the black middle class. These conflicts accelerated class tensions, though, even as all involved understood that the dual market and site selection were key instigators.

A SUCCESSFUL FAILURE

The racial turnover on Chicago's South Side revealed a great deal about the limits of racial liberalism in the second half of the twentieth century. Attitudes on race were clearly changing, but many behaviors were not. Integrationist liberals hoped that city neighborhoods would foster civic spirit and multiracial democracy. Yet no matter if they fled immediately to the suburbs, smashed windows, or worked to steady the neighborhood, nearly all whites eventually left, and they did so mostly for racial reasons. The racial turnover not only damaged cities such as Chicago, but the chances for American pluralism.

Though scholars have added context to the trend of "white flight," the transformation of middle-class areas on the South Side of Chicago reasserts the primacy of race.[198] The white middle class said many of the "right" things on race, but "equity" vanquished "principles." The stakes were more than just home values; it was all the privileges that came with living in a solidly white community. While the black middle class was constantly on trial, the white middle class rarely had to answer for anything. When they left, observers called it an understandable reaction to changing conditions, absolving them of any larger societal responsibilities.[199] The integration of places such as Chatham would not have solved all the discriminatory structural problems facing black Chicagoans. However, it would have gone a long way toward reversing the tide of departures and setting an example of integrated living.

The dramas of neighborhood life did not end as whites exited. Enforced segregation and continued migration made decent accommodations a prized commodity. The black middle class, wary of putting too much emphasis on elusive goals for integration, strategically shifted to maintaining a long-sought prestigious enclave. Borders were porous, though, and it took tremendous attention to maintain a neighborhood's character. Opposition to large-scale developments opened the middle class to amplified charges that they were "Black Babbitts." The reality was much more complicated, as high-status African Americans acted locally while also serving as the leadership cadre of citywide civil rights activities. When faced with complex issues, middle-class blacks usually chose engagement, a decision that made them divisive on some issues and a unifying force in others. American society expected a lot of the black middle class. As African Americans would soon learn, the same would be true in the corporate workplace. The era of the "super negro" had dawned.

CHAPTER 4

BLACK AMERICANS
IN WHITE COLLARS

"I wanna be somebody so bad. But something is holding me back. Is it because I'm black?"

—Syl Johnson, "Is It Because I'm Black?" 1969[1]

In 1956, Charles "Chuck" Harrison began searching for an industrial design career in Chicago. Armed with a bachelor's degree from the Art Institute of Chicago and a master's from the Illinois Institute of Technology, the Louisiana-born African American heard from a friend that a firm was hiring, but when Harrison showed up the next day they suddenly no longer needed help. "It seemed I was the answer to everyone's employment shortage problems!" he recalled. Former college classmates working at the venerable Chicago retailer Sears, Roebuck & Co. urged him to apply for an opening. The department manager, Carl Bjorncrantz, had a liberal reputation, and Harrison filled out the application and took a battery of personnel tests. On his next visit, however, Bjorncrantz regretfully informed him, "Chuck, I have to tell you. It turns out I can't hire you. I know you need an explanation and I'm going to tell it like it is: Sears has an unwritten policy against hiring black people." Harrison admired his rare frankness, and Bjorncrantz, who later became a friend, assisted Harrison in finding freelance jobs. Smaller design firms hired him, but the pay was low and benefits scarce. Harrison's reputation grew, and word spread that he was an agreeable coworker who, in his words, "didn't bite anybody." In 1961,

Bjorncrantz called back. "Well Chuck, we can hire you now." Harrison accepted, becoming the first black in a white-collar position at the company.[2]

Though Harrison had "arrived" by breaking the race barrier at Sears, in many ways his struggles had just begun. In the 1960s and 1970s black Americans initiated changes in employment practices. Blacks pressed forward into previously lily-white workplaces, forcing often-reluctant white coworkers and supervisors to accept them. For African Americans to make structural changes, though, activists argued that they needed to integrate the corporate workplace at all levels. This push was not just about giving deserving applicants opportunities, but fostering a class of decision makers in Chicago that could elevate the race. This was a tall order, putting an added layer of responsibility on individuals straining for acceptance.

Scholars have generally examined the push against employment discrimination from the perspective of government initiatives and the reactions of corporations, thus minimizing the role played by the primary actors.[3] Revisionist historians maintain that corporations were much more liberal on racial matters than they have been given credit for and played a leading role in opening the American workplace to minorities. By the mid-1980s, one historian argues, large corporations were "affirmative action's most credible champions" and "a real and powerful force for racial progress in the United States."[4] Perhaps some corporations fit this description, but most were reluctant and moved sluggishly. Many integrated only after the urban uprisings and government pressure compelled them, and they generally viewed black managers as nominal hires.

Though minorities could not have entered the corporate world without the help of some enlightened white gatekeepers, it was the trailblazers who shouldered the burden. The focus on governmental and corporate policy changes obscures how blacks were not only the most reliable "champions" of affirmative action, they were also the instigators. With the exceptions of a select few progressive corporations, big businesses either rejected equal opportunity or tried to evade it. Even when company leaders agreed to make hiring minorities a priority, junior executives and supervisors were often stubbornly resistant to change.[5] Getting hired meant that the battles had just begun, as black personnel were routinely shunted into marginal careers, denied promotions, and viewed as the products of unearned privilege by resentful white colleagues.

The changes wrought by civil rights initiatives also accelerated intraracial turmoil present since the First Great Migration. Class tensions were heightened during the 1960s and 1970s as civil rights groups hoped that blacks in corporations could make changes to bring more equity to the African American community, while also fretting that the successful would abandon the less afflu-ent.[6] Black managers struggled to make their ranks more inclusive, but could only watch as Chicago's industrial sector declined dramatically, hitting black manual workers especially hard.[7] There was no singular attitude or experience for black white-collar workers; some saw themselves as a part of the civil rights movement, while others wanted to deemphasize race and focus on their careers. Many did appeal for collective black actions to counter white racism and privi-lege, but black pioneers had to tread lightly as they negotiated frequently hostile workplaces while dealing with issues of racial authenticity, personal stress, and the costs of "the good life." Though black radicals and nationalists often dis-missed the blacks in white collars as privileged and pampered, in truth theirs was a long, hard road.

WHITE COLLARS FOR WHITES ONLY

The opening of the corporate workplace was a crucial breakthrough for African Americans. White-collar work in America was largely a white preserve, espe-cially in the private sector. While government agencies and the media generally focused on the blatant racism of craft unions, professional discrimination was more indirect. In 1957, the black magazine *Color* reported that the Department of Labor's *Dictionary of Occupational Titles* listed seventeen thousand jobs, but African Americans could realistically aspire to fill about one hundred of these. Headlines in the black press such as "Employs Negro on White Collar Job" tes-tified to the rarity of an African American in a salaried station. While blacks in the white-collar workforce grew by 87 percent in the 1950s, by 1960 they still only made up 3.7 percent of these positions. This near exclusion became even more calamitous as the country gradually shifted to a service-sector economy. Careers in the professions, management, clerical work, and sales accounted for 97 percent of the total increase in employment from the mid-1940s to the mid-1960s.[8] Throughout the civil rights decades, black leaders grasped that they must break through in corporate America, or "remain peripheral."[9]

In Chicago, white-collar job orders had traditionally been marked as "restricted" to indicate that they were white-only. While this practice dissi-pated in the post–World War II era, in 1953 at least 20 percent of corporate employment requests explicitly excluded blacks. When the *Chicago Defender* surveyed the hiring practices of Chicago's downtown shopping stores that year, it uncovered clear prejudice. A State Street store manager stated, "You can't jam this [integration] business down people's throats," but "maybe in another generation" employment procedures would change. Another manager earnestly asked if there was a way to keep Negroes in the South from coming to Chicago.[10] In 1959 the director of the Chicago Commission on Human Relations stated that businesses "maintain a closed door policy" for blacks in management, and a year later Chicago employment bureaus reported that 98 percent of white-collar job orders excluded African Americans.[11] Even as migrants continued to stream north, in 1964 *Business Week* branded the city "a laggard in providing job opportunity for the Negro," as a "miniscule" number attained salaried status.[12]

Education was supposed to be the ticket to success in America, but for black Americans high school and college degrees usually did not translate into befitting careers. Famed Chicago companies were notorious for using college-educated blacks as elevator operators or shoe shiners. Those applying for better positions were either bluntly denied, or more polite personnel managers gave them the "run around."[13] In 1947, Robert Span Browne graduated with a coveted Master's in Business Administration from the University of Chicago and began what he called the "traumatic experience" of job hunting. He received not a single interview.[14] Browne returned to Chicago after a stint in Houston, where he did a "daily battle with racism," including an arrest stemming from an altercation after a police officer addressed him as "boy." He landed a research position with the Chicago Urban League and organized a campaign to get banks to hire blacks. "Obviously," he recalled, "this was a personal vendetta from my days at the University of Chicago." He got an interview with the chair of First National Bank, who said that though he refused to hire African Americans, he did support the Urban League by donating his used carpeting to them. Browne drove home "nearly in tears," feeling "demeaned."[15]

Many white decision makers held that blacks could not supervise whites, arguing that whites would chafe at the subversion of the racial hierarchy and that African Americans were deficient in leadership and managerial qualities. The stereotype held African Americans back from achieving positions ranging from foreman to football quarterback.[16] Albert Miller hit the job market with degrees in political science and sociology. An encyclopedia firm hired him over the phone and told him to come in to discuss salary, but Miller felt it necessary to inform the personnel manager that he was black. The manager responded that while he was not prejudiced, Miller would be supervising whites, and he would have to check with his bosses. The next day Miller could not reach the manager, and no one at the firm could find him. "I often wonder what goes on in the mind of a prospective white employer who refuses to hire me because I am a Negro," Miller related. "I often wonder whether or not he thinks about me as human."[17] For African Americans, educational achievements frequently led to profound disappointments.

SMALL VICTORIES

Black Americans began a concerted push for a fair share of salaried careers soon after the end of World War II. In the late 1950s Chicagoans turned to an old tactic to specifically target racial barriers in the higher-paying ranks. The Negro Labor Relations League, an assertive organization that successfully led local "Don't Buy Where You Can't Work" boycotts in the 1930s, reemerged to demand careers in Chicago banks. Many industries maintained a color line, but banking was among the most stringent. In 1960, blacks made up less than 1 percent of banks' labor force nationally. After picketing brought early victories, the emboldened League set a deadline of thirty days for seventeen Chicago area banks to consider black applications or face demonstrations. Several firms caved after the League distributed two hundred thousand pieces of literature, sent five thousand letters, and used a sound truck to broadcast their demands. Gradually, activists in Chicago and nationwide made these "Don't Save Where You Can't Earn" and similar boycotts effective, as managers of banks and retail stores openly expressed fears of protests. In 1966, President Lyndon Johnson responded by prohibiting banks from handling federal funds if they discriminated in employment. By 1969, blacks made up 6 percent of employees in the nation's 1,700 largest banks.[18]

Chicago civil rights groups kept up the pressure. In Chatham, the CAPCC demanded that the local bank either hire African Americans or black residents would withdraw their accounts en masse. The Chicago Commission on Human Relations assisted in placing white-collar blacks at nine firms in 1963, and a year later Edwin Berry of the Chicago Urban League boasted that the demands had translated into opportunities for the educated at the foremost banks, with inroads in insurance and advertising. "We have noted that almost every major firm in Chicago is asking for some talented and skilled Negroes,"

Berry noted. "The young, well-trained Negro now has a chance to get into the mainstream of American economic life."[19]

The yawning racial gap in unemployment rates caught attention, yet black leaders also underscored the shoddy treatment afforded to the educated and skilled. In 1959, the median income of white male college graduates exceeded that of their nonwhite peers by an astounding 81 percent.[20] Calls for educational equality were pointless if the rewards for degrees were menial positions. Despite a swelling black middle class, a Student Nonviolent Coordinating Committee activist in Chicago charged that "no Negro mother in Chicago can guarantee that her daughter will not grow up to scrub Miss Ann's toilet bowl."[21] In one city after another, black groups insisted that they sought not just jobs, but *careers* for African Americans.[22] The problem was not just unemployment, Chicago labor activist Addie Wyatt stated, but "underemployment and underpayment. There is systematic exploitation of dark people. No matter how many Ph.D.'s a person may have, he is still exploited because he cannot get rid of the 'D' for 'Dark.'"[23]

These posts meant more than a salary boost; they conferred dignity. In a short story by Chicago author Cyrus Colter, the protagonist is proud that he "wore a necktie on the job, and made his inventory rounds with a ball-point pen and clipboard." His clerical position paid less than the Chicago steel mills, "but that kind of work was no good, undignified; coming home on the bus you were always so tired you went to sleep in your seat, with your lunch pail in your lap."[24] A twenty-five-year-old migrant from Mississippi with a fourth-grade education arrived in Chicago in 1953 and landed decent work as a hod carrier. For his son, though, he wanted "a clean job, to work in an office, to wear a clean shirt every day, and to be able to clean up a little after work so that he didn't have to ride home on the bus dirty and smelly."[25] Black protests over access to careers and education parity were not just about gaining immediate access, but securing intergenerational mobility. The white collar symbolized the triumph over relegation to backbreaking work.[26]

Blacks widely shared a desire for upward mobility into the white-collar ranks, but most instead realized that their lot in Chicago was not improving. Tensions festered as Chicago's political and economic power structure ignored black calls for inclusion. The riots of the 1960s were a visceral expression of ghetto dwellers' infuriation with how the city's veneer of liberalism veiled plantation politics, inhabitable living conditions, police brutality, and economic stagnation.[27] On the West Side, industrial jobs fled to the suburbs alongside white residents, leaving black residents confined in areas beset by unemployment and dissatisfaction. The West Side experienced racial conflagrations in 1965 and 1966, and the frustration culminated with a major disturbance after the death of Martin Luther King in 1968.[28] Meanwhile, the South Side remained relatively calm, in part because it was home to many of those finally getting a taste of integrated workplaces, better living, and political clout.

Chicago's business and political leaders responded to the uprisings by furthering the integration of upwardly mobile blacks. Company executives formed the Chicago Merit Employee Committee and claimed that equal opportunities in employment would be the decisive factor in stemming future riots.[29] The disturbances showed that Chicago needed an expansive desegregation plan and that ghetto areas required large and immediate structural investments. Instead, white elites wanted an empowered black middle class to, as one jaded observer noted, "discipline its unruly elements."[30]

By looking to the middle class to quell the unrest, whites badly underestimated the depth of support for radical measures. Glidden manager Percy Julian dressed down as an "ordinary Negro" to comprehend the anger bubbling up in ghetto areas. He noted that "stable" blacks were caught in the "web of bitterness" and listening to militant voices. "Painfully," he admitted, "I realized that there is a bit of Stokely Carmichael in nearly every American Negro, even in me."[31] Middle-class African Americans did not participate in the riots, but they often endorsed the sentiments. Many were no longer just comfortable attaining a degree of affluence and becoming an invisible buffer between the black poor and whites.[32] A black executive at Northern Illinois Gas got into a heated exchange with his boss over the riots, nearly souring their relationship. "But he had the problem, not me. Things eventually calmed down, and we ended up with a newer understanding of each other."[33] On a personal level, blacks appreciated that they often benefited from racial militancy. "Demonstrations do help," an account executive at a Chicago public relations firm noted. "They call attention to what people are trying to get across. Out of the Watts riots in Los Angeles have come many, many opportunities."[34] As panicked companies scrambled in response, blacks seized the moment. "The disorders in Chicago helped me," the owner of a new Anheuser-Busch distributorship remarked. He advised the young to begin their business careers in cities where the substantial racial disorders occurred.[35] The educated and qualified were especially fed up with the glacial pace of integration in corporate settings, and the threat of violence enhanced their bargaining power. A black banker said that without urban riots, "the bastards won't move. [The black community needs] some more Rap Browns and Stokely Carmichaels."[36]

The black middle-class response to riots was opportunistic in part because they knew that they could no more control the discontent than could the police. The uprisings were shocking to whites ignorant of the unbearable ghetto conditions, but the black middle class lived in close proximity to these areas. They saw the seething anger and realized how little they could do about it. A "leadership vacuum" existed in ghetto areas, the *Chicago Defender* noted in 1965, and was likely only be filled from within. The average black rioter associated the black middle class with the city's power structure and was distrustful of their shopworn assurances that improvements would only arrive through their access to white power brokers. As a letter writer noted, "All economic gains made in the civil rights movement have benefited only a few chosen individuals, and the masses of Negroes still live in the ghettoes," where they are "no better off than they were 10 years ago."[37] The black middle class was aware of this disparity, but also knew that the fires burned because of white decisions and were not about to "keep a lid" on situations for them. In 1968, blacks were 20 percent of Cook County's population, but held less than 3 percent of the county's nearly eleven thousand policy-making positions in private and public institutions.[38] If African Americans were to make a difference for the race, they needed more of these spots.

Black activists kept the heat on corporations to open salaried occupations, emboldened by white fears of continued uprisings. Many in positions of authority could trace their appointments as concessions to groups like Operation Breadbasket and Operation PUSH, both of which were spearheaded by civil rights leader Jesse Jackson.[39] For instance, in 1972 the Schlitz Brewing Company and Operation PUSH signed a historic agreement guaranteeing the black community a larger share of the firm's business, jobs, and profits. Schlitz made more than 15 percent of its sales to blacks nationally and was eager to avoid a boycott. Among other stipulations, the accord opened 185 white-collar jobs to African Americans and ensured a black person would fill at least one position on the board of directors.[40] Miller Brewing agreed to a covenant a year later, pledging to double the number of black managers and institute an internship program at black colleges.[41] As a black public relations director noted, a company doing business in Chicago needed to "be aware" of Jesse Jackson.[42]

CORPORATE INTRANSIGENCE

Even as they made gains, black applicants had good reason to doubt the earnestness of corporate America. Studies showed that most corporations were not

interested in equal opportunity but instead in "getting by" and "achieving min-
imum compliance" in order to avoid public relations disasters and government
sanctions.[43] The media dubbed 1964 the "year of the interview" as companies
hurried to previously ignored black colleges, but *Business Week* reported that
skepticism of the private sector led many black graduates to government posts
where they traditionally got a better shake from civil service.[44] An estimated 60
percent of black professional workers in Chicago in the 1960s were employed
in the public sector, compared to only 22 percent of whites.[45] While more
companies advertised themselves as "Equal Opportunity Employers," African
Americans referred to the help wanted section as the "funny pages."[46] They
recalled instances where they had shown up for interviews, only to be told "that
position has already been filled"—and then walked out of the personnel office
past a line of white prospects.[47] As an activist in Chicago noted in 1972, companies often made a "big to do" about recruiting at historically black colleges and
universities, but their actual results were meager.[48]

Companies were caught off guard by the black push to join corporate
America. Executives delighted in technical and production innovations, but
most of these same men were overwhelmingly conservative when it came to
social and political matters. Textbooks and management training assured
executives that certain groups were just not suited for Mahogany Row. Chester
Barnard's *The Functions of the Executive*, a staple of college management courses
in its eighteenth printing in 1968, stressed that decision makers must have
"social compatibility" and that minorities lacked the "fitness" for organizational
collaboration. Barnard instructed that irrespective of competence, social out-
siders "cannot be promoted or selected . . . because they 'do not fit.'"[49] In essence,
Barnard advised that companies create managerial ranks made up of well-educated Anglo-Saxon Protestant men. A study of top executives in 1975 found
that the upper ranks were becoming *more* homogeneous. They were exclusively
male and Caucasian, predominantly Protestant, Republican, of Eastern US ori-
gin, and almost all came from affluent families and a handful of select universities. As one critic quipped, corporate officers were "so inbred they resemble the
emperors of ancient Rome."[50]

Executives had varied reactions to the civil rights movement, yet most
remained deeply reluctant to bring African Americans and other minorities
aboard. Oblivious executives simply denied that racism existed, while others
recognized it at other firms but were "virtually blind" to discrimination in
their own companies.[51] A consultant candidly stated that "for many businesses,
an equal employment opportunity program is unpleasant, annoying, and

expensive." Recalcitrant executives made token hires and then privately asked, "When will they stop? How far will the civil rights people go?" Many were perplexed over why groups such as Jesse Jackson's PUSH fervently pressed them when they thought blacks already had made momentous advancements. The more hidebound business leaders simply fell back on their existing stereotypes to resist making changes.[52] "Let's face it," former Avis CEO Robert Townsend wrote. "The vast majority of corporations are still operating with dice loaded against Jews, black people, and women of all races and creeds."[53]

Businessmen provided a host of explanations for their intransigence. Common in the 1950s and early 1960s was the "third party" argument, where the executive claimed that while he was not personally racist, his customers and employees would not stand for blacks in white-collar positions. Worries over negative reactions to black employees virtually barred them from being hired in "sophisticated contact work," including banking, sales, and advertising. The ban served two purposes: it justified exclusion while distancing employers from its causes. "Personally I don't care if a man is black or white," a personnel manager declared. "But the man I hire is going to have to deal with a lot of people who would be uncomfortable if he were Negro. So I won't hire a Negro." Another cautious executive claimed employing minorities in contact positions would also make customers uneasy. While he admitted he could not cite a specific example, "it's just that we deal with so *many* companies that there is bound to be someone who feels this way."[54] Critics pointed out that managerial fears were often overblown, and integrationists urged executives not to pander to the lowest common denominator. As a *Harvard Business Review* writer noted, "Just because a Negro salesman can't sell bed sheets to the Ku Klux Klan does not mean that he can't sell sheets."[55]

More enlightened executives contended that while they wanted to hire blacks, there were just not enough in the labor pool. There was some credence to this claim. The legacies of racism produced educational shortcomings. College-educated African Americans preparing for careers that were open to them continued to train in the traditional professions of preaching and teaching. Throughout the 1960s and early 1970s, companies truly did have difficulty recruiting in science and technology, as historically black colleges produced only about 200 graduates in these fields per year.[56] In 1973, over 44,000 new engineers graduated from college, but only 405 were black.[57]

However, many executives pushed this argument too far, using questionable test results and doubts over qualifications as cover. Firms surveyed by *U.S.*

News & World Report in 1963 maintained they could not even locate African Americans suitable for entry-level, white-collar jobs. Civil rights activists scoffed at these reports, noting that employees could be easily trained, while black employment agencies declared that they had ready applicants for every kind of position. Though a 1963 *Business Week* article stated that the principal hurdle for black job seekers was "not prejudice based on the color of his skin but his lack of preparation," paradoxically the article also revealed that only 11 percent of whites with a year or more of college were laboring in low-skill, low-paid jobs, while 33 percent of blacks were confined to these stations, showing that many corporations were underutilizing black workers already on the payroll. In addition, a 1972 study showed that even if education levels were equal in the North, black workers would still be hired at levels a full third below parity with whites. When directors at the Chicago-based Motorola Corporation said they could not find qualified black candidates, Urban League Executive Director Edwin Berry lambasted them, saying the company "has been going almost nowhere in hiring Negroes for white-collar jobs. All Motorola has to do is issue job orders. It's that simple."[58] Contrary to popular opinion, the educational requirements for almost all white-collar jobs dropped from 1940 to 1970 due to the sector's expansion and a tight labor market.[59] While there was a supply-and-demand mismatch in employment for certain technical positions, companies aggravated the problem by failing to make and implement diligent recruitment, training, and promotion policies.

The civil rights drive called into question the entire merit-based edifice that corporate executives had supposedly created. As managers continued to insist that there simply were not enough competent African Americans to fill salaried openings and that affirmative action meant lowering standards, several candid executives admitted that the criteria for many administrative jobs were either so arbitrary or hard to define that any rationale could be used. Businesses overemphasized credentials when most duties were learned on the job, and the preponderance of corporate managers held titles not directly related to their major field of study in college. Most galling were companies such as Equitable Life Insurance, which claimed it could not find any black insurance salespeople even though that career had long been a point of pride for African Americans. Though personnel directors swore by it, "qualified" turned out to have decidedly subjective connotations, and employment officers divulged that there was no mixture of education, experience, and personality that predicted how an applicant would fare. Some top executives had themselves risen through the ranks

despite what might be judged as inadequate credentials and were thus hesitant
to characterize in detail what it meant to be "qualified." Aside from technical
abilities, one expert divulged, "'qualified' often means the measure of the human
chemistry that exists between interviewer and candidate." When pressed, other
executives confessed that the business world's boasted meritocracy had never
existed, but it was necessary to maintain the facade, for as a white vice president
of corporate affairs noted, "It's the myth that keeps the system going."[60]

Businesses that made a genuine effort to recruit and train African Americans
learned that the task was not nearly as insurmountable as some executives considered it. Firms that moved from a policy of "non-discrimination" to "affirmative action" discovered that after they hired blacks in jobs matching their
qualifications, they received an abundance of black applications. History taught
minority job seekers that openings advertised in the mainstream press were
"white" jobs, but when corporations tapped into the "Negro grapevine" of the
black media, churches, the Urban League, and historically black colleges, they
noticeably improved the size and composition of the prospective talent pool.[61]
Companies also hired black recruiters, putting African American job seekers
at ease and boosting minority hiring. After a company transferred one black
manager to the personnel office, his new coworkers constantly told him that "we
can't find any blacks" and carped over orienting and training the few African
Americans they had taken on. The manager pointed out the obvious: the personnel office had no black employees or black input in training programs. He
then set out on the recruiting trail. "I went out and found so many blacks in each
of the job areas they wanted that they had to force me to stop."[62] Entrepreneurs
also formed black-owned employment services in Northern cities, starting their
own networks within the corporate world.[63] These firms worked to dispel the
myth of the shortage of qualified African Americans. "Tell me about a job opening," a Chicago executive recruiter asserted, "and I'll find a black professional
who can meet its requirements."[64]

LIFE ON THE INSIDE

By the late 1960s, significant numbers of Africans Americans occupied offices
once off-limits to them. The declaration by an American Motors executive
that "the Negro is frequently unemployable except in the most menial jobs"
was proven false throughout the civil rights push, as black workers showed

themselves to be more than capable in a host of positions.[65] As a 1968 television special *A Black Man in a White Collar* related, it was a "new day" for the educated, and the time of being offered the "mop and broom" was over.[66] Blacks in salaried managerial positions went up 49 percent from 1962 to 1969. Almost all minorities acknowledged that affirmative action helped impel this transformation, but once inside corporate America their trials had just begun. Though both employers and fellow African Americans often expected them to "represent the race" and "set a good example," blacks in the salaried ranks were far from homogeneous. They varied in attitudes, goals, feelings toward the civil rights movement, and the significance of their racial identities.[67]

Many educated African Americans had been impatiently waiting and planning for opportunities in the mainstream. Despite centuries of racism, youths were often told by their elders to work hard, stay out of trouble, and opportunities will come. In contrast to E. Franklin Frazier's scathing view of the black middle class living in a world of "make-believe," parents were grooming their children for the changes ahead. What Frazier saw as self-delusion was considered dress rehearsal by some African Americans. As one college graduate remembered, *Ebony* magazine's articles detailing corporations selecting blacks for junior executive posts "was like hearing Jackie Robinson had hit another home run." Many young African Americans were cautiously optimistic and eager to meet the challenges ahead. As the first black hire in research at Chicago's General Foods in 1962 stated in *Ebony*, "There's no limit to how far I can go in the company."[68]

Confidence could only go so far, and corporate life was foreign for most people unfamiliar with the mores. Race added an extra level of pressure and discomfort. Though radical militants accused the middle class of blending into white society, as Albert Murray observed, "The minute a Negro moves into any integrated situation in the U.S. he becomes blacker than ever before."[69] Employers and coworkers often expected black managers to be "super-negroes." As a researcher found, whites wanted them to "combine pride and humility, wisdom and receptiveness, strength and tolerance, soberness and humor, aggressiveness and patience, ambition and satisfaction, and all this simultaneously and in delicate balance." Some of these expectations set up blacks to fail, and employers could claim that they had tried to diversify, but the hire had come up short.[70] Pioneers knew the spotlight was on them and that they usually would not be measured by the same standards as white peers.

Many encountered awkward interpersonal dealings. A marketing specialist noted that black hires were "constantly called on to interpret actions of all Negroes—the janitor to the secretary to Whitney Young to Rap Brown."[71] Interviewers and coworkers sometimes sincerely believed they were putting blacks at ease by asking them about "negro issues," but African Americans often wondered if they should tell them what they wanted to hear. Most did not consider themselves authorized to give the "black opinion" and blanched at the idea that blacks all thought alike on racial matters. "I developed the feeling that I was considered a black first and an individual second," a manager recalled. He also felt that he was constantly "on stage" for whites at the office, as they not only wanted to see how he would perform but also how he would react to racially sensitive situations in and out of the workplace.[72] An analyst at a suburban Chicago gas firm agreed, stating, "As a black man I feel we are constantly on a proving ground. Work performance is scrutinized more for blacks than for whites."[73] Management occupations emphasized the complicated equilibrium of individual achievement and teamwork. For African Americans this balance was even more knotty. Supervisors scrutinized their personal performance closely, and the employees knew that they were a test case for racial integration. It was a heavy cross to bear.

Predictably, fraught situations came up often. Entire levels of intimate and professional integration involved delicate negotiations. An African American man promoted to stock supervisor at Carson Pirie Scott was lauded for his ability to fit in, but his boss warned him about "integrating too fast," because white associates were unnerved by his invitations to join him for coffee breaks.[74] Due to these admonitions, black pioneers walked on eggshells, at once a part of the company and yet unsure if a casual gesture could violate racial taboos. Even senior black executives were cognizant they could be "put in their place" at any moment, whether through building security guards unnecessarily checking their credentials or being repeatedly mistaken for the delivery man.[75] Many black employees felt that they stuck out yet were invisible in so many ways.

White responses to black coworkers ranged from awkwardness to downright hostility. Even most liberals were clueless about how to treat, act around, or talk to blacks. At Sears, Chuck Harrison resigned himself to the realization that racist mind-sets were "ingrained" among most of his white coworkers. "Every day somebody said something out of order," Harrison recalled. "In most cases, they didn't even know what they were saying."[76] Some were transparently antagonistic. One black woman's exhilaration that she had been able to find work quickly after graduation turned to dismay when a male coworker cracked, "Well, that fills our quota for this month." Likewise, another new hire felt the prestige of his graduate degrees in engineering and business melt away on his first day as a coworker remarked, "Uh oh, there goes the neighborhood."[77] African American workers were almost certain to encounter the "nigger" joke, and a black manager noted that telling an ethnic gag was a "kind of ticket of admission to management meetings." Management consultants warned black novices that racial humor was inevitable, and they must walk the tightrope between coming off as the "Chairman of the Black Panther Party" or "Step 'n' Fetchit." Offending coworkers were frequently embarrassed in retrospect, but the damage was done. Some executives were unrepentant, pining for the days when their privileges included putting minorities and women "in their place" through risqué humor. A chagrined former executive at a Big Eight accounting firm recalled that in his day a business lunch meant a "good meal and good conversations with men of your own ilk. Now if you want to tell a joke, you have to look around the table first. One of your partners may be Negro, Spanish, a Jew or a woman. You know how sensitive they are."[78] For white male chauvinists, diversity meant a loss of their cherished camaraderie and signaled the end of the old order.

Once hired, black employees still often encountered the bigotry of low expectations and the belief that they had taken the position from a more qualified candidate. In the early 1960s, critics engaged in a "frontlash" against policy changes, alleging that employers were engaging in "bias against whites" and "reverse discrimination."[79] Employers went to extraordinary lengths to appease white employees during this period of transition. Personnel directors suggested that black hires should start in jobs beneath their capabilities to "insure peace."[80] Occasionally, executives thought the best approach to integration was "trial by fire," where the black novices were given the most challenging jobs to prove themselves to white coworkers.[81] Most blacks, however, experienced the opposite. Supervisors viewed them as "experiments" that needed the kid-gloves treatment. A vice president of human relations at Motorola admitted "we're attempting to place Negroes in white-collar jobs where they'll be a credit to their race."[82]

Too regularly, black recruits were company "showpieces," hired to blunt criticism from both civil rights activists and the hostility of white employees. In the early 1960s civil rights groups accused businesses of slotting blacks as mail room chiefs and in other managerial stations that were out of sight but could be touted when investigators came. Similarly, they worried that hires were merely "concessions." *Industrial Management* magazine remarked that companies sought the "instant negro" to work in "some nebulous capacity" without actual responsibilities. Comedian Dick Gregory joked that he saw a sign advertising

"Hertz Rent-a-Negro."[83] While broad-minded company executives expressed a genuine desire to hire minorities out of fairness, others were merely trying to avoid losing customers and government contracts. "Frankly and confidentially," a recruiter told the *Wall Street Journal*, "it's window dressing." Black managers were often uncertain of their roles and insecure over their status. "The worst things about being a black in the corporate world," an executive noted, "is that you never really know for sure whether they employed you for your color or your abilities, or whether you will be allowed to have any real influence."[84] One manager felt he was still on the outside despite his title. White employers hired him and other blacks because the Equal Employment Opportunity Commission was "looking at their ass and they know it," but these token workers were not decision-makers. "Sharing sensitive information or real company politics is not required by law," he noted. "And seeing me as a real person isn't either."[85] The underutilized employees collected their paychecks and seethed, knowing that they could not demonstrate their full capabilities.

Civil rights activists pushing for more black influence at the top echelons were disappointed as career paths regularly stalled. Most corporate promotions were not "posted" for application, and selections happened behind closed doors. In the cautious confines of the corporation, advancement came on the basis of "don't rock the boat," and even progressive firms struggled to break managers of discriminatory practices.[86] In Chicago, blacks held less than 5 percent of white-collar jobs in 1967, and about 80 percent of these were positions at the lower end of the salary scale.[87] *Ebony* reported that one firm suffered from 400 percent turnover among black professionals, as they believed they would be forever relegated to "paper shuffling."[88]

Top positions were especially out of reach. In 1967 the Illinois Fair Employment Practices Commission noted a "clear trend" in decreasing complaints over racial restrictions in hiring, but a sharp uptick in grievances by minority workers over training and upgrading. Whereas in earlier years some educated blacks were content just to have landed a salaried post, by the late 1960s they were demanding equal chances for promotions. A sampling of black executives in Chicago rated "opportunity for advancement" as the most significant factor in choosing their current job, with these prospects even outpacing salary concerns.[89] Cases involving advancement were hard to verify, and enforcement agencies generally focused on discrimination at the entry level. Yet, as a member of Chicago's Human Rights Commission learned, "Supervisors can, in subtle ways, throw blocks at a Negro."[90] In 1970, only about 25 blacks nationally had achieved vice presidencies in large corporations, and they were virtually nonexistent on corporate boards of directors.[91] A decade later, a survey of 13,000 managers ranked as department heads or higher by the Chicago Urban League found only 117 African Americans. After seeing the study, the Labor Department's Weldon Rougeau was dismayed. A long-time activist, he had graduated from Loyola University Chicago being expelled from Southern University after repeated arrests at civil rights demonstrations. "Deep in their hearts," he said, "many whites still can't accept the idea of equal opportunity."[92] For black workers, figuring out whether their employer would give them a chance was an integral part of their success equation.

Frustration became more evident as black careers stagnated. In 1972, a federal government study reported widespread unhappiness from American workers, and "the most dissatisfied group of American workers ... is found among young black people in white-collar jobs."[93] Earning a spot in the corporate world was not necessarily translating into fulfilling careers and decision-making authority. A survey of black managers concluded that 60 percent were more qualified in terms of formal education, technical skills, and managerial experience than their immediate supervisor.[94]

The problems of advancement persisted throughout the 1970s. In a 1978 letter to Continental Bank executives, a Chicago Urban League official thanked the bank for integrating but stressed the importance of upgrading more minorities in "professional industrial environments. If we are not placing our grads in this area, we are not meeting our goal."[95] Corporate spokespeople often retorted that promotions took time and that many black managers lacked experience. African American executives were skeptical about this gradualism. "People used to joke about 'the spook by the door'—the one black employee that many companies hired and put in a visible position to show they weren't prejudiced," Clark Burrus, a black senior vice president at Chicago's First National Bank, said in 1980. "If things have changed since then, I sure haven't seen it." Burrus, a mentor for African American professionals who had willed his way from handling the books for jazz singer Sarah Vaughan to becoming Chicago's first black city comptroller, expressed dismay that he was often the only black face in boardrooms.[96] Indeed, a 1979 survey of blacks in corporate America found that only 13 percent felt that they had a "high" chance to advance in their place of work.[97]

By hiring black managers to prevent future urban riots, corporations placed African Americans off the "executive escalator" from the start. Regardless of their training, companies shunted them into what one commentator called "The Relations": community, industrial, public, and personnel. While these could be important positions, they were not tied to the revenue-producing cores that prepped managers for the senior ranks.[98] As a black management trainee asked sardonically, "Who ever heard of a chief executive who got his job because he was brilliant in urban affairs?" African American employees worried that outright exclusion had been replaced by more understated forms of discrimination where companies, as one executive stated, "shelve their black employees and forget about them." Edward Williams, a black vice president at Chicago's Harris Trust & Savings, noted that "companies remain unwilling to put blacks in sensitive positions where they haven't been tested, where they can affect the bottom line. Better to put them in personnel or urban affairs, where the worst they can do is give out too many tickets to a baseball game."[99] As one black job seeker remarked, "I don't want to be hired as an engineer and then find myself assigned as the company's representative to Plans for Progress or some other government-sponsored program in the equal opportunity bag. Above all, deliver me from presiding over the company table at the annual Urban League dinner!"[100] Black employees had come a long way from the days of college-educated elevator operators, but they still worried about company motives. Several managers discovered that their supposed elevations meant tamping down black rank-and-file dissent or firing disgruntled workers because supervisors were afraid to deal with racial discontent.[101]

Most had no interest in doing company dirty work, and not surprisingly, many African Americans were disappointed with these "relations" positions. In a 1972 study, 63 percent of black managers in race-related departments reported low job satisfaction, while 80 percent of blacks in profit-making branches indicated high satisfaction. Seven years later, Urban League studies discovered that workers in "staff" positions removed from the company bottom line were much more likely to feel blocked from fully achieving their goals. Possibly because so many African Americans ended up in these posts, the survey found that the majority of black managers thought they were in marginal positions in their respective companies.[102] The writer Orde Coombs, hired in 1968 at Western Electric as a "Senior Public Relations Specialist" even though he had no familiarity with the field, noted that he "could have done the job with both eyes closed and my pen between my teeth." His task, he soon detected, was to "unwrinkle the public face of the company," a post that only reinforced his belief that he was a showpiece for the corporation.[103] This marginality also meant black managers occupied precarious perches. As sociologist Sharon Collins shows, the "functional segregation" of black professionals "locked them into limited and fragile career paths" as economic downturns and the conservative backlash against civil rights made these jobholders "economically expendable."[104] In the 1980s, as corporations merged and looked to get "lean," black managers were more vulnerable to layoffs as corporations deemed relations departments unessential.[105]

Yet while companies were spurred to hire in reaction to racial tensions and race politics were an ever-present reality at the workplace, corporate cultures expected blacks to conform and leave their "blackness" behind. Sometimes companies took this color preference quite seriously, hiring only light- and brown-skinned African Americans. Others stressed selecting hires with compatible personalities.[106] Whites extolled black employees who discarded supposed negative "black" traits. For instance, associates of an African American manager at Carson Pirie Scott were so impressed by his drive and talents that they "never [thought] of him as being 'colored.'" Not only had this employee became an honorary white man, but his coworkers evidently believed that ambition and skill were not common black characteristics. Even well-meaning tutorials for the aspiring at times trafficked in broad stereotypes to encourage cultural whitening, such as warning against keeping "colored people's time" and stating that in order to succeed they must eliminate "jive behavior."[107] The message was straightforward: employees would need to adapt to white standards if upper management was going to regard them as "team players." A degree of nonconformity by whites could be idiosyncratic, a black banking vice president noted, but "anything that's different when you're black just makes you stand out more."[108]

Activists wanted black managers and executives to assist with racial uplift, but companies usually expected them to keep their viewpoints on civil rights and black power to themselves. As *Ebony* magazine observed in 1966, corporate America was looking for the "acceptable Negro." As in the past, "the white man is still putting a premium on docility and obedience—not only on the job but in everyday life."[109] Corporations obsessed with how beginners would "fit" wanted black personnel who left their politics out of the office. A brochure written by the director of personnel at Owens-Illinois counseled that the first minority workers "must be selected carefully" for "appraisal of the person's attitude as well as abilities. People with a chip on the shoulder should be avoided."[110] Managers learned to avoid the tag "militant" as if it were the plague, as it "will get all kinds of doors shut for you." One corporate attorney had his career turn for the worse after he was elected spokesperson for the company's black caucus. "I did the speaking and after that the word was out on me," he recalled. "I was a militant, I hated white people, you should have heard the rumors that were spread on me." The silence on civil rights issues was especially difficult because whites often ran to black workers for their "take" as the dramas unfolded in the media. Yet African Americans needed to keep their opinions close to their vests, especially when anger bubbled up. "One thing they wouldn't deal with is an angry black man," a manager said about his supervisors, "so you had to be very careful even about the tone of your voice."[111] While black Americans often called for white-collar African Americans to be community leaders, their employers urged them to mute their activism.

Black corporate pioneers had mixed responses to these competing demands. Though they usually conceded that racism existed, ardent individualists urged others to underplay race and move forward. They assumed African Americans could only rise by maintaining a positive attitude, assimilating, and persevering. Advancing "the race" was not their priority, at least in any explicit fashion. One manager said he had thrived by staying aloof from "movements and organizations" and thinking of himself as "an individual, not as a classification." While he recognized that he had encountered racism, "I don't let discrimination stand in my way. . . . Now my reputation goes before me."[112] Richard Jackson, the vice president of engineering at Chicago's Gits Brothers, counseled his peers to adapt to white professional norms. He dismissed "black power" as a futile distraction. "There is only one form of power and that's green power, and the only way the black guy is going to do anything is to get associated with that power."[113] Though these managers seemed out of step with the cultural currents of the era, in some cases this style of resolve may have been the only effective way of flourishing, or at least surviving, on the job. Many firms made it quite clear to black employees that malcontents and militants would be dismissed or buried.

In contrast, others scolded their assimilationist peers, insisting that they had larger duties. They objected to the notion that equal opportunity meant measuring oneself by white standards and conforming to white styles. One manager worried his company was stripping him of his sartorial choices, humor, and identity, the "existential things that are part of your racial heritage."[114] As many critics had warned, integration often appeared to be a one-way street. A purchasing agent for Kaiser Aluminum and Chemical believed that "the problems concerning blacks in private industries are white problems. It's about time the whites went through some of the changes, rather than sending us through them all."[115] The industrial psychologist Stuart Taylor argued that it was mentally unhealthy to be black while trying to be "white" at the same time. He advised African American employees that they would be both more productive and at ease if they stayed true to themselves.[116]

Yet for many black white-collars, preserving their black cultural characteristics and advancing up the ladder were incompatible. A Chicago banking supervisor sensed a strong pull to sit next to other African Americans in the cafeteria so he could "'feel black' for just 45 minutes." But he did not want coworkers to "refer to it as the 'black table'" and believed that he had to sit with whites. "This is unnatural; it is unnatural to turn yourself away from that with which you feel most comfortable."[117] Listening to coworkers discuss water sports and skydiving at the all-important after-hours events left a weary black manager "bored as hell," but he knew that he would have to endure these situations if he expected to be promoted.[118] As Bayard Rustin noted, much of the criticism of middle-class blacks came from peers dealing with their own guilt and anxieties over racial authenticity. "The lower classes," Rustin noted, "are too busy trying to become middle class to feel guilty about their aspirations." Yet even Rustin acknowledged that many of the successful felt "uneasily suspended" between the black masses and white elites, while simultaneously trying to please both groups.[119] Racial identity struggles became even more complex as black managers tried to decipher the corporate world's unwritten rules.

THE SHADOW CORPORATION

One of the most confounding and discriminatory elements of corporate life was the "shadow corporation." This informal structure existed in nearly every large company, though one would never find it in the employee handbook. It was the after-work schmoozing, the gatherings at country clubs, and the networking that not only played a fundamental role in company business, but in Chicago's power structure as well. Blacks achieved more managerial posts, but their inability to crack into select circles showed the limits of their abilities to make substantial changes.

Membership in exclusive clubs was nearly a prerequisite for success in the corporate world, placing the member and his family among the local elite. For generations, Americans announced that they had "made it" through acceptance to the country club. The country club was more than a place to broadcast status, though, as it was also vital to business dealings and contacts. By the 1950s, businessmen made country clubs as important to operations as the adding machine and Rolodex. "The club is really a kind of grease, like a fraternity," a Chicago executive stated. "It makes it easier for you to pick up business."[120] The club was also a prime site to angle for jobs and promotions, as most businesses hired according to the referral system.[121]

The problem of the club became more acute as the pace of integration sped up and companies struggled to bring black workers into the entirety of corporate life. Oftentimes, their initial responses were clumsy at best, transparently discriminatory at worst. For example, executives at Chicago's American National Bank decided to keep their Christmas outing at a white-only country club and give cash to black employees barred from attending.[122] As *Ebony* magazine noted, blacks were blocked from making strides in salaried positions not only by outright prejudice but also by "subtle detours" that barred them from membership in business organizations and clubs. "Because a junior executive job depends largely upon acceptance in country club circles, few Negro employees become junior executives."[123] A manager candidly admitted that he used to play basketball, but he took up golf after realizing that staff meetings would end with someone saying, "Let's work out the details on the 19th green." On the course, "I got into the free-flowing communications. I learned a lot by socializing . . . things I never learned in school."[124]

Calculating executives used informal criteria to mask discrimination, claiming that they were not denying jobs and promotions because of race, but because African Americans were "different" and did "not fit well into the necessary social aspects of the job."[125] As late as 1980, Bernard Anderson, a black economist with the Rockefeller Foundation, said that the paucity of African Americans in the executive ranks was due to unfamiliarity with "corporate culture": the social contacts, corporate politicking, and technical expertise that propelled careers.[126] While this was certainly true, black employees were deficient in these areas because of the racism inherent in the corporate club system. White male executives at ease with people like them deflected attempts by others to join their elite circles.

In addition, black and white managers did not live and travel together, as discrimination created extra barriers, diminished interracial socialization, and scuttled promotions. From 1958 to 1969, Chicago gained a mere 37,000 jobs, while its suburbs added a whopping 584,000.[127] Capital flight was especially pronounced on the majority-black South and West Sides, which actually lost jobs during this economic expansion.[128] A steel industry executive charged that this was not just the result of market factors, as many firms were moving to the suburbs "in order to assure themselves of a white workforce."[129] The "Chicago Wall" meant that many blacks lived a great distance from these new opportunities, college graduates turned down opportunities to move to the area because of limited housing prospects, and employees did not dwell in the same neighborhoods as their white coworkers.[130] Black dissatisfaction with their careers often stemmed from the realization that they could not attain the same housing, education, and consumer goods that their white peers attained. "Spatial mismatch," the problem of living far from suitable employment, not only plagued low-income African Americans, but educated blacks looking for high-status positions. In one telling example, executives at Allstate deemed their minority recruitment program a success. Several African Americans had landed permanent posts. However, a downside was that two black female interns had four-hour daily commutes to Allstate's suburban offices.[131]

Promotions often required relocating to another city, but blacks knew that this would mean another painful search for a new residence. As a black home seeker stated, this process made him feel "as something less than human." Many declined the offers, feeling that the added stress was not worth it.[132] Business trips, especially to the South, meant searching for accommodating hotels and restaurants, and black workers sometimes had agonizing racial incidents when just trying to find a meal or a bed.[133] Though African Americans made inroads into the corporate workplace, their careers were often slowed by factors whites did not have to contemplate.

While blacks struggled to break into this side of the business scene, they learned that the effort was nearly as convoluted as getting hired in the first place. "Many of these people can be treacherous when they've had a few drinks," a scarred manager observed after experiencing club life. "Ugly remarks and incidents are not uncommon under these circumstances. You've got to rationally weigh those risks when deciding whether accepting an invitation to join the club will produce enough career benefits to justify the aggravation of socializing with many people you would just as soon have nothing to do with you off the job."[134] For reasons like this, hesitant black managers declined social invitations though they knew they would be further distanced from vital company decisions occurring over cocktails and on putting greens.

PRESSURE AND PERSEVERANCE

The impediments to African Americans entering corporate America were met by a striking perseverance from pioneers. Walter Clark came to Chicago with an accounting degree in 1951 but received no offers. Disturbed but undaunted, he enrolled in master's degree courses at DePaul University while taking odd jobs. He finally landed an accounting clerk position at First Federal Savings and Loan in 1955, the company's first black employee. Though better educated than any of his coworkers, he stagnated at the entry level. His immediate boss had not even finished high school. "When your supervisors come to you for help with simple calculations," Clark recalled, "you know you're getting screwed." No one was willing to show him the ropes. "It was like being thrown into water loaded with barracudas. My options were to swim faster than hell or be eaten alive. I swam." Many coworkers saw him as a threat, and the personnel director constantly inquired about his marital status and scolded him after he danced with a white woman at a company function. Clark finally began to move up in the company after seven years, and then, after self-educating himself in bond trading, he convinced First Federal's board to let him set up a highly profitable trading unit inside the firm. Yet the shadow corporation stymied him, as he could not bring clients to white-only clubs. The chair suggested he make alternative arrangements, but Clark refused. In response, the chair sponsored him for the Union League Club in 1971, where Clark became the second black member. By 1974 Clark's patient persistence proved worthwhile as he was the senior vice president in charge of First Federal's investment program.[135]

For newcomers such as Clark, pioneering was a paradox. It entailed heavy burdens, but the payoff in terms of legacy and personal rewards could be profoundly satisfying. Despite the stress, the determined took pride in the role of trailblazer.[136] The first executive in the American airline industry felt "I had to develop an image which would make it difficult, if not impossible, for an individual to say that a black man could not hold down an executive position with a major airline."[137] Many blacks also felt they were indebted to previous generations who had sacrificed to give them these opportunities, whether through civil rights agitation or plain hard work.[138] The onus was well-defined; these men and women were test cases for the future of minority employment. While some black managers were initially intimidated by their new surroundings, once inside the scales fell from their eyes. They had underestimated their own potential and overestimated the capabilities of white coworkers, and they tapped the hidden reservoirs of the black experience, such as how to cunningly but doggedly resist power and handle the racist behavior of others.[139]

Black white-collars acclimatized to corporate life using a variety of approaches. Among the most essential was thick skin. To be successful, black managers could not be derailed by the racial prejudice of others. They were not self-deluded, but they had to implement a mind-set that racism was the bigot's problem.[140] Service organizations such as Chicago's Royal Coterie of Snakes were not only beneficial to advancement, they also allowed members to vent and discuss "survival tactics." "The only thing that keeps my head intact is the chance to get with other [black executives] now and then and talk that talk," a black personnel recruiter admitted. "It's a mental-health device, to be able to call the Man a motherfucker once in a while."[141]

This resolve could lead to gratifying careers for African Americans in corporate America. Though nearly all encountered racially motivated slights, they knew staying in "the system" had rewards.[142] Some in managerial careers reported coworkers and supervisors had accepted them with "surprisingly little fuss."[143] While promotions remained a problem, certain executives were sincerely committed to tapping into burgeoning minority markets, an attitude that jibed with the ideology of risk-taking black professionals. "There's only one color that the business is interested in," an engineering manager at General Electric discovered. "It is not white or Negro but green. If you can make the southeast corner of the balance sheet come out right, industry, as I have seen it, doesn't really give a hoot who you are or what you are."[144] Despite the numerous extra struggles white-collar blacks faced, they knew that their prospects had improved significantly, as just years earlier the best that many with education could hope for was the post office or segregated businesses.

In addition, corporate work became increasingly lucrative as the knowledge economy boomed. Managerial positions imparted the ability to indulge in prosperity and to enhance prospects for their children. "They give you the good bucks and a taste of the good life and it's hard to leave it," one executive affirmed. "You get caught up in that bag and you assimilate in order to enjoy the benefits."[145] Even those who served in oft-frustrating "penciled-in" positions occasionally conceded that the remuneration made it worthwhile. A stymied manager recognized that while he was the company's "spook who sat by the door," he "charged them well for it."[146] Money, leisure time, and job security usually could not overcome dissatisfied feelings about their careers, but they kept many black workers from quitting.

IDENTITY ISSUES

This persistence opened doors for future black hires, but the activists who pushed for inclusion had more expansive goals, and skeptical African Americans questioned whether entering the system benefited the race. Chicago Urban League executive director Edwin Berry relished the gains made in the white-collar ranks, but warned that while the privileged were being offered "access to the total society," the mass of Chicago's blacks were left out.[147] As the middle class expanded and its fortunes blossomed, civil rights leaders charged that while the movement had decidedly improved conditions for them, it had not done much for the poor.[148] Critics noted that the rise of a viable black middle class coincided with the collapse of the black working class as automation and capital flight decimated the blue-collar workforce.

Intrarace class divisions widened, and vociferous black power militants dismissed mainstream success as "selling out." The concern that black managers would lose touch with their race was evident from the initial breakthroughs. *Ebony*, which enthusiastically cheered advancements, also warned that these pioneers must maintain their dignity, lauding "the white collar worker who refused to tom."[149] Commentators worried that through adopting corporate values, black managers were "unconsciously devaluing" the less fortunate and, ultimately, themselves. More militant cynics charged that staying authentically black in business attire was an inherent contradiction, or that blacks were being promoted mainly into "flak-catching" positions as intermediaries to keep protest under wraps. "The rift has reached the point where some low-income Negroes are calling any Negro with a decent white-collar job an 'Uncle Tom,'" *Jet* magazine reported in 1967.[150]

Corporate blacks were fully aware of this tension and often felt they were in a no-win situation. Some reported that other African Americans, including their own children, "tested" them to see whether they were maintaining their "racial fidelity." "Believe me," a drained manager stressed, "it's an effort to maintain my integrity, moving up in management and at the same time being black."[151] A 1967 Operation Breadbasket report indicated fears that integration diluted African American culture and that applicants would need to be like white people. However, white-collar careers were exploding, and "a substantial proportion of these upgraded vocations and job opportunities must be absorbed by Negroes if they are ever to 'catch up.'"[152] When engaged in negotiations on hiring and promotions with Continental Baking that same year, Jesse Jackson

fired off a heated missive to chair of the board R. Newton Laughlin for sending Sam Simmons, whom Jackson termed "Continental's 'Negro,'" to a summit.
According to Jackson, "it became obvious to us that Mr. Simmons had neither
a future within the present structures of Continental nor the power to use and
create with the information at his disposal." Laughlin emphatically objected to
Jackson's portrayal of Simmons, calling him "not a public relations employee but
a member of our sales department who has worked his way up to the position
of Assistant Sales Manager with responsibilities which include many important
accounts. This is far from a dead end job."[153] Regardless of Simmons's actual role,
the episode demonstrated the distrust of corporations and the blacks in their
employ, even as civil rights groups attempted to place more African Americans
in these positions. Activists with Operation PUSH, which effectively pressured
companies to hire black managers, simultaneously worried that "the best black
minds" were "locked into the job system in the white corporate structure" and
unwilling to take on black nationalist objectives.[154] Publications such as *Ebony*
and *Negro Digest*, while singing the praises of strivers, nearly always posed the
question if they were "giving back."[155] The articles implied a degree of mistrust
toward the high achieving, a pointed reminder that they had bigger responsibilities than their white peers.

Many managers insisted that they were advancing both their personal
interests and those of the race through their careers. Through their example,
black white-collars had defied the erroneous perceptions that the race lacked
the necessities to make it in the corporate world, and their groundbreaking
actions were an essential, if underappreciated, part of the freedom movement.
"My professional life," Xerox executive Barry Rand audaciously asserted, "was
as much a part of the civil rights struggle as the bus boycotts and lunch counter
sit-ins of a few years earlier."[156] Ron Sampson, a Chicago advertising executive, engaged in sit-ins as a student, but now tried to set an example for others
by establishing himself professionally. "Quite frankly, I felt like I walked the
picket line every morning when I started to work."[157] In Chicago, 45 percent of
high-status blacks belonged to a civil rights organization, the highest percentage
of any socioeconomic group.[158] Some of the well-off strongly objected to the
assertion that they were not carrying their weight, pointing out that they were
the "backbone" of the movement organizationally and financially. "The children think they invented civil rights," a prominent black Chicagoan sarcastically
remarked.[159] A study of sixty black executives and entrepreneurs in 1970 and
1971 found that 47 percent were active in protest movements, and not just with

conventional organizations such as the NAACP and Urban League. Almost a quarter of these businesspeople had been involved with more militant groups such as Operation Breadbasket, the Congress of Racial Equality, and the Black Panthers.[160] A *Fortune* journalist found that many in the black middle class were adopting standpoints far more aggressive than their predecessors, "views sometimes just as bristling and hostile as those held by all but the most extreme of his black brothers."[161]

Black managers' association with black power organizations seemed an unlikely match. However, while whites often correlated black power with violence, most blacks, even those in corporate America, thought of it as the solidification of their communal power.[162] By the mid-1970s the country was suffering from integration exhaustion, and many Americans turned from assimilation toward identity politics.[163] African Americans in corporate positions were not immune from this shift, especially since white coworkers had consistently resisted integration while blacks were apprehensive over the price of conformity.

If black white-collars were in "the system," for most of them it continued to be an unnerving existence. Charles Harrison, the first African American manager at Sears, remembered that from the day he was hired until he retired in 1993, "I was always reminded that I could not take my guard down, that I was in a hostile environment every day. Every day!" When materials disappeared from the laboratory, Harrison, despite his ten-year tenure at the firm, was the only executive investigated by an outside detective agency. After two white technicians were discovered as the culprits, Harrison's embarrassed supervisor gave him his largest pay increase, a bittersweet end to another in a long line of excruciating workplace incidents. Harrison and a black colleague carpooled from their South Side residences to the office. Each morning, prior to entering, they paused and donned imaginary "gasmasks" to mentally prepare themselves for the "toxic" environment ahead.[164]

MANAGERIAL DILEMMAS

Despite the endeavors by African American networking organizations, the indirect discrimination of the "shadow corporation" remained a hindrance to black advancement. Critics charged that affirmative action had undermined the merit system by making it "relativistic."[165] In reality, the black experience in management exposed the phony claims of color-blind merit. Blacks encountered a host of frustrating traps and impediments that had nothing to do with their talents or capabilities. By the mid-1980s, media reports suggested that numerous African Americans were ditching their "dead-end" jobs in corporations.[166] A manager who left a bank to found a consulting firm said, "Capability and performance were important in corporate promotion, but equally important was the old-boy network—and race plays a significant part in limiting access to the network."[167] Though activists expended a great deal of energy to convince corporations to hire blacks in white-collar positions, the struggles of these employees began again as they reached their desks.

Indeed, the tensions reflected the larger burdens borne by black managers. Activists wanted them to usher large-scale changes into the economic climate of Chicago. Companies hired them mostly to tamp down dissent. The managers themselves were often just trying to survive. In a sense, they emerged at an inopportune time. If they had materialized in the *Ebony* magazine–era of the long 1950s or the Reagan 1980s, they would have been lauded. Instead, blacks entered corporate America just as black power and calls for racial authenticity were at their height. Dr. James Comer, the son of a steelworker from East Chicago who became a Yale psychologist, contended that more than any other ethnic group, middle-class African Americans were "desperately concerned" about their poor brethren and strongly wanted to do something for the whole community. But because black poverty was structural and the nascent black middle class had neither the capital nor the clout to produce extensive change, "there just isn't much they can do.... There are many who feel that frustration."[168] While American society threw up repeated obstacles for the black middle class, they also expected more from this group than perhaps any other. Blaming the dormant condition of black Chicago on decisions made by the African American middle class not only fed unrealistic expectations, but ignored the depth of their struggles.

CONCLUSION

In 2009, the *New York Times* reported that job-seeking African Americans were "whitening" their job résumés. For example, businesses were not returning calls for job interviews to Tahani Tompkins, a Chicagoland resident. A friend advised her to change her name to T. S. Tompkins to better her chances. Another Chicagoan deleted information on her bachelor's degree from Hampton University, a historically black college. Additionally, she removed details on a previous position at an African American nonprofit and reshuffled her references to ensure that that the top names were not black-sounding. According to the article, the practice of hiding or downplaying blackness was common among college-educated African Americans.[1]

"Whitening" the résumé was not a choice born in paranoia or deceit, but rather an often-agonizing compromise to the American racial order. One study of hiring practices in Boston and Chicago in 2004 showed that applicants with "black" names received half as many callbacks as people with "white" names.[2] In 2009, the unemployment rate for black male college graduates twenty-five and older was close to double that of white male college graduates.[3] The Great Recession worsened the employment outlook for young African Americans. By 2013, the unemployment rate for whites who did not finish high school was *lower* than that for blacks with some college education.[4] Though many Americans believed that affirmative action and government quotas mandated that employers give preferences to minorities, in truth blacks had to contend with severe disadvantages in hiring. Three generations after employers compelled European immigrants to "whiten" their résumés to be considered for mainstream occupations, black Americans still felt this burden.[5]

The measures taken by African Americans to find employment were not rejections of their racial heritage. In response to persistent disparities, many middle-class blacks perceived that their life chances were intertwined with those of other African Americans.[6] Blackness was not a liability; rather, the affluent enjoyed being black and being part of a larger community, and they were determined to maintain their racial identities.[7] Moreover, in spite of their accomplishments, most blacks could not escape their race even if they wanted to. Offhand remarks, slights, tokenism, and incidents of blatant racism connected them—distressingly—to a larger African American experience of marginality. Additionally, blacks faced resounding pressure to take responsibility for their less fortunate brethren, a compulsion that white ethnics discarded as they assimilated into the middle class.

As black Americans arrived in Chicago, they encountered blatant racism that made it tremendously challenging to achieve their educational, occupational, and residential objectives. The emotional weight they carried in their bruising struggle for upward mobility led to imaginative schemes to get ahead, and they formed a modified rendering of the American Dream that openly acknowledged the extra burdens of achieving success in a society that did not want them to succeed. Many were frustrated by the seemingly insurmountable barriers, and those that made good often faced criticism for their decisions that Chicagoans of other races never had to consider.

Class divisions were present since the earliest days of Chicago's Black Belt, but they widened significantly with civil rights triumphs in the 1950s and 1960s as educated black Chicagoans pushed open doors. Nonetheless, severe discrimination continued to constrain their search for full inclusion and unencumbered opportunity, and societal pressures insisted that the black middle class take on responsibility for racial progress. Some rejected this obligation and sought to distance themselves physically from the poor and psychologically from the burden of elevating the entire race. Others advocated the time-honored mantra of "lifting while we climb," but they could do only so much to improve the prospects of blacks confronting deep-seated systemic impediments. The black middle class grew, but in the 1970s the black working class began collapsing. Deindustrialization, government cutbacks, automation, and enduring discrimination deprived many African Americans of the springboard of working-class stability.[8] Any fixes to the crisis in the jobless ghetto went far beyond the resources of the black middle and upper classes.[9] By the turn of the century, many began to give up on what was once called the "Promised Land." From 2000 to 2010, Chicago lost 181,000 black residents, with many relocating to the suburbs or back to the South.[10]

As urban neighborhoods faltered, the black middle class continued the long tradition of attempting to move away from the disorder and limited means of high-poverty areas and carve out exclusive residential spaces.[11] In 1987, *Ebony* magazine noted that Chatham, the South Side middle-class incubator, was "more than just a neighborhood. It's a symbol of hopes, dreams and progress, and it has been that way for the 30 or so years that the Black middle class has occupied the area." There was tremendous demand for homes in the community, which ranged from affordable bungalows at $50,000 to luxurious mansions that fetched $500,000.[12] Though almost all whites left, black residents had largely succeeded in preserving it as a desirable place to live.

Twenty years later, black Chathamites felt besieged as the city dismantled public housing and the country largely discarded strategies to alleviate poverty. Maryellen Drake, whose parents moved to Chatham as part of the short-lived experiment in integration in 1957, had served as vice president of the Chatham–Avalon Park Community Council, then in existence for fifty years. In 2011, though, Drake saw a troubled neighborhood. "This is a class issue," Drake concluded. "It's not just about income. It's about the standards that you are accustomed to.... Barbecue grills on the front lawn. Ten and 12 people piled up on the front porch. Opening fire hydrants instead of going in the backyard and getting in the pool or under a hose." She was not sure where the newcomers were coming from, but "I know that—by the way they behave—although they look like me, we are very different."[13] Blacks were not immune to the politics of personal responsibility, and many blamed the poor for their difficulties. Additionally, middle-class blacks often held themselves responsible for not achieving parity with their white peers, reflecting a broader neoliberal focus on individual solutions for social problems.[14]

However, the emphasis on personal agency masked the profound structural issues plaguing the black middle class. For Chicagoans in "gilded ghettos," the legacies of segregation, redlining practices by financial institutions, and capital flight made their neighborhoods perilous and diminished investments in housing. Between 1980 and 1983, Chicago's suburbs got twice as many home loans and three times more loan money as the city, even though the suburban population was only one-third larger than the city's. All twenty-two Chicago neighborhoods classified as "credit-starved" were predominantly minority, including Chatham and three other black middle-class communities with median family incomes at or appreciably above the citywide average.[15] Black families accrued much less return on their residential assets, which contributed significantly to the generational wealth gaps between the black and white middle classes.[16] Laverne Hayes owned a two-bedroom bungalow in Avalon Park. It had nearly doubled in value from 1990 to 2005, but Hayes estimated that if her home were in another neighborhood, it would be worth considerably more. Her assumption was correct, as similar homes in a white community on the Northwest Side sold for 126 percent above those in Avalon Park.[17] In Chatham, the impact of demolishing public housing high-rises, the sluggish economy, and a disintegrating housing market led to more crime, a jump in unemployment, and decisions to leave. The low points came in 2010, when Chicago police officer Thomas Wortham IV was shot to death at his parents' house by thieves attempting to steal his new motorcycle. Three months later, assailants shot and killed another Chicago cop, Michael Bailey, in front of his home while he polished his new car.[18] The homicides were stark reminders of the hazards middle-class blacks faced in places once considered havens.

The disparities between the black middle class and its white counterpart starkly demonstrated that race still mattered and that the country had not entered a post-racial era. The African American middle class doubled in size in the 1960s as agitation and equal employment laws opened new opportunities.[19] While some optimists stated that blacks had achieved economic parity by the early 1970s and the media often featured accomplished African Americans in glossy spreads and television specials, civil rights lawyer Vernon Jordan cautioned that "the vast majority of blacks are still far from middle-class status. Let us not forget that the gains won are tenuous ones, easily shaken from our grasp by an energy crisis, a recession, rampant inflation, or nonenforcement of hard-won civil-rights laws."[20] Jordan's warning was prescient, as economic malaise and a conservative counterreaction pushed back progress in education, in the workplace, and in residential capital.

Education, which helped propel so many into the middle class in the twentieth century, has remained inequitable for most African Americans.[21] Intractable whites blocked true school integration in Northern cities during the period of civil rights momentum. The Supreme Court gradually retreated from and terminated integration plans, while the Reagan and Bush administrations expressed hostility to desegregation orders. In 2011–12, a study of education sixty years after *Brown v. Board* related that the states of New York and Illinois were the most segregated for black students. The Chicago area, the study reported, "combines extremely high residential segregation and a metropolitan area fragmented into hundreds of separate school districts with a sharply declining white share of the school age population."[22]

Segregated inner-city schools not only denied students opportunities for networking, but tended to have strikingly fewer resources, third-rate facilities, and more inexperienced teachers.[23] The white privilege of middle-class flight had lasting negative effects for educational equity. When whites left, urban areas lost social, political, and economic capital, producing large gaps between urban and suburban districts.[24] Public education "reformers" responded by subjecting urban systems to market-based standards, including touting charter schools and supporting private school vouchers.[25] Increasingly, elites raised doubts on the value of a broad education for the masses while doing everything in their power to assure that their own children had access to the best instruction possible.

Momentum in the workplace also subsided. Blacks made stunning gains in the late 1960s and early 1970s in the corporate world through the power of social movements, government action, and the tenacity of qualified blacks seizing the moment.[26] However, this burst was brief, slowed by a stumbling economy and shifting political tides. Black careers in corporate America stagnated or even regressed in the 1980s, and many frustrated managers left to start their own firms.[27] Even as the number of African American managers grew, companies still placed most of them in less influential positions.[28] Moreover, black male college graduates experienced an acute decline in relative earnings in the late 1970s and the 1980s.[29] New Right and neoliberal cuts to government employment hit the black middle class hard, as African Americans had long been overrepresented in these jobs due to lower levels of discrimination and growing urban political clout.[30] Blacks in corporate jobs advised young aspirants that their work must be "impeccable," as employers still expected blacks to be "super-negroes." As a frustrated executive remarked in 1987, "We are still playing on an uneven playing field."[31]

Political support for redressing racial discrimination ran dry in the 1980s. The Reagan administration's disdain for affirmative action emboldened recalcitrant managers. One consultant observed that many were contemptuous of black men, and they ascribed African American advancement to "reverse discrimination."[32] A pharmaceutical executive noted that at discussions over diversity, white supervisors asked, "Why are we doing this when the outside environment has cooled to these programs? Why are we wasting the money?" Strikingly, the challenges faced by black managers were familiar to the pioneers of the 1960s. At a company cocktail party, an official told a black executive, "Most of my people would find it extremely difficult, almost counterproductive, to work for a minority individual."[33] This frankness made it clear why many blacks could not attain promotions: truculent whites still could not tolerate blacks in authority positions. As *Wall Street Journal* reporters concluded in 1992, white-collar blacks "walk a tightrope in corporate America, where they're expected to blend with a culture that never fully accepts them."[34] Few black managers rose to the top spots, and the historian and real estate magnate Dempsey Travis's interviews with Chicago's black executives revealed that not one was a member of an establishment country club or could lay claim to being a part of the city's "good old boys network."[35]

Affirmative action programs became politically untenable, easing the bureaucratic impulse for change. Aggrieved whites generally succeeded in convincing the public that they tainted merit-based processes by artificially inserting race. Some African American managers, seeking to conform to the corporate ethos, also questioned the wisdom of affirmative action.[36] Corporations shifted to "diversity" and "inclusion" rather than targeted advancement programs, contending that the presence of minority employees was not as important as being "culturally competent" and making everyone feel valued.[37] Black initiative, though vital to entry into the economic mainstream, could only go so far.

Residential integration also foundered, despite some notable exceptions in areas where denizens overcame long-standing restrictive practices and integrated through the managed strategies proposed by liberals such as Thomas Gaudette in the late 1950s.[38] These hard-won bright spots served as evidence that equal-status contact worked, while often eliding the excruciating process.[39] In most cases, Chicagoland remained stubbornly segregated. The patterns of pioneering, panic, and flight in suburban Matteson in the mid-1990s remained eerily similar to those in previous decades. An influx of black middle-class home buyers led to a mass sell-off by whites, even though the newcomers were of the same, if not higher, socioeconomic status. Those exiting reflexively claimed that the schools were getting worse and crime was rising, despite test scores and crime rates remaining unchanged. The debacle attracted the attention of the national media, startled by the realization that most whites were still unwilling to live next to blacks.[40]

African Americans had torn down the "Chicago Wall" and moved into a host of suburbs, yet recurring white flight meant that these relocations were not a panacea. Suburban middle-class blacks usually lived in areas with sluggish home values, less access to good schools, and greater distance to high-paying careers. A study in the mid-2000s found that 94 percent of blacks dwelt in "low-opportunity" suburbs around Chicago, compared to 44 percent of whites.[41] Indeed, to maintain diverse communities residents needed to pay close attention to anxieties over schools, delinquency, and commercial vitality, because whites perceived integration to be risky and unstable. In an attempt to stabilize housing markets and sustain diversity, Matteson residents launched an aggressive marketing plan to woo white home buyers, turning back to a strategy employed thirty years earlier.[42] Meanwhile, skeptical African Americans suffered from integration fatigue, tired of the repetitive cycles of flight and having to prove themselves as "acceptable."[43] Though many Americans still believed in equal-status contact, research indicated that increasing neighborhood diversity did not necessarily produce hostility, but rather mounting distrust of neighbors and social withdrawal, regardless of class.[44] Throughout the twentieth century, blacks persistently moved to communities to upgrade their living conditions and gain access to resources, only to watch those amenities fade into renewed segregation.

The resulting inequalities in the workplace, neighborhood, and schools calcified the stubborn American racial divide. Since the 1950s, Americans regularly judged racial progress by the size of the black middle class. The visible presence of minorities that "made it" was crucial to the country's legitimacy as a place of egalitarian ideals and fair play. In times of crisis, whites turned to them as "reasonable" junior partners with a stake in the system. But as journalist Ta-Nehisi Coates bluntly stated, "America does not really want a black middle class."[45] Whites often claimed that if blacks only achieved a higher status and adopted more customary behaviors, then they would find acceptance. Yet they denied blacks access to housing, schools, and jobs that secured upward mobility. The contradiction was hardly new to the United States, but it was difficult for a nation that prided itself on merit, hard work, and tolerance to acknowledge.

Many whites looked back on their own journeys to the middle class as the model and faulted African Americans for not taking these routes, thereby erasing how earning whiteness had been a major factor in their achievements.[46]

Even as they faced stubborn prejudice, the American Dream still enjoyed wide currency among black Americans.[47] Moving on up emerged as gospel for the aspirational classes. They could look back at centuries of subjugation and inequality, yet still marvel at the developments at hand, including the election of Chicago's own Barack Obama. The confidence in advancement exerted a strong force, urging Chicagoans to emulate and strive for the feats of the city's black elite. Unlike white Americans accustomed to the skewed benefits of racialized state capitalism, blacks had a more clear-eyed view of what it took to get ahead.[48] Neoliberalism, austerity, and deindustrialization changed the social and economic landscape for many whites, but African Americans had long been aware of the harshest edges of free enterprise. The United States always promised more than it could deliver. Yet faith continued, spurred on by triumphant examples. Their achievements suggested that if they played the game right and caught a break, blacks could move up and move out.

NOTES

NOTES TO INTRODUCTION

1. Marylin Bender, "Black Capitalist: Listing of His Concern on Amex Marks a 'First,'" *New York Times*, January 24, 1971, F2.

2. *Wall Street Journal*, "Chatham Bank, Chicago, Is Being Liquidated," August 22, 1963, 6; *Chicago Defender*, "$1,243,360 Paid Off by FDIC for Chatham," September 5, 1963, 3; Beverly Jensen, "Independence Bank of Chicago," *Black Enterprise*, June 1977, 106.

3. Timuel D. Black Jr., *Bridges of Memory: Chicago's First Wave of Black Migration, an Oral History* (Evanston, IL: Northwestern University Press, 2003), 375.

4. A. L. Foster, "Other People's Business: Charter for That Bank," *Chicago Defender*, June 6, 1964, 6.

5. William Robbins, "Takeovers Lift Standing of Largest Black Bank," *New York Times*, July 24, 1979, D1.

6. Nelson Algren, *Chicago: City on the Make* (Garden City, NY: Doubleday and Co., 1951).

7. Randi Storch, *Red Chicago: American Communism at Its Grassroots, 1928–1935* (Urbana: University of Illinois Press, 2007); Preston H. Smith II, *Racial Democracy and the Black Metropolis: Housing Policy in Postwar Chicago* (Minneapolis: University of Minnesota Press, 2012); Jeffrey Helgeson, *Crucibles of Black Empowerment: Chicago's Neighborhood Politics from the New Deal to Harold Washington* (Chicago: University of Chicago Press, 2014); Adam Green, *Selling the Race: Culture, Community, and Black Chicago, 1940–1955* (Chicago: University of Chicago Press, 2007); Davarian L. Baldwin, *Chicago's New Negroes: Modernity, the Great Migration, and Black Urban Life* (Chapel Hill: University of North Carolina Press, 2007); Bill V. Mullen, *Popular Fronts: Chicago and African-American Cultural Politics, 1935–46* (Urbana: University of Illinois Press, 1999); Jakobi Williams, *From*

the Bullet to the Ballot: The Illinois Chapter of the Black Panther Party and Racial Coalition Politics in Chicago (Chapel Hill: University of North Carolina Press, 2013).

8. Glenda Elizabeth Gilmore, *Gender and Jim Crow: Women and the Politics of White Supremacy in North Carolina, 1896–1920* (Chapel Hill: University of North Carolina Press, 1996); Evelyn Brooks Higginbotham, *Righteous Discontent: The Women's Movement in the Black Baptist Church, 1880–1920* (Cambridge, MA: Harvard University Press, 1993); Stephanie Shaw, *What a Woman Ought to Be and Do: Black Professional Women Workers during the Jim Crow Era* (Chicago: University of Chicago Press, 1996).

9. Willard B. Gatewood, *Aristocrats of Color: The Black Elite, 1880–1920* (Bloomington: Indiana University Press, 1990); Charles T. Banner-Haley, *The Fruits of Integration: Black Middle-Class Ideology and Culture, 1960–1990* (Jackson: University of Mississippi Press, 1994); Touré F. Reed, *Not Alms But Opportunity: The Urban League and the Politics of Racial Uplift* (Chapel Hill: University of North Carolina Press, 2008).

10. E. Franklin Frazier, *Black Bourgeoisie: The Rise of a New Middle Class* (New York: Free Press, 1957); Nathan Hare, *The Black Anglo-Saxons* (New York: Marzani and Munsell, 1965); Harold Cruse, *The Crisis of the Negro Intellectual: Historical Analysis of the Failure of Black Leadership* (New York: Morrow, 1967), 90, 312; Albert Murray, *The Omni-Americans: New Perspectives on Black Experience and American Culture* (New York: Outerbridge & Dienstfrey, 1970), 86–90; Stokely Carmichael and Charles V. Hamilton, *Black Power: The Politics of Liberation in America* (New York: Random House, 1967), 53; Harold Cruse, *Plural but Equal: Blacks and Minorities in America's Plural Society* (New York: William Morrow and Co., 1987), 389.

11. Nicholas Lemann, *The Promised Land: The Great Black Migration and How It Changed America* (New York: Knopf, 1991); Martin Kilson, "Political Change in the Negro Ghetto, 1900–1940's," in *Key Issues in the Afro-American Experience*, vol. 2, Nathan Huggins, Martin Kilson, and Daniel Fox, eds. (Chicago: Harcourt Brace Jovanovich, Inc., 1971), 171; Adam Green, *Selling the Race: Culture, Community, and Black Chicago, 1940–1955* (Chicago: University of Chicago Press, 2007); George Lipsitz, *How Racism Takes Place* (Philadelphia: Temple University Press, 2011), 57.

12. William Julius Wilson, *The Truly Disadvantaged: The Inner City, the Underclass, and Public Policy* (Chicago: University of Chicago Press, 1987), 7, 49–61; John Bauman, Norman Hummon, and Edward Muller, "Public Housing, Isolation, and the Urban Underclass: Philadelphia's Richard Allen Homes, 1941–1965," *Journal of Urban History* 17 (May 1991): 264–92; William J. Grimshaw, *Bitter Fruit: Black Politics and the Chicago Machine, 1931–1991* (Chicago: University of Chicago Press, 1992), 43; Alan Ehrenhalt, *The Lost City: Discovering the Forgotten Virtues of Community in the Chicago of the 1950s* (New York: Basic Books, 1995), 140; Robert G. Spinney, *City of Big Shoulders: A History of Chicago* (DeKalb: Northern Illinois University Press, 2000), 207–8; Eugene Robinson, *Disintegration: The Splintering of Black America* (New York: Doubleday, 2010), 20–21, 38–39, 49.

13. Mary Pattillo-McCoy, *Black Picket Fences: Privilege and Peril among the Black Middle Class* (Chicago: University of Chicago Press, 1999); Lynne Feldman, *A Sense of Place: Birmingham's Black Middle-Class Community* (Tuscaloosa: University of Alabama Press, 1999); Bruce D. Haynes, *Red Lines, Black Spaces: The Politics of Race and Space in a Black Middle-Class Suburb* (New Haven, CT: Yale University Press, 2001); Marcus Anthony Hunter, *Black Citymakers: How the Philadelphia Negro Changed Urban America* (New York: Oxford University Press, 2013); Todd M. Michney, *Surrogate Suburbs: Black Upward Mobility and Neighborhood Change in Cleveland, 1900–1980* (Chapel Hill: University of North Carolina Press, 2017).

14. Kevin K. Gaines, *Uplifting the Race: Black Leadership, Politics, and Culture in the Twentieth Century* (Chapel Hill: University of North Carolina Press, 1996), xiv, xxi.

15. For a concise contemplation, see Bill E. Lawson, "Uplifting the Race: Middle-Class Blacks and the Truly Disadvantaged," in *The Underclass Question*, Bill E. Lawson, ed. (Philadelphia: Temple University Press, 1992), 90–113.

16. Mahalia Jackson with Evan McLeod Wylie, *Movin' On Up*, (New York: Hawthorn Books, 1966), 46.

17. James R. Grossman, *Land of Hope: Chicago, Black Southerners, and the Great Migration* (Chicago: University of Chicago Press, 1989), 94–97; Thomas Philpott, *The Slum and the Ghetto: Neighborhood Deterioration and Middle-Class Reform in Chicago, 1880–1930* (New York: Oxford University Press, 1978), 116–17.

18. Jackson, *Movin' On Up*, 46.

19. Arnold Hirsch, *Making the Second Ghetto: Race and Housing in Chicago, 1940–1960* (Chicago: University of Chicago Press, 1998); William Julius Wilson, *When Work Disappears: The World of the New Urban Poor* (New York: Knopf, 1996).

20. Rick Halpern, *Down on the Killing Floor: Black and White Workers in Chicago's Packinghouses, 1904–1954* (Urbana: University of Illinois Press, 1997); James R. Ralph Jr., *Northern Protest: Martin Luther King, Jr., Chicago, and the Civil Rights Movement* (Cambridge, MA: Harvard University Press, 1993); Arvarh E. Strickland, *History of the Chicago Urban League* (Urbana: University of Illinois Press, 1966); Christopher Robert Reed, *The Chicago NAACP and the Rise of Black Professional Leadership, 1910–1966* (Bloomington: Indiana University Press, 1997).

21. Michelle Mitchell, *African Americans and the Politics of Racial Destiny after Reconstruction* (Chapel Hill: University of North Carolina Press, 2004).

22. W. E. B. Du Bois, "Three Centuries of Discrimination," *The Crisis*, December 1947, 363.

23. Smith II, *Racial Democracy and the Black Metropolis*, xii, 8.

24. Robert Weems, *Black Business in the Black Metropolis: The Chicago Metropolitan Assurance Company, 1925–1985* (Bloomington: Indiana University Press, 1996); Christopher Robert Reed, *The Rise of Chicago's Black Metropolis, 1920–1929* (Urbana: University of Illinois Press, 2011); Robert Weems and Jason Chambers, *Building the Black Metropolis: African American Entrepreneurship in Chicago* (Urbana: University of Illinois Press, 2017).

25. For works on the creation of segregated Chicago, see Chicago Commission on Race Relations (CCRR), *The Negro in Chicago: A Study of Race Relations and a Race Riot* (Chicago: University of Chicago Press, 1922); Allan H. Spear, *Black Chicago: The Making of a Negro Ghetto, 1890–1920* (Chicago: University of Chicago Press, 1967); Philpott, *Slum and the Ghetto*, 113–14; Sylvia Hood Washington, *Packing Them In: An Archaeology of Environmental Racism in Chicago, 1865–1954* (New York: Lexington Books, 2005); Hirsch, *Making the Second Ghetto*.

26. For examples that put pioneers at the center of the story, see L. K. Northwood and Ernest A. T. Barth, *Urban Desegregation: Negro Pioneers and Their White Neighbors* (Seattle: University of Washington Press, 1965); Kevin Boyle, *Arc of Justice: A Saga of Race, Civil Rights, and Murder in the Jazz Age* (New York: Henry Holt and Co., 2004); Andrew Wiese, *Places of Their Own: African American Suburbanization in the Twentieth Century* (Chicago: University of Chicago Press, 2004); Beryl Satter, *Family Properties: Race, Real Estate, and the Exploitation of Black Urban America* (New York: Henry Holt & Co., 2009); Todd M. Michney, *Surrogate Suburbs: Black Upward Mobility and Neighborhood Change in Cleveland, 1900–1980* (Chapel Hill: University of North Carolina Press, 2017).

27. Gordon W. Allport, *The Nature of Prejudice*, (Reading, MA: Addison-Wesley Publishing Co., 1954); Selwyn James, "We Refused to Give Up Our Homes," *Redbook*, December 1955; Ellsworth Rosen, "When a Negro Moves Next Door," *Saturday Evening Post*, April 1959, 32–33, 139–42; Ralph Bass, "Prejudice Won't Make Us Sell Our House!" *Coronet*, July 1959, 103–7.

28. Stephen Grant Meyer, *As Long as They Don't Move Next Door: Segregation and Racial Conflict in American Neighborhoods* (New York: Rowman & Littlefield Publishers, Inc, 2000); Amanda Seligman, *Block by Block: Neighborhoods and Public Policy on Chicago's West Side* (Chicago: University of Chicago Press, 2005); Eileen M. McMahon, *What Parish Are You From? A Chicago Irish Community and Race Relations* (Lexington: University Press of Kentucky, 1995); Gerald Gamm, *Urban Exodus: Why the Jews Left Boston and the Catholics Stayed* (Cambridge, MA: Harvard University Press, 1999).

29. St. Clair Drake, "Folkways and Classways within the Black Ghetto," in *The Making of Black America: Essays in Negro Life and History*, vol. 1, August Meier and Elliot Rudwick, eds. (New York: Atheneum, 1969), 448.

30. Wilson, *The Truly Disadvantaged*; Lemann, *Promised Land*; Kenneth Karst, *Belonging to America* (New Haven, CT: Yale University Press, 1989).

31. Sidney Kronus, *The Black Middle Class* (Columbus, OH: Charles E. Merrill Publishing, 1971), 51; Alan B. Anderson and George W. Pickering, *Confronting the Color Line: The Broken Promise of the Civil Rights Movement in Chicago* (Athens, GA: University of Georgia Press, 1986), 87–89; Ralph Jr., *Northern Protest..*

32. Bart Landry, *The New Black Middle Class* (Berkeley: University of California Press, 1987).

33. For exceptions, see Theresa A. Hammond, *A White-Collar Profession: African American Certified Public Accountants since 1921* (Chapel Hill: University of North Carolina Press, 2002); George Davis and Glegg Watson, *Black Life in Corporate America: Swimming in the Mainstream* (Garden City, NY: Anchor Press, 1982); Edward D. Irons and Gilbert W. Moore, *Black Managers: The Case of the Banking Industry* (New York: Praeger, 1985); Jason Chambers, *Madison Avenue and the Color Line: African Americans in the Advertising Industry* (Philadelphia: University of Pennsylvania Press, 2008).

34. Robin D. G. Kelley, *Race Rebels: Culture, Politics, and the Black Working Class* (New York: Free Press, 1996); Roger Horowitz, *"Negro and White, Unite and Fight": A Social History of Industrial Unionism in Meatpacking, 1930-1990* (Urbana: University of Illinois Press, 1997); Bruce Nelson, *Divided We Stand: American Workers and the Struggle for Black Equality* (Princeton, NJ: Princeton University Press, 2001); Nancy MacLean, *Freedom Is Not Enough: The Opening of the American Workplace* (Cambridge, MA: Harvard University Press, 2006), 342; William P. Jones, *The March on Washington: Jobs, Freedom, and the Forgotten History of Civil Rights* (New York: W. W. Norton & Co., 2013).

NOTES TO CHAPTER 1

1. Frank Marshall Davis, *Livin' the Blues: Memoirs of a Black Journalist and Poet* (Madison: University of Wisconsin Press, 1992), 57–58.

2. Horace R. Cayton, *Long Old Road* (New York: Trident Press, 1965), 243; Elmer Irey as told to William J. Slocum, *The Tax Dodgers: The Inside Story of the T-Men's War with America's Political and Underworld Hoodlums* (New York: Greenberg, 1948), 187–89.

3. *Time*, "Business in Bronzeville," April 18, 1938, 70–71.

4. *Chicago Tribune*, "Police Raid Swank Policy Racket Depot," October 1, 1949, 1.

5. Orville Dwyer, "Policy Racket Pays Million in Protection," *Chicago Defender*, May 14, 1946, 1; Roger Biles, *Big City Boss in Depression and War: Mayor Edward J. Kelly of Chicago* (DeKalb: Northern Illinois Press, 1984), 91.

6. *Chicago Tribune*, "Roe Bosses Huge Policy Empire; Defies Syndicate," June 20, 1951, 2.

7. *Time*, "The Conglomerate of Crime," August 22, 1969, 31; Mark H. Haller, "Illegal Enterprise: A Theoretical and Historical Interpretation," *Criminology* 28, no. 2 (1990): 218.

8. Raymond Grow, "De King Is Daid!" *American Mercury*, October 1939, 212–15.

9. *Chicago Defender*, "Threats of Death Sent to Jones Boys," May 4, 1940, 2.

10. *Chicago Sun*, "Policy King's Release Seen as Kin Arrive," May 15, 1946, 1; Lester Velie, "The Capone Gang Muscles into Big Time Politics," *Colliers*, September 30, 1950, 18; William J. Grimshaw, *Bitter Fruit: Black Politics and the Chicago Machine, 1931–1991* (Chicago: University of Chicago Press, 1992), 82–84.

11. *Time*, "Emperor Jones," May 27, 1946, 25; *Time*, "Lucky Ted," August 8, 1952, 20.

12. *Chicago Defender*, "Jones Kidnap Starts Drive against Racket," June 8, 1946, 8.

13. Albert N. Votaw, "Chicago: 'Corrupt and Contented'?" *New Republic*, August 25, 1952, 12–13; *Chicago Tribune*, "Ted Roe, Policy Boss, Slain," August 5, 1952, 1; Lee Blackwell, "Midnight Street Echoes Dread Tale Roe Is Dead—You Can't Beat Mob," *Chicago Defender*, August 16, 1952, 4.

14. Special Committee to Investigate Organized Crime in Interstate Commerce, *The Kefauver Committee Report on Organized Crime* (New York: Didier, 1951), 38–39.

15. Preston H. Smith II, *Racial Democracy and the Black Metropolis: Housing Policy in Postwar Chicago* (Minneapolis: University of Minnesota Press, 2012); Lisa Krissoff Boehm, *Making a Way Out of No Way: African American Women and the Second Great Migration* (Jackson: University of Mississippi Press, 2009).

16. Richard Wright, "The Shame of Chicago," Dec. 1951, Richard Wright Papers, Box 6, Folder 140, Beineke Library, Yale University.

17. Robert Weems, *Black Business in the Black Metropolis: The Chicago Metropolitan Assurance Company, 1925–1985* (Bloomington: Indiana University Press, 1996), 93.

18. Leon Litwack, *Trouble in Mind: Black Southerners in the Age of Jim Crow* (New York: Knopf, 1998), 150–63, 312–22; Tim Madigan, *The Burning: Massacre, Destruction, and the Tulsa Race Riot of 1921* (New York: St. Martin's Press, 2001), 179–82.

19. Christopher Robert Reed, *The Rise of Chicago's Black Metropolis, 1920–1929* (Urbana: University of Illinois Press, 2011), 9.

20. Richard Wright, *Later Works* (New York: Library of America, 1991), 880.

21. *Chicago Whip*, "Forward, Let's Go!" December 9, 1922, 8.

22. Reed, *Rise of Chicago's Black Metropolis*, 3.

23. Emmett Scott, *Negro Migration during the War* (New York: Oxford University Press, 1920), 17; James R. Grossman, *Land of Hope: Chicago, Black Southerners, and the Great Migration* (Chicago: University of Chicago Press, 1989), 35, 81–82; Louise Venable Kennedy, *The Negro Peasant Turns Cityward* (New York: Columbia University Press, 1930), 53–54; Otis and Beverly Duncan, *Chicago's Negro Population: Characteristics and Trends* (Chicago: University of Chicago Press, 1956), 2.

24. George E. Haynes, "Negro Migration," *Opportunity*, October 1924, 303; *Opportunity*, "Chicago," March 1929, 69; National Committee on Negro Housing, "The Physical Aspect of Negro Housing," July 1931, Irene McCoy Gaines Papers (IMG), Box 1, Folder

10, Chicago History Museum; Scott, *Negro Migration during the War*, 112–17; William M. Tuttle Jr., *Race Riot: Chicago in the Red Summer of 1919* (New York: Atheneum, 1970), 95.

25. *Chicago Defender*, "Overstepping the Bounds," August 4, 1917, 12; Ben Baker, "A Few Do and Don'ts," *Chicago Defender*, July 13, 1918, 16.

26. August Wilson, *The Piano Lesson* (New York: Dutton, 1990), 4.

27. E. Franklin Frazier, "Chicago: A Cross Section of Negro Life," *Opportunity*, March 1929, 70–73.

28. "Houses," 4, Illinois Writers Project: "Negro in Illinois" Papers (IWP), Box 37, Folder 3, Vivian G. Harsh Research Collection of Afro-American History and Literature, Carter G. Woodson Regional Library; Gunnar Myrdal, *An American Dilemma: The Negro Problem and Modern Democracy* (Harper & Brothers, 1944), 652; Robert Roberts, "Negro-White Marriages in Chicago," Unpublished MA Thesis, University of Chicago, 1939, 19; W. Lloyd Warner, Buford H. Junker, and Walter A. Adams, *Color and Human Nature: Negro Personality Development in a Northern City* (Washington, DC: American Council on Education, 1941), 149.

29. Allan H. Spear, *Black Chicago: The Making of a Negro Ghetto, 1890–1920* (Chicago: University of Chicago Press, 1967); Thomas Philpott, *The Slum and the Ghetto: Neighborhood Deterioration and Middle-Class Reform in Chicago, 1880–1930* (New York: Oxford University Press, 1978).

30. *Inter-Ocean*, "Landlords Seek to Eject Woman," September 28, 1894, 1; *Chicago Record*, "Race War Campaign Planned," May 5, 1897; *Inter-Ocean*, "Woodlawn Wages War on Negroes," February 12, 1902, 2; *Inter-Ocean*, "Would Bar Colored Family," July 25, 1902, 1; *Inter-Ocean*, "Refuse Negro Club Home," December 15, 1904, 1; *Chicago Herald*, "Neighbors Bar Door against Negro Owner," May 2, 1915; clippings in IWP, Box 37, Folder 12; *Broad Ax*, "The White Residents of Kenwood, Hyde Park and Woodlawn Are Up in Arms," August 28, 1909, 1; *Broad Ax*, "Negroes and Property Values," September 18, 1909, 2; *Chicago Tribune*, "Oak Park Negro, Home Set Afire, Sees White Man," March 8, 1916, 15; M. M. Cummings, "History of Woodlawn," Paper for Sociology 234, 1932, Ernest W. Burgess Papers (EWB), Box 159, Folder 2, Regenstein Library, University of Chicago.

31. St. Clair Drake and Horace R. Cayton, *Black Metropolis: A Study of Negro Life in a Northern City* (New York: Harcourt, Brace and Company, 1945), 74–75.

32. *Chicago Whip* quoted in Willard B. Gatewood, *Aristocrats of Color: The Black Elite, 1880–1920* (Bloomington: Indiana University Press, 1990), 124; Warner, Junker, and Adams, *Color and Human Nature*, 85.

33. Scott, *Negro Migration during the War*, 13.

34. St. Clair Drake, "Churches and Voluntary Associations in the Chicago Negro Community: Report of the Official Project 465-54-386 conducted under the auspices of the Work Projects Administration," (Chicago: Work Projects Administration, 1940), 214.

35. Carter Woodson, *Free Negro Heads of Families in the United States in 1830* (Washington, DC: The Association for the Study of Negro Life and History), xxxvi. Carole Marks estimates that skilled blacks outnumbered skilled whites in the South at the end of the Civil War by a five to one margin. Carole Marks, "The Social and Economic Life of Southern Blacks during the Migration," in *Black Exodus: The Great Migration from the American South*, Alferdteen Harrison, ed. (Jackson: University Press of Mississippi, 1991), 38–41.

36. Merah Stuart, *An Economic Detour: A History of Insurance in the Lives of American Negroes* (New York: Wendell Malliet & Co., 1940), 321–22.

37. Davis Joseph, "That Dixie Monster," *Half-Century Magazine*, January 1919, 13.

38. Marks, "The Social and Economic Life of Southern Blacks during the Migration," 38–41; Emmett J. Scott, "Letters of Negro Migrants of 1916–1918," *Journal of Negro History* 4 (July 1919): 293, 295, 298–302, 309–11, 329, 332, 334–37; Emmett J. Scott, "Additional Letters of Negro Migrants of 1916–1918," *Journal of Negro History* 4 (October 1919): 416, 422, 427, 433, 436, 441, 445, 448; Peter Gottlieb, *Making Their Own Way: Southern Blacks' Migration to Pittsburgh, 1916–30* (Urbana: University of Illinois Press, 1987), 98.

39. Walter White, *A Man Called White: The Autobiography of Walter White* (New York: The Viking Press, 1948), 42–43.

40. Paul A. Gilje, *Rioting in America* (Bloomington: Indiana University Press, 1996), 104.

41. *Half-Century Magazine*, "Going North," September 1919, 2; "The Migrants Keep Coming," IWP, Box 33, Folder 1; H. A. Phelps, "Negro Life in Chicago," *Half-Century Magazine*, May 1919, 12–13; Scott, "Letters of Negro Migrants of 1916–1918," 308; *Chicago Defender*, "Northern Drive to Start," February 10, 1917, 3; Carter G. Woodson, *The Negro Professional Man and the Community* (New York: Negro Universities Press, 1969 [1934]), 117; Grossman, *Land of Hope*, 94–96; Scott, *Negro Migration during the War*, 24–25.

42. According to the 1940 census, 22 percent of black out-migrants had a high school degree as opposed to only 6 percent who stayed in the South. James N. Gregory, *The Southern Diaspora: How the Great Migrations of Black and White Southerners Transformed America* (Chapel Hill: University of North Carolina Press, 2005), 30–31.

43. Carl Sandburg, *The Chicago Race Riots* (New York: Harcourt, Brace and Howe, 1919), 10.

44. Roi Ottley, *The Lonely Warrior: The Life and Times of Robert S. Abbott* (Chicago: Henry Regnery Co., 1955), 6–7, 77–78.

45. Davis, *Livin' the Blues*, 103.

46. Grossman, 3, 36.

47. Charles S. Johnson, *The Negro in American Civilization* (New York: Henry Holt and Company, 1930), 297–98; John Bodnar, Roger Simon, and Michael P. Weber, *Lives of Their Own: Blacks, Italians, and Poles in Pittsburgh, 1900–1960* (Urbana: University of Illinois Press, 1982), 35, 143; Suzanne W. Model, "Work and Family: Blacks and Immigrants from South and East Europe," in *Immigration Reconsidered: History, Sociology, and Politics*, Virginia Yans-McLaughlin, ed. (New York: Oxford University Press, 1990), 134; John J. Bukowczyk, *And My Children Did Not Know Me: A History of the Polish-Americans* (Bloomington: Indiana University Press, 1987), 12–13, 32.

48. Scott, "Letters of Negro Migrants of 1916–1918," 301.

49. E. Franklin Frazier, *The Negro Family in Chicago* (Chicago: University of Chicago Press, 1932), 130; "The Exodus Train," IWP, Box 33, Folder 1; George Arthur, "The Young Men's Christian Association Movement among Negroes," *Opportunity*, March 1923, 16–18; Scott, "Additional Letters," 432–38; Warner, Junker, and Adams, 94; John H. Johnson with Lerone Bennett Jr., *Succeeding against the Odds* (New York: Warner Books, 1989), 22; Alden Bland, *Behold a Cry* (New York: Charles Scribner's Sons, 1947), 104.

50. Grossman, 246–49; A. Albertine Wetter, "A Glimpse into an Unusual Night School," *Chicago Schools Journal*, June 1921, 132–34.

51. Letitia Merrill, "Children's Choice of Occupation," *Chicago Schools Journal*, December 1922, 156.

52. Charles Johnson, *The Negro College Graduate* (Chapel Hill: University of North Carolina Press, 1938), 185–86.

53. Langston Hughes, "Mother to Son," *Vintage Hughes* (New York: Vintage, 2004), 7–8.

54. *Half-Century Magazine*, "A Monument to Negro Thrift and Industry: The Overton Building," January–February, 1923, 13; Reed, *Rise of Chicago's Black Metropolis*, 87.

55. Johnson, *Succeeding against the Odds*, 63.

56. *Chicago Defender*, "What the Defender Has Done," February 2, 1918, 11; Tuttle, *Race Riot*, 91.

57. Harold F. Gosnell, *Negro Politicians: The Rise of Negro Politics in Chicago* (Chicago: University of Chicago Press, 1935), 339; Sterling D. Spero and Abram L. Harris, *The Black Worker: The Negro and the Labor Movement*, (New York: Atheneum, 1968 [1931]), xv, 398.

58. Saunders quoted in Neal Samors and Michael Williams, *Chicago in the Fifties: Remembering Life in the Loop and the Neighborhoods* (Chicago: Chicago's Neighborhoods, Inc., 2005), 9; Travis quoted in Neal Samors and Michael Williams, *The Old Chicago Neighborhood: Remembering Life in the 1940s* (Chicago's Neighborhoods, Inc., 2003), 110.

59. Abram Harris, *The Negro as Capitalist: A Study of Banking and Business among American Negroes* (Philadelphia: The American Academy of Political and Social Science, 1936), ix–x; Juliet E. K. Walker, *The History of Black Business in America: Capitalism, Race, Entrepreneurship*, 2nd ed. (Chapel Hill: University of North Carolina Press, 2009), 183; Jonathan Scott Holloway, *Confronting the Veil: Abram Harris Jr., E. Franklin Frazier, and Ralph Bunche, 1919–1941* (Chapel Hill: University of North Carolina Press, 2002), 72–73.

60. William L. Evans, "The Negro in Chicago Industries," *Opportunity*, February 1923, 15–16; Junius Wood, "Southerners Soon Readjusted," *Chicago Daily News*, April 7, 1917; Henry M. Hyde, "Half a Million Darkies from Dixie Swarm the North to Better Themselves," *Chicago Tribune*, July 8, 1917, 8.

61. *Half-Century Magazine*, "Money Bleaches," July–August 1922, 3.

62. L. L. Davis, "That Thorn in the Flesh," *Half-Century Magazine*, January–February 1925.

63. *Chicago Daily News*, "Time and Security Needed: Negro to Solve Own Housing Problems, Slum Parley Told," February 5, 1954; Oscar Handlin, *The Newcomers: Negroes and Puerto Ricans in a Changing Metropolis* (Garden City, NY: Doubleday, 1959), 120–21. Handlin concluded that these migrants "followed the general outline of the experience of earlier immigrants." Neoconservatives such as Nathan Glazer and Irving Kristol stubbornly held to this belief even though many black "newcomers" called the city home for many years and were still mired at the bottom socioeconomically. See Nathan Glazer, "Blacks and Ethnic Groups: The Difference, and the Political Difference It Makes," in *Key Issues in the Afro-American Experience*, vol. 2, Nathan Huggins, Martin Kilson, and Daniel Fox, eds. (Chicago: Harcourt Brace Jovanovich, Inc., 1971), 193–211; Irving Kristol, "The Negro Today Is Like the Immigrant of Yesterday," *New York Times Magazine*, September 11, 1966, 51–52, 124–42.

64. Scott, *Negro Migration during the War*, 114.

65. For the creation of the segmented labor market, see David M. Gordon, Richard Edwards, and Michael Reich, *Segmented Work, Divided Workers: The Historical Transformations of Labor in the United States* (New York: Cambridge University Press, 1982), ix–x, 3, 174.

66. Scott, *Negro Migration during the War*, 113–14; Myra Hill Colson, "Home Work among Negro Women in Chicago," Unpublished MA Thesis, University of Chicago, 1928, 66; "The Migrants Keep Coming," 10, IWP, Box 32, Folder 1; "Negro Migration in 1916–17," 5, IWP, Box 33, Folder 4; Woodson, *Negro Professional Man and the Community*, 330; N. C. Jenkins, "What Chance Has the Trained Student?" Washington Intercollegiate Club, *The Negro in Chicago*, vol. 2, 193; Warner, Junker, and Adams, 180, 242.

67. Irene McCoy Gaines fundraising letter for the YWCA, Jan. 27, 1922, IMG, Box 1, Folder 6.; Jenkins, "What Chance Has the Trained Student?" 89; Walter Reckless, *Vice in Chicago* (Chicago: University of Chicago Press, 1933), 25, 29.

68. Warner, Junker, and Adams, 100.

69. Carroll Binder, *Chicago and the New Negro: How the City Absorbed the Huge Post-war Migration from the South, and What Economic, Social and Civic Changes Were Wrought Thereby* (Chicago: Chicago Daily News, 1927), 8–10.

70. Rick Halpern, *Down on the Killing Floor: Black and White Workers in Chicago's Packinghouses, 1904–1954* (Urbana: University of Illinois Press, 1997), 40, 94; Lizabeth Cohen, *Making a New Deal: Industrial Workers in Chicago, 1919–1939* (New York: Cambridge University Press, 1990), 165–67; Gottlieb, *Making Their Own Way*, 99–100.

71. Oscar Douglas Hutton, "The Negro Worker and the Labor Unions," Unpublished MA Thesis, University of Chicago, 1939, 90.

72. Alma Herbst, *The Negro in the Slaughtering and Meat-Packing Industry in Chicago* (New York: Houghton Mifflin Company, 1932), 5–6; 61–62, 70; Scott, *Negro Migration during the War*, 117; Hutton, "The Negro Worker and the Labor Unions," 13–15; Colson, "Home Work among Negro Women in Chicago," 67.

73. William Broonzy, as told to Yannick Bruynoghe, *Big Bill Blues* (London: Cassell & Company, Ltd., 1955), 59.

74. Weems, *Black Business in the Black Metropolis*, 93; Hylan Garnet Lewis, "Social Differentiation in the Negro Community," Unpublished MA Thesis, University of Chicago, 1936, 97.

75. William L. Evans, "The Negro in Chicago Industries," *Opportunity*, February 1923, 15–16; Claude Barnett, "We Win a Place in Industry," *Opportunity*, March 1929, 82–86. For the limited clerical and business opportunities open to college-educated blacks, see David King Cherry, "Vocational Activities of Educated Negroes," Unpublished MA Thesis, University of Chicago, 1931, 25–27; Hutton, 8.

76. Claude Barnett, "We Win a Place in Industry," *Opportunity*, March 1929, 82–86; Chicago Commission on Race Relations (CCRR), *The Negro in Chicago: A Study of Race Relations and a Race Riot* (Chicago: University of Chicago Press, 1922), 229–30; Jenkins, "What Chance Has the Trained Student?" 89, 201; Letter from Council for Job Equality on State Street, Gerald Bullock, Chair, to Irene McCoy Gaines, Dec. 19, 1947, IMG, Box 2, Folder 6; "Negro Employees in Chain Stores," IWP, Box 35, Folder 10; Stephen Breszka, "And Lo! It Worked," *Opportunity*, November 1933, 342.

77. *Chicago Whip*, February 18, 1939, "Don't Spend Your Money Where You Can't Work," IWP, Box 41, Folder 7.

78. Grossman, 258. As late as 1959, the incomes of white male college graduates exceeded that of nonwhite college graduates by 81 percent, whereas whites with grade school educations had an advantage of 46 percent over their nonwhite peers. Richard B. Freeman, *Black Elite: The New Market for Highly Educated Black Americans* (New York: McGraw-Hill, 1976), xix.

79. Shaw quoted in Southside Community Committee, *Bright Shadows in Bronze-town: The Story of the Southside Community Committee* (Chicago: 1949), 8–9.

80. Larry Tye, *Rising from the Rails: Pullman Porters and the Making of the Black Middle Class* (New York: Henry Holt and Co., 2004), 80; *Chicago Whip*, "Under the Lash of the Whip," July 22, 1922, 8.

81. Letitia Merrill, "Children's Choice of Occupation," *Chicago Schools Journal*, December 1922, 157.

82. Letter from Stanley B. Norvell to Victor Lawson, August 22, 1919, 4, 7, Julius Rosenwald Papers (JRP), Box 6, Folder 3, Regenstein Library, University of Chicago.

83. Lewis A. H. Caldwell, "The Policy Game in Chicago," Unpublished MA Thesis, Northwestern University, 1940, 29.

84. J. Winston Harrington, "Let 'em, Policy," *Chicago Defender*, November 25, 1939, 13; "Effect of the Depression on Insurance Business," 1934–1935, EWB, Box 134, Folder 1; Caldwell, "Policy Game in Chicago," 58–59.

85. Gosnell, *Negro Politicians*, 115; "Effect of the Depression on Insurance Business," 1934–1935, EWB, Box 134, Folder 1; *Chicago Defender*, "Chicago's Underworld Shaken by Vice Probe: Gambling on South Side under Fire," August 25, 1928, 1; Caldwell, "Policy Game in Chicago," 3, 48, 87–88; J. Winston Harrington, "Let 'em, Policy," *Chicago Defender*, November 25, 1939, 13.

86. *Chicago Defender*, "Arrest Minister's Sons as Policy Racketeers: Mayor Issues Order in Clean-Up of All Policy Racket Dens," September 26, 1931, 1; Harold Gosnell, "The Negro Vote in Northern Cities," *National Municipal Review* 30, no. 5 (May 1941), 4.

87. Humbert S. Nelli, *Italians in Chicago, 1880–1930* (New York: Oxford University Press, 1970), 138–39; *Chicago Whip*, "Find Vice Den near YWCA Home for Girls," August 5, 1922, 1. For a scathing critique of policy, see David Camelon, "The Number Racket," *Negro Digest* (March 1950), 46–49.

88. "Policy: Negro Business," 15–17, IWP, Box 35, Folder 11; J. Winston Harrington, "Let 'em, Policy," *Chicago Defender*, November 25, 1939, 13.

89. Bricktop with James Haskins, *Bricktop* (New York: Atheneum, 1983), 29; Katherine Dunham, *A Touch of Innocence* (New York: Harcourt, Brace and Company, 1959), 178; Roi Ottley, *New World a-Coming* (Boston: Houghton Mifflin, 1943), 159; Enoch P. Waters, *American Diary: A Personal History of the Black Press* (Chicago: Path Press, 1987), 74–77.

90. *Hyde Park–Kenwood Voices*, "Gangs: Their Evolution and Essence" [1969?], Leon Despres Papers, Box 94, Folder 7, Chicago History Museum.

91. Sandburg, *Chicago Race Riots*, 59–61; Caldwell, "Policy Game in Chicago," 53; "Interview with Harris B. Gaines," Aug. 1, 1938, IWP, Box 43, Folder 17; Waters, *American Diary*, 74–77, Drake and Cayton, *Black Metropolis*, 487; *Chicago Defender*, "'Policy' Sam Rites Held Friday," May 29, 1937, 5; J. Winston Harrington, "Let 'em, Policy," *Chicago Defender*, November 25, 1939, 13; Orville Dwyer, "Policy Racket Pays Million in Protection," *Chicago Defender*, May 14, 1946, 1.

92. Ruth Evans Pardee, "A Study of the Functions of Associations in a Small Negro Community in Chicago," Unpublished MA Thesis, University of Chicago, 1937, 24.

93. "Policy" [1932?], EWB, Box 37, Folder 5; Julius J. Adams, "Policy, Once a Big Industry, Hits Skids: Defender Reporter Spills the 'Inside' Dope on Rise and Fall of Numbers," *Chicago Defender*, April 22, 1933, 11; Mark Haller, "Policy, Gambling, Entertainment, and the Emergence of Black Politics: Chicago from 1900 to 1940," *Journal of Social History* 24, no. 4 (1991): 733.

94. Letter from Stanley B. Norvell to Victor Lawson, Aug. 22, 1919, 4, JRP, Box 6, Folder 3; Davis, 128.

95. Herbert Morrisohn Smith, "Three Negro Preachers in Chicago: A Study in Religious Leadership," Unpublished MA Thesis, University of Chicago, 1935, 42; Samuel Strong, "Social Types in the Negro Community of Chicago: An Example of the Social Type Method," Unpublished PhD Dissertation, University of Chicago, 1940, 118–19.

96. South Side Community Committee, "Are These Our Children?" [1942?] and Untitled Journal, South Side Community Committee, May 13, 1942, Chicago Area Project Papers, Box 98, Folder 1, Chicago History Museum; Chicago Defender, "James Knight Rites Saturday," January 6, 1962, 3.

97. Chicago Defender, "Pick 'Miss Bronze America' and Bronzeville Mayor on Sept. 22," September 22, 1934, 21. The four candidates were James Knight, Ily Kelly, Levirt Kelly, and Ed Jones.

98. "Policy: Negro Business," 2, 11–12, 15–17, IWP, Box 35, Folder 11; Weems, Black Business in the Black Metropolis, xii.

99. Caldwell, "Policy Game in Chicago," 60.

100. "Policy: Negro Business," 15–17, IWP, Box 35, Folder 11.

101. Cornelia Tilford, "Report of Mrs. Cornelia Tilford, work relief employee assigned through the Urban League, 1934–1935," 15, EWB, Box 134, Folder 1; Colson, 93; Gareth Canaan, "'Part of the Loaf': Economic Conditions of Chicago's African-American Working Class during the 1920's," Journal of Social History 35, no. 1 (2001): 157–58.

102. Chicago Defender, "Chicago's Underworld Shaken by Vice Probe: Gambling on South Side under Fire," August 25, 1928, 1; Caldwell, "Policy Game in Chicago," 27–29; Claude McKay, Harlem: Negro Metropolis (New York: E. P. Dutton & Co., 1940), 112–13.

103. A. J. Jaffe, "Policy" [1932?], EWB, Box 132, Folder 6.

104. Caldwell, "Policy Game in Chicago," 32–33; J. Saunders Redding, "Playing the Numbers," The North American Review 238, no. 6 (December 1934): 536.

105. A. J. Jaffe, "The Negro as Customer" [1932?], EWB, Box 132, Folder 6; Cornelia Tilford, "Report of Mrs. Cornelia Tilford, work relief employee assigned through the Urban League, 1934–1935," 15, EWB, Box 134, Folder 1; J. Saunders Redding, "Playing the Numbers," The North American Review 238, no. 6 (December 1934): 535.

106. Rufus Schatzberg and Robert J. Kelly, African-American Organized Crime: A Social History (New York: Garland Publishing, 1996), xvii; Victoria W. Wolcott, "The Culture of the Informal Economy: Numbers Runners in Inter-War Black Detroit," Radical History Review 69 (Fall 1997): 46–75; Khalil Gibran Muhammad, The Condemnation of Blackness: Race, Crime, and the Making of Modern Urban America (Cambridge, MA: Harvard University Press, 2010), 10, 193, 208.

107. Richard Wright, "The Shame of Chicago," c. 1949, Richard Wright Papers, Box 6, Folder 140, Beinecke Library, Yale University.

108. Will Cooley, "Jim Crow Organized Crime: Black Chicago's Underground Economy in the Twentieth Century," in Building the Black Metropolis: African-American Entrepreneurship in Chicago, Robert Weems and Jason Chambers, eds. (University of Illinois Press, 2017), 147–70.

109. Drake, "Churches and Voluntary Associations in the Chicago Negro Community," 142; Harriet Choice, "The Good News of Gospel," Chicago Tribune, January 22, 1978, H40.

110. W. E. B. Du Bois, The Souls of Black Folk (Chicago: A. C. McClurg & Co., 1903), 190.

111. Melvin Van Peebles, *Bear for the FBI* (New York: Trident Press, 1968), 16.

112. "And Churches," 7, IWP, Box 45, Folder 1; Vattel Elbert Daniel, "Ritual in Chicago's South Side Churches of Negroes," Unpublished PhD Dissertation, University of Chicago, 1940, 13, 93–94, 125–26; Wallace D. Best, *Passionately Human, No Less Divine: Religion and Culture in Black Chicago, 1915–1952* (Princeton, NJ: Princeton University Press, 2005), 55–59; Arna Botemps and Jack Conroy, *Anyplace but Here* (New York: Hill and Wang, 1966), 173.

113. Ethel R. Harris, "A Study of Voluntary Social Activity among the Professional Negroes in Chicago," Unpublished MA Thesis, University of Chicago, 1937, 58–59; Strong, "Social Types in the Negro Community of Chicago," 204–5.

114. Ira De Augustine Reid, "Let Us Prey!" *Opportunity*, September 1926, 277–78.

115. Interview with Rev. J. Langston Poole, St. Paul AME, Jan. 19, 1934, and interview with Rev. S. A. Bryant, New Hope Baptist Church, Feb. 2, 1934, EWB, Box 89, Folder 5; Strong, 219.

116. Laura B. Richardson, "Essay on African-American Conflict and Self-Organization in the Early Twentieth Century," IWP, Box 32, Folder 4; Estelle Hill Scott, *Occupational Changes among Negroes in Chicago* (Chicago: Work Projects Administration, 1939), 218; Drake and Cayton, 629–32.

117. Johnson, *Negro College Graduate*, 263.

118. Daniel, "Ritual in Chicago's South Side Churches of Negroes," 37–39, 58–59, 69–72; Drake, "Churches and Voluntary Associations in the Chicago Negro Community," 190.

119. R. F. C. Tonelle, "Effect of the Depression on Spiritualism," 1934–1935, EWB, Box 134, Folder 1; A. J. Jaffe, "Negro Music" [1932?], EWB, Box 132, Folder 6; David W. Kellum, "First Church of Deliverance Largest of Its Kind in U.S: Rev. Clarence H. Cobbs Closes Ninth Anniversary Celebration at the Noted Institution," *Chicago Defender*, June 4, 1938, 23; "Spirituals of Today," 2, 17–19, IWP, Box 49, Folder 24; Laurraine Goreau, *Just Mahalia, Baby* (Waco, TX: Word Books, 1975), 55–56, 119.

120. Ira De Augustine Reid, "Let Us Prey!" *Opportunity*, September 1926, 275; Laura B. Richardson, "Essay on African-American Conflict and Self-Organization in the Early Twentieth Century," IWP, Box 32, Folder 4.

121. Best, *Passionately Human, No Less Divine*, 40–43; "And Churches," 7, IWP, Box 45, Folder 1.

122. Smith, "Three Negro Preachers in Chicago," 18.

123. Daniel, 11, 44–45.

124. "A Brief History of Provident Baptist Church," June 18, 1941, IWP, Box 5, Folder 17; "And Churches," 16–17, IWP, Box 45, Folder 1; "The History of Good Shepherd Congregational Church," June 18, 1941, IWP, Box 5, Folder 18.

125. Interview with Rev. S. A. Bryant, New Hope Baptist Church, Feb. 2, 1934, and interview with Rev. E. Harris, Assistant Pastor of Union MB Church, Jan. 18, 1934, EWB, Box 89, Folder 5; Drake, "Churches and Voluntary Associations in the Chicago Negro Community," 198–201.

126. David W. Kellum, "First Church of Deliverance Largest of Its Kind in U.S: Rev. Clarence H. Cobbs Closes Ninth Anniversary Celebration at the Noted Institution," *Chicago Defender*, June 4, 1938, 23; R. F. C. Tonelle, "Effect of the Depression on Spiritualism," 1934–1935, EWB, Box 134, Folder 1.

127. *Chicago Defender*, "And Speaking of Folks Going Places . . . and Doing Things," May 21, 1938, 13; *Chicago Defender*, "Local Leaders to Head Lobby Fight Committee," June

14, 1941, 2; *Chicago Tribune*, "NAACP Unit Installs Its New Officers," January 4, 1958, 12; Ted Coleman, "Clerics Meet Wilson on Wabash Shakeup," *Chicago Defender*, May 4, 1963, 2; Chicago Urban League Papers (CUL), Series II, Box 241, Folder 2406, CUL memo from Idarae Jackson and Lauretta Travis to Task Force Directors, Aug. 4, 1970, Daley Library, University of Illinois at Chicago.

128. Cayton, *Long Old Road*, 243.

129. Best, 4–5.

130. Spear, *Black Chicago*, 112; Lewis, "Social Differentiation in the Negro Community," 82–83; *Chicago Tribune*, "C. S. Funk Sued for $50,000," May 6, 1914, 3; H. A. Phelps, "Negro Life in Chicago," *Half-Century Magazine*, May 1919, 12–13.

131. Gosnell, *Negro Politicians*, 169, 177; *Chicago Defender*, "Banker Binga in Jail Hospital: Held for $300,000 Embezzlement," March 14, 1931, 2; Carl Osthaus, "The Rise and Fall of Jesse Binga, Black Financier," *Journal of Negro History* 58 (1973): 42.

132. Binder, *Chicago and the New Negro*, 6; Waters E. Turpin, *O Canaan!* (New York: Doubleday, Doran & Company, Inc., 1939), 43.

133. Alice Quan Rood, "Study of Social Conditions among the Negroes on Federal Street between Forty-Fifth Street and Fifty-Third Street," Unpublished MA Thesis, University of Chicago, 1924, 33–36; Rev. Harold Kingsley, Minutes of Interracial Committee Meeting of Women's City Club, Nov. 23, 1931, and National Committee on Negro Housing, "The Physical Aspect of Negro Housing," July 1931, IMG, Box 1, Folder 10; "Effect of Depression on Religion," 1934–1935, interview with Rev. J. B. Redmond, St. Mark's Methodist Episcopalian, EWB, Box 134, Folder 1; *The Crisis*, "Iron Ring of Housing," July 1940, 205, 210.

134. Gwendolyn Brooks, "kitchenette building," in *Blacks* (Chicago: The David Company, 1987), 20; Richard Wright, *12 Million Black Voices: A Folk History of the Negro in the United States* (New York: Arno Press, 1969 [1941]), 106.

135. Elwood Fife, "High Rent on the Throne," *Half-Century Magazine*, June 1919, 17; Edith Abbott, *The Tenements of Chicago, 1908–1935* (Chicago: University of Chicago Press, 1936), 124, fn 55.

136. *Chicago Whip*, "We Live Like Dogs and Pay Like Princes," January 28, 1939.

137. *Chicago Defender*, "Hansberry Is Plaintiff in $50,000 Suit," January 7, 1939, 6; *The Crisis*, "Iron Ring of Housing," July 1940, 205, 210; *The Crisis*, "The Hansberrys of Chicago: They Join Business Acumen with Social Vision," April 1941, 106–7; Truman Gibson, *Knocking Down Barriers: My Fight for Black America* (Evanston, IL: Northwestern Press, 2005), 44–48.

138. CCRR, *Negro in Chicago*, 217; T. J. Woofter Jr., *Negro Problems in Cities* (Garden City, NY: Doubleday, Doran & Company, Inc., 1928), 132–33. See also National Committee on Negro Housing, "The Physical Aspect of Negro Housing," July 1931, IMG, Box 1, Folder 10. Among the many prominent blacks who invested in real estate as landlords were Carl Hansberry, Harris Gaines, Clarence Cobbs, and Mahalia Jackson. See Gladys Priddy, "Flock Will Aid Me Stay Out of Jail," *Chicago Tribune*, May 6, 1951, S6; Letter from Harris Gaines to Alderman Claude Holman, Mar. 21, 1963, IMG, Box 6, Folder 6; Mahalia Jackson with Evan McLeod Wylie, *Movin' On Up* (New York: Hawthorn Books, 1966), 119–22.

139. Interview with Grace Garnett, July 30, 1941, IWP, Box 37, Folder 25.

140. Leonard Pearson interview with William Neighbors, secretary of the Negro Chamber of Commerce, Sept. 30, 1937, IWP, Box 25, Folder 15; Gosnell, *Negro Politicians*, 347; Christopher Robert Reed, *The Chicago NAACP and the Rise of Black Professional Leadership, 1910–1966* (Bloomington: Indiana University Press, 1997), 85.

141. Robert Weaver, *The Negro Ghetto* (New York: Harcourt, Brace, 1948), 52–57.

142. Drake and Cayton, 83.

143. Cohen, *Making a New Deal*, 205–6, 242.

144. *Chicago Tribune*, "Reds Riot; 3 Slain by Police," August 4, 1931, 1; Dempsey J. Travis, *An Autobiography of Black Politics* (Chicago: Urban Research Institute, 1987), 89–90; Randi Storch, *Red Chicago: American Communism at Its Grassroots, 1928–1935* (Urbana: University of Illinois Press, 2007), 99–100; Drake, "Churches and Voluntary Associations in the Chicago Negro Community," 258.

145. James O'Donnell Bennett, "Plans, Work, Binga's Secret for Success," *Chicago Tribune*, May 8, 1927, 1; Inez V. Cantey, "Jesse Binga," *The Crisis*, December 1927: 329.

146. Drake and Cayton, 64; *Chicago Tribune*, "Bomb No. 6 Only Annoys Binga; Hurts Neighbors," November 24, 1920, 1; *Chicago Tribune*, "Binga's Guard Tries Gun Play after Bombing: Blast Rocks Negro's Home 7th Time," August 26, 1921, 13.

147. CCRR, *Negro in Chicago*, 131.

148. *Chicago Tribune*, "City Sues Many under Fire Laws," April 21, 1910, 4; *Chicago Tribune*, "Two Bombs Smash Homes of Negroes," March 20, 1919, 1; *Chicago Tribune*, "Bomb at Home of Colored Real Estate Dealer," December 4, 1919, 19; Harris, *Negro as Capitalist*, 153–59; Spear, 112–13.

149. *Chicago Defender*, "Jesse Binga Adds New Land Mark to City's South Side," February 16, 1929, 2; *Chicago Defender*, "Demand That Stockholders Pay in Binga Bank Crash: Stockholders' Cash to Aid Depositors in Defunct Bank," August 12, 1933, 1; Ottley, *Lonely Warrior*, 259.

150. *Chicago Defender*, "Binga State Bank Stockholders Meet: New Interest Manifested in Banking among Our People," April 24, 1920, 13.

151. Quoted in Osthaus, "The Rise and Fall of Jesse Binga, Black Financier," 50.

152. Dewey R. Jones, "Chicago Claims Supremacy," *Opportunity*, March 1929, 92–94.

153. Lucius C. Harper, "Binga Represented a Business Era That Was Crude, Rough, Uncultured," *Chicago Defender*, June 24, 1950, 7.

154. Dewey R. Jones, "Chicago Claims Supremacy," *Opportunity*, March 1929, 92–94; *Opportunity*, "A Negro Bank Closes Its Doors," September 1930, 264; Spear, 197.

155. Osthaus, 50.

156. *Chicago Defender*, "Banker Binga in Jail Hospital: Held for $300,000 Embezzlement," March 14, 1931, 2; Lewis, "Social Differentiation in the Negro Community," 107–8. Binga's downfall mirrored his white banking counterpart on the South Side, John Bain, whose chain of twelve banks collapsed in the early 1930s. Bain, like Binga, used his bank presidents as "rubber stamps, yes men, and office boys" to manipulate bank finances for personal gain before speculating with depositor funds led to his downfall. But unlike Binga, Bain's failure was not perceived as having implications for the white race, demonstrating the extra pressure and different set of circumstances facing black businessmen. *Chicago Tribune*, "State Says Bain Used Presidents as Office Boys," July 2, 1932, 7.

157. *Chicago Defender*, "Binga Bank Had Only 2 Accounts of Over $10,000," October 31, 1931, 3; William Oswald Morrison, "To Whom Shall We Go?" *Chicago Defender*, July 25, 1931, 15.

158. *Chicago Defender*, "3 Chicago Banks Closed: South Side Hit Hard When Institutions Shut Doors," August 9, 1930, 1; *Chicago Defender*, "Banker Binga in Jail Hospital: Held for $300,000 Embezzlement," March 14, 1931, 2; Drake and Cayton, 465; "Interview

with Harris B. Gaines, Republican former member of the Illinois House of Representatives," Aug. 1, 1938, IWP, Box 43, Folder 17.

159. Davis, 293; *Chicago Defender*, "Jim Crow in Chicago," November 11, 1939, 15; Kathleene Simmons, "Negroes Exploit Own Workers," *Chicago Defender*, February 26, 1944, 12.

160. Letter from Irene McCoy Gaines to Lewis Caldwell, July 6, 1937, IMG, Box 1, Folder 12.

161. Earl Richard Moses, "Community Factors in Negro Delinquency," Unpublished MA Thesis, University of Chicago, 1932, 16–17.

162. Quoted in Caldwell, "Policy Game in Chicago," 58–59.

163. Leon Forrest, *The Furious Voice for Freedom: Essays on Life* (Wakefield, RI: Asphodel Press, 1994), 52.

164. *Our World*, "Chicago: Money Capital of Negro America," September 1951, 15–16.

165. Turpin, *O Canaan!* 127–28. See also Frank London Brown, *The Myth Maker* (Chicago: Path Press, 1969), 110–11; Gwendolyn Brooks, "Maud Martha" in *Blacks* (Chicago: The David Company, 1987), 309–10.

166. Gosnell, *Negro Politicians*, 169.

NOTES TO CHAPTER 2

1. Gwendolyn Brooks, *The World of Gwendolyn Brooks* (New York: Harper & Row, 1971), 360–62.

2. *Chicago Defender*, "What 'Oak Leaves' Said. Attempted Murder: Fiends Set Fire to Citizen's Home—Block Front and Back Door—Arrests to Be Made," April 25, 1914, 7; *Chicago Tribune*, "Women Called to Explain Fire: Oak Park 'Gossipers' Will Be Summoned before State Marshal Tomorrow," April 22, 1914, 10; *Chicago Tribune*, "Women Would Tar Negro," April 24, 1914, 8.

3. *Chicago Defender*, "Oak Park in Disgrace," April 25, 1914, 8; *Chicago Defender*, "Oak Park Needs Missionaries: Oak Park Incendiaries Attempt to Burn Jefferson Family Alive," April 25, 1914, 1.

4. *Chicago Tribune*, "Suspect Oak Park Women of Arson: State Fire Marshal to Investigate Burning of Negro's House," April 19, 1914, 1.

5. *Chicago Defender*, "Oak Park Needs Missionaries: Oak Park Incendiaries Attempt to Burn Jefferson Family Alive," April 25, 1914, 1; Jon C. Teaford, *City and Suburb: The Political Fragmentation of Metropolitan America, 1850–1970* (Baltimore, MD: Johns Hopkins University Press, 1979), 22–23.

6. *Daily Jewish Courier*, "Due to Prejudice," April 22, 1914.

7. *Chicago Defender*, "Oak Park Needs Missionaries: Oak Park Incendiaries Attempt to Burn Jefferson Family Alive," April 25, 1914, 1.

8. *Chicago Tribune*, "Oak Park Negro, Home Set Afire, Sees White Man," March 8, 1916, 15.

9. For examples of race relations and neighborhood racial change mainly from the vantage point of whites, see Eileen M. McMahon, *What Parish Are You From? A Chicago Irish Community and Race Relations* (Lexington: University Press of Kentucky, 1995); Thomas Sugrue, *Origins of the Urban Crisis: Race and Inequality in Postwar Detroit* (Princeton, NJ: Princeton University Press, 1996); Arnold Hirsch, *Making the Second Ghetto: Race*

and Housing in Chicago, 1940-1960 (Chicago: University of Chicago Press, 1998); Gerald Gamm, *Urban Exodus: Why the Jews Left Boston and the Catholics Stayed* (Cambridge, MA: Harvard University Press, 1999); Stephen Grant Meyer, *As Long as They Don't Move Next Door: Segregation and Racial Conflict in American Neighborhoods* (New York: Rowman & Littlefield Publishers, Inc., 2000); Amanda Seligman, *Block by Block: Neighborhoods and Public Policy on Chicago's West Side* (Chicago: University of Chicago Press, 2005); David M. P. Freund, *Colored Property: State Policy and White Racial Politics in Suburban America* (Chicago: University of Chicago Press, 2007). For one of the few studies that depicts the entire process of neighborhood change, see Rachel A. Woldoff, *White Flight/Black Flight: The Dynamics of Racial Change in an American Neighborhood* (Ithaca, NY: Cornell University Press, 2011).

10. William Julius Wilson, *The Truly Disadvantaged: The Inner City, The Underclass, and Public Policy* (Chicago: University of Chicago Press, 1987), 7, 49-61.

11. See, for example, Richard Lacayo, "Between Two Worlds," *Time*, March 13, 1989, 58-64; Dawn Turner Trice, "Community's Woes May Not Be a Matter of Class," *Chicago Tribune*, July 17, 2006; Leon Dash, *Rosa Lee: A Mother and Her Family in Urban America* (New York: Basic Books, 1996), 252-56.

12. Terri Schultz, "Suburban Negroes Probe Ways, Means to Build toward Significant Integration," *Chicago Tribune*, January 30, 1969, S1; Dempsey J. Travis, *I Refuse to Learn to Fail: The Autobiography of Dempsey J. Travis* (Chicago: Urban Research Press, 1992), 2-3, 14; Timuel D. Black Jr., *Bridges of Memory: Chicago's First Wave of Black Migration* (Evanston, IL: Northwestern University Press, 2003), 117. For a refutation of the "golden age" thesis, see Norman Fainstein and Susan Nesbitt, "Did the Black Ghetto Have a Golden Age? Class Structure and Class Segregation in New York City, 1949-1970, with Initial Evidence for 1990," *Journal of Urban History* 23 (November 1996): 3-28; Michelle R. Boyd, *Jim Crow Nostalgia: Reconstructing Race in Bronzeville* (Minneapolis: University of Minnesota Press, 2008), xii, 79-80.

13. Earl Richard Moses, "Community Factors in Negro Delinquency," Unpublished MA Thesis, University of Chicago, 1932, 109-10; Mary Pattillo-McCoy, *Black Picket Fences: Privilege and Peril among the Black Middle Class* (Chicago: University of Chicago Press, 1999), 23.

14. Portions of this chapter previously appeared in Will Cooley, "Moving On Out: Black Pioneering in Chicago, 1915-1950," *Journal of Urban History* 36, no. 4 (July 2010): 485-506.

15. Franc Lewis McCluer, "Living Conditions among Wage-Earning Families in Forty-One Blocks in Chicago," Unpublished PhD Dissertation, University of Chicago, 1928, 71.

16. *Chicago Defender*, "'Black Belts' Cause Chicago's Bank Failures," August 23, 1930, 13; Roi Ottley, *New World a-Coming* (Boston: Houghton Mifflin, 1943), 84; Alden Bland, *Behold a Cry* (New York: Charles Scribner's Sons, 1947), 124. The Dillingham Commission found that one in three blacks reported home employment, usually taking in laundry, a trend that continued as discrimination confined black women to domestic work. See The United States Joint Immigration Commission, *Immigrants in Cities*, vol. 26 (Washington, DC: Government Printing Office, 1911), 94.

17. Edith Abbott, *The Tenements of Chicago, 1908-1935* (Chicago: University of Chicago Press, 1936), 121; John T. Clark, "When the Negro Resident Organizes," *Opportunity*, June 1934, 168.

18. Katherine Johnson, "Can the Southside Be Cleaned Up for the World's Fair?" Washington Intercollegiate Club, *The Negro in Chicago*, vol. 2, 60–61; Carroll Binder, *Chicago and the New Negro: How the City Absorbed the Huge Post-war Migration from the South, and What Economic, Social and Civic Changes Were Wrought Thereby* (Chicago: Chicago Daily News, 1927), 24.

19. H. L. Harris Jr., "Negro Mortality Rates in Chicago," *Social Science Review* 1 (March 1927): 58–60; William M. Tuttle Jr., *Race Riot: Chicago in the Red Summer of 1919* (New York: Atheneum, 1970), 164.

20. Roi Ottley, *The Lonely Warrior: The Life and Times of Robert S. Abbott* (Chicago: Henry Regnery Co., 1955), 295–97.

21. David McBride, *From TB to AIDS: Epidemics among Urban Blacks since 1900* (Albany: State University of New York Press, 1991), 36–37.

22. L. B. Anderson, "Facts to Show We Came Here First and Are Here to Stay," *Chicago Defender*, February 7, 1920, 20.

23. Ottley, *Lonely Warrior*, 295–97. In 1921 the death rate for blacks in Illinois was 18.1 per 1,000; by contrast, black mortality rates in Mississippi and Louisiana were 13.5 and 13.9. McBride, *From TB to AIDS*, 36.

24. Langston Hughes, *The Big Sea* (New York: Knopf, 1945), 33.

25. Walter Reckless, *Vice in Chicago* (Chicago: University of Chicago Press, 1933), 3–5; Chicago Commission on Human Relations (CCRR), *The Negro in Chicago: A Study of Race Relations and a Race Riot* (Chicago: University of Chicago Press, 1922), 343.

26. *Chicago Defender*, "To Indict in Vice Probe: Special Jury Quiz to Hit South Side: Find Politicians Got Huge Sum," September 15, 1928, 1; Carl Sandburg, *The Chicago Race Riots* (New York: Harcourt, Brace and Howe, 1919), 59–61; Joseph Spillane, "The Making of an Underground Market: Drug Selling in Chicago, 1900–1940," *Journal of Social History* (Fall 1998): 27–28.

27. Sophonisba Breckinridge, "The Color Line in the Housing Problem," *Survey*, February 1, 1913, 575–76.

28. Ottley, *New World a-Coming*, 158.

29. Bricktop with James Haskins, *Bricktop* (New York: Atheneum, 1983), 8.

30. Bricktop, *Bricktop*, 57.

31. Sylvester Russell, "Mayor Thompson's Reform Policy: The Mayor's Actions in Dealing with Vice Seems to Be Wrought with Astounding Inconsistency," *Indianapolis Freeman*, April 1, 1916, 1; Ben Hecht, *A Child of the Century* (New York: Simon and Schuster, 1954), 181.

32. For examples of African Americans using the cultural sphere of Chicago for self-expression, including vice spots, see Davarian L. Baldwin, *Chicago's New Negroes: Modernity, the Great Migration, and Black Urban Life* (Chapel Hill: University of North Carolina Press, 2007), 115, 165.

33. *Broad Ax*, "Begins New Vice War," September 11, 1909, 2; G. W. Lambert of the Property Owners Improvement Association letter to the Chicago Chief of Police, June 25, 1935, quoted in Lewis A. H. Caldwell, "The Policy Game in Chicago," Unpublished MA Thesis, Northwestern University, 1940, 73, 79.

34. *Chicago Whip*, "Under the Lash of the Whip," August 5, 1922, 8.

35. *Indianapolis Freeman*, "The 'Red Light' Rumor: Chicago Colored Citizens Alarmed over the Social Evil Coming into Their Residence District," March 11, 1916, 1; *Chicago Whip*, "Find 'Buffet Flats' Near Best Homes," August 26, 1922, 1; Johnson,

"Can the Southside Be Cleaned Up for the World's Fair?" 65; W. Lloyd Warner, Buford H. Junker, and Walter A. Adams, *Color and Human Nature: Negro Personality Development in a Northern City* (Washington, DC: American Council on Education, 1941), 45, 110–11.

36. The Vice Commission of Chicago, *The Social Evil in Chicago: A Study of Existing Conditions* (Chicago: Gunthorp-Warren Printing, 1911), 38–39, 239; Reckless, *Vice in Chicago*, 86–87.

37. Paul G. Cressey, *The Taxi-Dance Hall: A Sociological Study in Commercialized Recreation and City Life* (Chicago: University of Chicago Press, 1932), 44; Richard R. Wright Jr., *87 Years behind the Black Curtain: An Autobiography* (Philadelphia: Rare Book Company, 1965), 104–5; *Chicago Tribune*, "Black and Tan Vice," December 1, 1921, 8; Edward E. Wilson, "The Responsibility for Crime," *Opportunity*, March 1929, 95–97; Reckless, 25–29.

38. *Chicago Tribune*, "Black and Tan Vice Wide Open in Old Levee: South Side Police Captains Face Investigation Following Raids," August 25, 1917, 13.

39. *Chicago Defender*, "Chicago's Underworld Shaken by Vice Probe" August 25, 1928, 1.

40. *Chicago Defender*, "Uplifters Use Smoked Glasses to View Vice: Thrasher and the So-Called 'Clean-Up' Committee Still Show Rank Prejudice," June 10, 1922, 2; Kevin J. Mumford, *Interzones: Black/White Sex Districts in Chicago and New York in the Early Twentieth Century* (New York: Columbia University Press, 1997), 180.

41. *Chicago Whip*, "Under the Lash of the Whip," December 3, 1921, 8; *Chicago Whip*, "Nab 'Black and Tan' Lovers," December 24, 1921, 1; *Chicago Whip*, "Under the Lash of the Whip," July 8, 1922, 8; *Chicago Whip*, "Underworld Color Line Laid Bare," December 2, 1922, 1; *Chicago Whip*, "Under the Lash of the Whip," July 8, 1922, 8.

42. *Chicago Whip*, "Vice May Cause More Riots," December 23, 1922, 1; *Chicago Defender*, "Chicago's Underworld Shaken by Vice Probe," August 25, 1928, 1.

43. Abbott, *Tenements of Chicago*, 325; Johnson, "Can the Southside Be Cleaned Up for the World's Fair?" 61; Clarence Cunningham and Bertram Moss, "Commission on Intercommunity Relationship and Hyde Park–Kenwood Council of Churches and Synagogues," 21–22, January 24, 1940, Metropolitan Housing and Planning Commission Papers (MHPC), Accession 74-20, Box 16 (supplement II), Folder 184, Daley Library, University of Illinois at Chicago; Binder, *Chicago and the New Negro*, 16–17.

44. *Chicago Whip*, "Church of God next to Vice Den," July 22, 1922, 1; *Chicago Whip*, "Find Vice Den near YWCA Home for Girls," August 5, 1922, 1; *Chicago Whip*, "Vice Is a Menace to Morals of Children," December 2, 1922, 1; *Chicago Whip*, "Orientals Easy Prey to Ropers," August 12, 1922, 1; William Hall Thomas, "Prostitutes Operate on Indiana Ave.," *Chicago Whip*, July 29, 1922, 3; Raymond Lee Gibbs, "The Life Cycle of Oakland Community," Unpublished MA Thesis, University of Chicago, 1937, 179–83; Robert Taylor, "Effect of the Depression on Tenants of Michigan Blvd. Garden Apartments," 1935, EWB, Box 134, Folder 1; Raymond De Orro, "Why Not Clean Up This Vice?" *Chicago Defender*, October 12, 1935, 16.

45. Ethel R. Harris, "A Study of Voluntary Social Activity among the Professional Negroes in Chicago," Unpublished MA Thesis, University of Chicago, 1937, 13–14; Warner, Junker, and Adams, *Color and Human Nature*, 121; St. Clair Drake, "Churches and Voluntary Associations in the Chicago Negro Community: Report of the Official Project

465-54-386 conducted under the auspices of the Work Projects Administration," (Chicago: Work Projects Administration, 1940), 190, 207.

46. "Sermon of S. E. J. Watson, Pilgrim Baptist Church," Mar. 12, 1922, Robert E. Park Papers (REP), Box 2, Folder 5, Regenstein Library, University of Chicago; Vattel Elbert Daniel, "Ritual in Chicago's South Side Churches of Negroes," Unpublished PhD Dissertation, University of Chicago, 1940, 80.

47. *Chicago Defender,* "Worthless People," July 10, 1915, 8; CCRR, *Negro in Chicago,* 158, 164–65; St. Clair Drake and Horace R. Cayton, *Black Metropolis: A Study of Negro Life in a Northern City* (New York: Harcourt, Brace and Company, 1945), 658; Southside Community Committee, *Bright Shadows in Bronzetown: The Story of the Southside Community Committee* (Chicago: 1949), 31–32; Warner, Junker, and Adams, 145, 199–200. Strong's research on pimps found a gender divide, as only one of thirty-eight women interviewed deemed the figure as a credit to the race, while twelve of thirty-nine men believed it was a credible occupation. Samuel Strong, "Social Types in the Negro Community of Chicago: An Example of the Social Type Method," Unpublished PhD Dissertation, University of Chicago, 1940, 250–51.

48. Dempsey J. Travis, *An Autobiography of Black Chicago* (Chicago, Urban Research Institute, 1987), 43–44; Enoch P. Waters, *American Diary: A Personal History of the Black Press* (Chicago: Path Press, 1987), 166–67. For other examples of visible prostitution in residential areas of the Black Belt, see E. Franklin Frazier, *The Negro Family in Chicago* (Chicago: University of Chicago Press, 1932), 100–101; Drake and Cayton, *Black Metropolis,* 656–57.

49. Harold F. Gosnell, *Negro Politicians: The Rise of Negro Politics in Chicago* (Chicago: University of Chicago Press, 1935), 115, 119; Reckless, 192. *Chicago Bee* quoted in Binder, 16–17.

50. Willard B. Gatewood, *Aristocrats of Color: The Black Elite,* 1880–1920 (Bloomington: Indiana University Press, 1990), 189.

51. Hylan Garnet Lewis, "Social Differentiation in the Negro Community," Unpublished MA Thesis, University of Chicago, 1936, 131.

52. Warner, Junker, and Adams, 34; Waters, *American Diary,* 71; Drake and Cayton, 516; Daniel, "Ritual in Chicago's South Side Churches of Negroes," 99–100; Lewis, "Social Differentiation in the Negro Community," 77; Carter G. Woodson, *The Negro Professional Man and the Community* (New York: Negro Universities Press, 1969 [1934]), xi; Harris, "A Study of Voluntary Social Activity among the Professional Negroes in Chicago," 7, 17–18, 21–22; "The History of Good Shepherd Congregational Church, Chicago," June 18, 1941, IWP, Box 5, Folder 18.

53. Fannie Barrier Williams, "Social Bonds in the 'Black Belt' of Chicago," in *The New Woman of Color: The Collected Writings of Fannie Barrier Williams, 1893–1918,* Mary Jo Deegan, ed. (DeKalb: Northern Illinois Press, 2002), 118.

54. Touré F. Reed, *Not Alms but Opportunity: The Urban League and the Politics of Racial Uplift* (Chapel Hill: University of North Carolina Press, 2008), 31.

55. Warner, Junker, and Adams, 168.

56. Southside Community Committee, *Bright Shadows in Bronzetown,* 29; Harold Gibbard, "The Status Factor in Residential Succession," *American Journal of Sociology* 46, no. 6 (May 1941): 838; Charles S. Johnson, *The Negro in American Civilization* (New York: Henry Holt and Co., 1930), 199.

57. Frank Marshall Davis, *Livin' the Blues: Memoirs of a Black Journalist and Poet* (Madison: University of Wisconsin Press, 1992), 133.

58. *Broad Ax*, "Afro-Americans, Including Many Members of the Sporting Element," September 4, 1909, 1; *Chicago Defender*, "East of State Street," May 30, 1914, 8.

59. Walter Farmer, "An Open Letter to a Republican Municipal Judge," *Broad Ax*, September 18, 1909, 2; CCRR, *Negro in Chicago*, 173–74.

60. "Houses," IWP, Box 37, Folder 3; T. J. Woofter Jr., *Negro Problems in Cities* (Garden City, NY: Doubleday, Doran & Company, Inc., 1928), 107–8, 163; CCRR, *Negro in Chicago*, 138; Washington Intercollegiate Club of Chicago, *The Negro in Chicago*, vol. 1 (Chicago: 1927), 229. Frazier reported that in 1920 there were 1,912 black homeowners in Chicago, 7.4 percent of the black population. Frazier, *Negro Family in Chicago*, 73.

61. Evelyn M. Kitagawa and Karl E. Taeuber, eds., *Local Community Fact Book: Chicago Metropolitan Area, 1960* (Chicago: City of Chicago, 1963), 164.

62. CCRR, *Negro in Chicago*, 107, 137–38; "Morgan Park and Its Changes," IWP, Box 37, Folder 24; The Chicago Plan Commission, *Forty-Four Cities in the City of Chicago*, (Chicago: 1942), 76–77.

63. *Chicago Tribune*, "Police to Guard Flats; Rented to Negroes?" July 20, 1917, 1; *Chicago Tribune*, "Negroes Help Morgan Park to Calm Itself," July 21, 1917, 13; *Chicago Tribune*, "City Takes Hand In Morgan Park 'Negro Invasion,'" July 22, 1917, 13; *Chicago Tribune*, "Negro Owner of Flat House to 'War' Back," July 27, 1917, 3; *Chicago Tribune*, "Court Blocks Morgan Park Negro Invasion: Injunction to Halt Move until Improvements Are Put In," August 2, 1917, 9; Davis, *Livin' the Blues*, 114–15. Resakes was identified as a "Greek" by both the *Tribune* and the *Defender*.

64. *Chicago Defender*, "Mrs. Ray Proves Traitor in Morgan Park Trouble," July 28, 1917, 5.

65. Following the Chicago School's theory of radial expansion, Frazier divided the Black Belt into seven zones with varying class compositions. Frazier, *Negro Family in Chicago*, 100–107. See also CCRR, *Negro in Chicago*, 155; Drake and Cayton, 382, 604–5.

66. National Committee on Negro Housing, "The Physical Aspect of Negro Housing," July 1931, IMG, Box 1, Folder 10.

67. *Chicago Defender*, "East of State Street," May 30, 1914, 8; *Broad Ax*, "Afro-Americans, Including Many Members of the Sporting Element," September 4, 1909, 1.

68. Frazier, *Negro Family in Chicago*, 111–12; Drake, "Churches and Voluntary Associations in the Chicago Negro Community," 276.

69. Christopher Van Buren, "Interview with Hattie E. Lawrence," July 27, 1937, IWP, Box 32, Folder 2; Mahalia Jackson with Evan McLeod Wylie, *Movin' On Up*, (New York: Hawthorn Books, 1966), 47; National Committee on Negro Housing, "The Physical Aspect of Negro Housing," July 1931, IMG, Box 1, Folder 10; "Notes on the Michigan Boulevard Garden Apartments, from Rosenwald annual reports, 1935, 1937," Nov. 14, 1940, to Dec. 6, 1940, IWP, Box 37, Folder 27.

70. *Broad Ax*, "Some Afro-Americans Residing in the 37th Street Block on Forest Avenue," September 18, 1909, 1; CCRR, *Negro in Chicago*, 19, 186–88; Mrs. M. W. Newman, "Trouble Makers," *Half-Century Magazine*, June 1920, 17; Southside Community Committee, 65.

71. *Chicago Daily News*, "How Some Blocks Keep Blight Away," July 13, 1953.

72. *Chicago Defender*, "Defender to Give Prizes for Best Kept Lawns," June 4, 1921, 8; Mrs. George H. Graham, "Editor's Mail," *Chicago Defender*, May 14, 1921, 16; *Half-Century*

Magazine, "Here and There," September–October 1924, 6; Rebecca Stiles Taylor, "Federated Clubs: Block Organizations Are Becoming Popular," *Chicago Defender*, June 5, 1948, 7.

73. *Chicago Defender*, "Defender to Give Prizes for Best Kept Lawns," June 4, 1921, 8; *Chicago Defender*, "Neighborhood Improvement," January 17, 1920, 12.

74. Arthur Evans, "Housing Still Chief Problem of Negro Here: Little Done to Meet Rise in Population," *Chicago Tribune*, August 25, 1924, 3; Kenneth T. Jackson, *Crabgrass Frontier: The Suburbanization of the United States* (New York: Oxford University Press, 1985), 197–98, 206–9.

75. *Chicago Defender*, "Neighborhood Pride," September 29, 1923, 12; Drake and Cayton, 663–64.

76. *Chicago Defender*, "Citizens Head World in Business," May 3, 1930, 10; CCRR, *Negro in Chicago*, 155, 158, 164–65; National Committee on Negro Housing, "The Physical Aspect of Negro Housing," July 1931, IMG, Box 1, Folder 10. In 1920, 29.8 percent of blacks in Woodlawn and 25 percent of blacks in Englewood owned their homes, compared to zero homeowners in the northernmost zone of the Black Belt. Frazier, *Negro Family in Chicago*, 127, 135, fn1.

77. *Half-Century Magazine*, "Stagnation," November–December 1923, 6; Alice Quan Rood, "Study of Social Conditions among the Negroes on Federal Street between Forty-Fifth Street and Fifty-Third Street," Unpublished MA Thesis, University of Chicago, 1924, 50; Abbott, 118; *Chicago Defender*, "The Negro in Chicago," July 24, 1943, 14; George Nesbitt, "Break Up the Black Ghetto?" *The Crisis*, February 1949, 48; Oscar DePriest, "Today's Negroes Have No Guts," *Negro Digest*, March 1950, 87.

78. *Inter-Ocean*, "Landlords Seek to Eject Woman," September 28, 1894, 1; *Chicago Record*, "Race War Campaign Planned," May 5, 1897; *Inter-Ocean*, "Woodlawn Wages War on Negroes," February 12, 1902, 2; *Inter-Ocean*, "Would Bar Colored Family," July 25, 1902, 1; *Inter-Ocean*, "Refuse Negro Club Home," December 15, 1904, 1.

79. J. Saunders Redding, *No Day of Triumph* (New York: Harper & Brothers, 1942), 17.

80. Gibbard, "The Status Factor in Residential Succession," 837–38; *Chicago Defender*, "'Black Belts' Cause Chicago's Bank Failures," August 23, 1930, 13; National Committee on Negro Housing, "The Physical Aspect of Negro Housing," July 1931, IMG, Box 1, Folder 10.

81. CCRR, *Negro in Chicago*, 124; Rose Helper, *Racial Policies and Practices of Real Estate Brokers* (Minneapolis: University of Minnesota Press, 1969), 78, 156.

82. *Chicago Defender*, "Bomb Wrecks Nurses' Home: Assassin Plants Dynamite in Doorway while Girls Sleep," April 30, 1921, 1.

83. CCRR, *Negro in Chicago*, 126.

84. CCRR, *Negro in Chicago*, 122–27; *Half-Century Magazine*, "That Bombing Crusade against Colored People," May 1919, 1, 16; *Chicago Defender*, "27 Bombings Hit Chicago Negro Homes: Local Police Flayed for Failure to Act in Reign of Terror," July 6, 1946, 1, 6; "Community Forum Meeting on Trumbull Park," May 23, 1954, IMG, Box 4, Folder 1; Hirsch, *Making the Second Ghetto*, 69–72; Lawrence Rieser, "An Analysis of the Reporting of Racial Incidents in Chicago, 1945 to 1950," Unpublished MA Thesis, University of Chicago, 1951, 48–51, 64, 77; Chicago Council Against Racial and Religious Discrimination, "Attacks on the Person and Property of Negroes Moving into So-Called 'White' Communities in Chicago during 1948," IMG, Box 2, Folder 8.

85. Irene McCoy Gaines note, [1931?], IMG, Box 1, Folder 10.

86. *Broad Ax*, "Object to Race Segregation," September 25, 1909, 2; CCRR, *Negro in Chicago*, 3, 34; *Chicago Tribune*, "Two Bombs Smash Homes of Negroes," March 20,

1919, 1; *Chicago Defender,* "Bomb Wrecks Nurses' Home: Assassin Plants Dynamite in Doorway while Girls Sleep," April 30, 1921, 1; Binder, 3; DePriest quoted in Gosnell, *Negro Politicians,* 177, 193.

87. L. B. Anderson, "Facts to Show We Came Here First and Are Here to Stay," *Chicago Defender,* February 7, 1920, 20.

88. Mary McDowell, "Hovels or Homes," *Opportunity,* March 1929, 74–77, 100.

89. J. S. Brookins, "Voice of the People: Negro Reaction to Evanstonian Objection," *Chicago Tribune,* March 1, 1923, 8.

90. *Chicago Defender,* "Meet to Halt Evils of Kenwood Rebels," January 31, 1920, 16; Harris Gaines state senate campaign brochure, 1922, IMG, Box 1, Folder 6; Warner, Junker, and Adams, 199–200; Otis Dudley Duncan and Beverly Duncan, *The Negro Population of Chicago: A Study of Residential Succession* (Chicago: University of Chicago Press, 1957), 106; *Chicago Defender,* "Launch Drive to Halt Segregation: Thousands to Gather at 8th Armory and Formulate Plans of Operation," February 7, 1920, 1; Woofter, *Negro Problems in Cities,* 73; Charles Duke, *The Housing Situation and the Colored People of Chicago* (Chicago, 1919), 16.

91. Interview with A. L. Scott of Lincoln Memorial Congregational Church [1929?], EWB, Box 135, Folder 1.

92. Robert J. Blakely with Marcus Shepard, *Earl B. Dickerson: A Voice for Freedom and Equality* (Evanston, IL: Northwestern University Press, 2006), 104; Clement E. Vose, *Caucasians Only: The Supreme Court, the NAACP, and the Restrictive Covenant Cases* (Berkeley: University of California Press, 1959), 55.

93. *Chicago Defender,* "Race Mobilizes to Fight for Its Rights," January 17, 1920, 13; *Chicago Defender,* "Protective Circle on Path of Hyde Parkers," March 6, 1920, 17.

94. Jane Jones, "Links in the Chain," *Half-Century Magazine,* July–August 1923, 4.

95. W. E. B. Du Bois, "The Challenge of Detroit," *The Crisis,* November 1925, 7–10; *The Crisis,* "The Hansberrys of Chicago: They Join Business Acumen with Social Vision," April 1941, 106–7; Oscar DePriest, "Today's Negroes Have No Guts," *Negro Digest,* March 1950, 84–88.

96. David Lilienthal, "Has the Negro the Right to Self-Defense?" *The Nation,* December 23, 1925, 724–25; Lenore Mummy and Dorothy Phillips, "A Dream Come True," *Negro Digest,* May 1944, 55.

97. Egbert Schietinger, "Real Estate Transfers during Negro Invasion: A Case Study," Unpublished MA Thesis, University of Chicago, 1948, 27–29.

98. Rudolph Fisher, *The Walls of Jericho* (New York: Knopf, 1928), 37, 41.

99. *Chicago Tribune,* "Lawyer Warns Negroes Here to Arm Selves: Former Prosecutor Sees Danger of Riots in Chicago," July 4, 1917, 2; Sundiata Cha-Jua, "'A Warlike Demonstration': Legalism, Violent Self-help and Electoral Politics, in Decatur, Illinois, 1894–1898," *Journal of Urban History* 26 (July 2000): 591–629; Mark Robert Schneider, *"We Return Fighting": The Civil Rights Movement in the Jazz Age* (Boston: Northeastern University Press, 2002), 7, 27–28; Sterling D. Spero and Abram L. Harris, *The Black Worker: The Negro and the Labor Movement,* (New York: Atheneum, 1968 [1931]), 386.

100. *Chicago Defender,* "Robey Street Mob Slays Innocent Man: Charles Jackson Meets Death at Hands of White Hoodlums," July 5, 1919, 1.

101. CCRR, *Negro in Chicago,* 46–47.

102. *Half-Century Magazine,* "Race Riots in Chicago," September 1919, 18; Joseph Dalton, "Drowning Those Returning South," G. T., "Giving a Punch for a Punch," and Ethan Jackson, "Thrilling the South," *Half-Century Magazine,* October 1919, 21.

103. *Chicago Tribune*, "Angry Negroes Blast Harmony in Housing Plan: Bolt Meeting at Realty Board with Threats of 'Fight,'" April 17, 1917, 12; *Chicago Daily News*, "Turns Away Protestors," June 4, 1919, 2; CCRR, *Negro in Chicago*, 130; *Chicago Tribune*, "Hyde Parkers Meet Negroes on Home Plan: Parley Holds Hope of Settling the Trouble," October 25, 1919, 1.

104. CCRR, *Negro in Chicago*, 481.

105. Kevin Boyle, *Arc of Justice: A Saga of Race, Civil Rights, and Murder in the Jazz Age* (New York: Henry Holt and Co., 2004), 25–26.

106. Katherine Dunham, *A Touch of Innocence* (New York: Harcourt, Brace and Company, 1959), 15–16.

107. CCRR, *Negro in Chicago*, 127–28.

108. Lorraine Hansberry, *To Be Young, Gifted, and Black* (Englewood Cliffs, NJ: Prentice-Hall, Inc., 1969), 20–21.

109. Leon Forrest, *The Furious Voice for Freedom: Essays on Life* (Wakefield, RI: Asphodel Press, 1994), 55–60, 115, Arnold Shankman, *Ambivalent Friends: Afro-Americans View the Immigrant* (Westport, CT: Greenwood Press, 1982), 50; Louise Venable Kennedy, *The Negro Peasant Turns Cityward* (New York: Columbia University Press, 1930), 218–19; Alden Bland, *Behold a Cry*, 185.

110. Drake and Cayton, 57; *Chicago Defender*, "No Niggers Live in This Section," May 29, 1926, A2.

111. Raymond Jenkins, "Would Urge Education," *Half-Century Magazine*, December 1920, 17. For other examples of this sentiment, see *Half-Century Magazine*, "Here and There," July–August 1924, 6; Harriette Hall, "Says Negroes' Problem Is Economic Not Social," *Chicago Defender*, November 17, 1945, 14.

112. L. Hollingsworth Wood, "Some Happy Results of Race Contacts," *Opportunity*, June 1924, 185–86. See also letter from Stanley B. Norvell to Victor Lawson, Aug. 22, 1919, 4, JRP, Box 6, Folder 3; Raymond Jenkins, "Would Urge Education," *Half-Century Magazine*, December 1920, 17; CCRR, *Negro in Chicago*, 495–97.

113. CCRR, *Negro in Chicago*, 127–28. For more evidence of middle-class whites hiring "thugs" to enforce the color line when more "polite" methods failed, see *Chicago Tribune*, "Race War Fades—Flares Up Again," May 4, 1915; *Chicago Defender*, "Hunt for DePriest Bombers," April 9, 1921, 1.

114. *Broad Ax*, "The Hyde Park Improvement Protective Club at Its Annual Meeting," September 18, 1909, 1; *Chicago Defender*, "Bomb Goes Off after Whites Meet," October 16, 1920, 12; CCRR, *Negro in Chicago*, 116–22; *Chicago Defender*, "Launch Drive to Halt Segregation: Thousands to Gather at 8th Armory and Formulate Plans of Operation," February 7, 1920, 1; Postcard dated July 6, 1944, from Hyde Park–Kenwood Association to Irene McCoy Gaines, IMG, Box 2, Folder 3.

115. *Broad Ax*, "The White Residents of Kenwood, Hyde Park and Woodlawn Are Up in Arms," August 28, 1909, 1; *Chicago Defender*, "Bomb Goes Off after Whites Meet," October 16, 1920, 12. For more on the rhetorical strategy of publicly questioning white "civilization," see Gail Bederman, *Manliness & Civilization: A Cultural History of Gender and Race in the United States, 1880–1917* (Chicago: University of Chicago Press, 1995), ch. 2.

116. *Chicago Defender*, "Battle of the Ghettos," August 4, 1945, 12.

117. Waters, *American Diary*, 27; Seligman, *Block by Block*, 79–82; Irving Cutler, *The Jews of Chicago: From Shtetl to Suburb* (Urbana: University of Illinois Press, 1996), 231–33. As Gerald Gamm shows, Jews in the urban North fled black incursions earlier, faster, and

more thoroughly than white Catholics, but did not attack their black neighbors. Gamm, *Urban Exodus*, 8-13.

118. Lawrence Ward, "America's Leading Soya Bean Expert," *Opportunity*, March 1941, 68-71; *Time*, "The New Neighbor," December 4, 1950, 18-19.

119. Drake and Cayton, 738-39, 763; Christopher Robert Reed, *The Chicago NAACP and the Rise of Black Professional Leadership, 1910-1966* (Bloomington: Indiana University Press, 1997), 146; Letter from United States delegation to the United Nations to the Chicago Council of Negro Organizations, June 7, 1945, IMG, Box 2, Folder 4; Travis, *An Autobiography of Black Politics*, 303-5.

120. Robert Weaver, *The Negro Ghetto* (New York: Harcourt, Brace, 1948), 78-81.

121. Sugrue, *Origins of the Urban Crisis*; Freund, *Colored Property: State Policy and White Racial Politics in Suburban America*; Robert O. Self, *American Babylon: Race and the Struggle for Postwar Oakland* (Princeton, NJ: Princeton University Press, 2003); Kevin Kruse, *White Flight: Atlanta and the Making of Modern Conservatism* (Princeton, NJ: Princeton University Press, 2005); Josh Sides, *L.A. City Limits: African American Los Angeles from the Great Depression to the Present* (Berkeley: University of California Press, 2003); Jason Sokol, *All Eyes Are upon Us: Race and Politics from Boston to Brooklyn* (New York: Basic Books, 2014).

122. Weaver, *Negro Ghetto*, 87; Hirsch, 4-5; *Chicago Daily News*, "Growing Negro Districts Need Housing," February 1, 1949.

123. Chicago Council Against Racial and Religious Discrimination, "Against Discrimination," 3, no. 1 (August 3, 1946), MHPC, Accession 74-20, Box 16 (supp. II), Folder 185.

124. Hirsch, 54-55, 74-75; Homer Jack, "Chicago's Violent Armistice," *The Nation* (December 10, 1949), 571-72.

125. *Chicago Defender*, "Julians Overcome Hostile Neighbors," October 21, 1950, 1; *Chicago Tribune*, "Vandals Fail in Plot to Burn Dr. Julian Home," November 23, 1950, 7; *Chicago Defender*, "Guard Dr. Julian's Home: Chicagoan of the Year's House Target of Vandals," December 2, 1950, 1; *New York Times*, "Arson Fails at Home of a Negro Scientist," November 23, 1950, 29. For the demographic composition of postwar riots in Chicago, see Hirsch, 84-85.

126. *New York Times*, "Negro's Suburban Home Bombed," June 14, 1951, 20; *Chicago Defender*, "Dr. Julian Target of New Attack," June 23, 1951, 4; *Chicago Defender*, "Say FBI May Probe Threat against Julian," July 7, 1951, 12.

127. *Chicago Defender*, "Guard Dr. Julian's Home: Chicagoan of the Year's House Target of Vandals," December 2, 1950, 1.

128. *Time*, "The New Neighbor," December 4, 1950, 18-19; Felicia Lee, "Reclaiming a Black Research Scientist's Forgotten Legacy," *New York Times*, February 6, 2007, E1; Carl Rowan, "Why Negroes Move to White Neighborhoods," *Ebony*, August 1958, 17-22.

129. Confidential Memo from James Cassels, August 5, 1952, American Friends Service Committee Papers (AFSC), Box 88, Folder 9, Daley Library, University of Illinois at Chicago.

130. Ernestine Cofield, "Oak Park Fought Battle for Percy Julian Family," *Chicago Defender*, October 8, 1962, 9.

131. Confidential Memo from James Cassels, August 7, 1952, AFSC, Box 88, Folder 9. Despite the violent incidents that marred the Julians' and subsequent black moves into Oak Park, the suburb gradually earned a reputation as relatively tolerant. Indeed, some

liberal whites expressed indignation at the violent events, and some even offered to guard the Julian home themselves. The city set up a human relations commission and labored greatly to maintain a fragile racial balance. See Betty Jane Merrill, "Oak Park Board Orders Probe in New Bus Route," *Chicago Tribune*, December 3, 1950, W8; Albert Barnett, "Brotherhood—Effective Antidote to the Virus of Jim Crow," *Chicago Defender*, July 14, 1951, 7; Andrew Wiese, *Places of Their Own: African American Suburbanization in the Twentieth Century* (Chicago: University of Chicago Press, 2004), 240.

132. *Chicago Tribune*, "An Outrage," June 14, 1951, 12.

133. *Time*, "Ugly Nights in Cicero," July 23, 1951, 10–11; Charles Abrams, "The Time Bomb That Exploded in Cicero," *Commentary*, November 1951, 407–14; Walter White, "This Is Cicero," *The Crisis*, August–September 1951: 436; Homer Jack, "Cicero Nightmare," *The Nation*, July 28, 1951, 64–65; Ernestine Cofield, "Oak Park Fought Battle for Percy Julian Family," *Chicago Defender*, October 8, 1962, 9.

134. *Chicago Defender*, "Bar Julian from Chicago Club: Retract Bid to Union League Fete," July 28, 1951, 11.

135. Langston Hughes, "Do Big Negroes Keep Little Negroes Down?" *Negro Digest*, November 1951, 79, 82; E. Franklin Frazier, "Some Aspects of Negro Business," *Opportunity*, October 1924, 293–97.

136. *Chicago Daily News*, "Negroes Tell Race Struggle in Oak Park," July 19, 1958; Carl Rowan, "Why Negroes Move to White Neighborhoods," *Ebony*, August 1958, 17–18; James Q. Wilson, *Negro Politics: The Search for Leadership* (Glencoe, IL: Free Press, 1960), 198–99. For Percy Julian's leadership roles in the black community, see, e.g., *Chicago Defender*, "Julian Hits Silence on Race Crime," April 24, 1958, 27; Austin Wehrwein, "Biracial Unit Set Up in Chicago with 2 U.S. Judges as Members," *New York Times*, July 26, 1963, 12.

137. James N. Gregory, *The Southern Diaspora: How the Great Migrations of Black and White Southerners Transformed America* (Chapel Hill: University of North Carolina Press, 2005), 271.

138. "Significant presence" is defined here as more than one hundred black residents in the census tract. Data derived from the National Historical Geographic Information System. NHGIS.org, accessed May 16, 2013.

NOTES TO CHAPTER 3

1. *Chicago Tribune*, "Profile: Chatham," June 7, 1998.

2. Mae Gregory, *Chatham 1856–1987: A Community of Excellence* (Chicago: Chicago Public Library, 1989), 26–28.

3. *Chicago Tribune*, "Profile: Chatham," June 7, 1998.

4. Stephen Grant Meyer, *As Long as They Don't Move Next Door: Segregation and Racial Conflict in American Neighborhoods* (New York: Rowman & Littlefield Publishers, Inc., 2000); Amanda Seligman, *Block by Block: Neighborhoods and Public Policy on Chicago's West Side* (Chicago: University of Chicago Press, 2005); Eileen M. McMahon, *What Parish Are You From? A Chicago Irish Community and Race Relations* (Lexington: University Press of Kentucky, 1995); Gerald Gamm, *Urban Exodus: Why the Jews Left Boston and the Catholics Stayed* (Cambridge, MA: Harvard University Press, 1999).

5. *Chicago Daily News*, "A Neighborhood Can Integrate—And Peaceably: Honor Jew, Catholic, Protestant for Chatham–Avalon Pk. Work," February 19, 1959; *Chicago Tribune*, "Biracial Unit Wins a Battle: Year's Fight to Stop Blight Is Success," October 6, 1960, 1;

Chicago Daily News, "It Resisted the Irresistible and Won," July 21, 1962; *Chicago Tribune*, "North Avalon Plans Model for Integration of Races," September 22, 1963, S1. For an example of this outside of Chicago, see James E. Cebula, "Creating a Multiracial Community in Post–World War II Cincinnati," *Ohio Valley History* 7, no. 3 (Fall 2007): 32–48.

6. Rev. James Walsh, address to inaugural Southeast Community Organization Congress, October 6, 1960, Thomas A. Gaudette Papers (TAG), Box 2, Folder 1, Von der Ahe Library, Loyola Marymount University, Los Angeles.

7. *Chicago Daily News*, "A Middle-Class Problem," August 24, 1963.

8. Gordon W. Allport, *The Nature of Prejudice* (Reading, MA: Addison-Wesley Publishing Co., 1954).

9. James W. Prothro and Charles W. Grigg, "Fundamental Principles of Democracy," *Journal of Politics* 22 (Spring 1960): 276–94; G. H. Smith, "Liberalism and Level of Information," *Journal of Educational Psychology* 39 (1948): 65–82; James G. Martin and Frank R. Westie, "The Tolerant Personality," *American Sociological Review* 24 (August 1959): 521–28; Samuel Stouffer, *Communism, Conformity, and Civil Liberties: A Cross-Section of the Nation Speaks Its Mind* (Garden City, NY: Doubleday, 1955), 89–105.

10. Robin Williams, "Racial and Cultural Relations," in *Review of Sociology: Analysis of a Decade*, Joseph B. Gittler, ed. (New York: Wiley & Sons, 1957), 434; Bruno Bettelheim and Morris Janowitz, *Social Change and Prejudice, Including Dynamics of Prejudice* (New York: Free Press, 1964), 198, 272; Allport, *The Nature of Prejudice*, 371–72; Arthur Kornhauser, *Detroit as the People See It: A Survey of Attitudes in an Industrial City* (Detroit: Wayne University Press, 1952), 86–88; Herbert H. Hyman and Paul B. Sheatsley, "Attitudes toward Desegregation," *Scientific American*, December 1956, 39; Mildred A. Schwartz, *Trends in White Attitudes toward Negroes* (Chicago: National Opinion Research Center, 1967), 54, 119.

11. Confidential Memo from James Cassels [1952?], AFSC, Box 88, Folder 9; Julia Abrahamson, *A Neighborhood Finds Itself* (New York: Harper & Brothers, 1959), 299–300.

12. Thomas J. Sugrue, "Jim Crow's Last Stand: The Struggle to Integrate Levittown," in *Second Suburb: Levittown, Pennsylvania*, Dianne Harris, ed. (Pittsburgh: University of Pittsburgh Press, 2010), 180.

13. Hugh Hough, "9 Years Later: A Look at Trumbull Park," *Chicago Sun-Times*, September 30, 1962, 50.

14. Louis Rosen, *The South Side: The Racial Transition of an American Neighborhood* (Chicago: Ivan R. Dee, 1998), 97, 99–100.

15. St. Clair Drake and Horace R. Cayton, *Black Metropolis: A Study of Negro Life in a Northern City* (New York: Harcourt, Brace and Company, 1945), 281–84.

16. Drake and Cayton, *Black Metropolis*, 283.

17. Weaver was the leading exponent of class replacing race as an acceptable basis of community formation. Quote from Robert C. Weaver, "Class, Race and Urban Renewal," *Land Economics*, August 1960, 243. See also Robert C. Weaver, "Race Restrictive Housing Covenants," *The Journal of Land & Public Utility Economics* XX, no. 3 (August 1944), 183–93, and Robert C. Weaver, "Integration in Public and Private Housing," *Annals of the American Academy of Political and Social Science* 304 (March 1956): 86–97.

18. Selwyn James, "We Refused to Give Up Our Homes," *Redbook*, December 1955; Ellsworth Rosen, "When a Negro Moves Next Door," *Saturday Evening Post*, April 1959, 32–33, 139–42; Ralph Bass, "Prejudice Won't Make Us Sell Our House!" *Coronet*, July 1959, 103–7.

19. *Chicago Report, 1957,* WBBM (Chicago, 1957), Peabody Awards Collection Archives (PAC), University of Georgia Library, Athens, GA.

20. Thomas Gaudette, "Urban Crisis: Conserving the Community," *New World,* May 12, 1961, TAG, Series 1, Box 2, Folder 1. See also Statement of Saul Alinsky, Civil Rights Housing Hearing, Commission on Civil Rights, May 5, 1959, Industrial Areas Foundation Papers (IAF), Folder 34, Daley Library, University of Illinois at Chicago; Robert Colby Nelson, *Christian Science Monitor,* "Negro Upsurge in Decade Vies for Chicago Housing Locations," February 18, 1960, 3.

21. Chatham–Avalon Park Community Council, "Community Future Discussed," *Hi, Neighbor,* May 1956, TAG, Series 1, Box 1, Folder 2.

22. Chatham Village as Mutual Ownership Organization, Dec. 14, 1959, John Egan Papers (CJEG), Box 24, Hesburgh Library, Notre Dame University, South Bend, IN.

23. Chicago Commission on Human Relations, "Chatham Apartment Project Tries Open Occupancy," *Human Relations News of Chicago* 2:2, May 1960, AFSC, Box 94, Folder 5.

24. Sterling D. Spero and Abram L. Harris, *The Black Worker: The Negro and the Labor Movement* (New York: Atheneum, 1968 [1931]), 386; Herman H. Long and Charles S. Johnson, *People vs. Property: Race Restrictive Covenants in Housing* (Nashville, TN: Fisk University Press, 1947), 73.

25. Rose Helper, *Racial Policies and Practices of Real Estate Brokers* (Minneapolis: University of Minnesota Press, 1969), 78.

26. United States Commission on Civil Rights, *Report of the United States Commission on Civil Rights* (Washington, DC: US Government Printing Office, 1959), 431.

27. Albert H. Miller, "Negro in the North," *Ave Maria,* Jan. 24, 1959, 6, Daniel Cantwell Papers, Box 30, Folder 5, Chicago History Museum.

28. New York State Commission for Human Rights, *In Search of Housing: A Study of Experiences of Negro Professional and Technical Personnel in New York State* (New York: State of New York, 1965), 42.

29. Preston H. Smith II, *Racial Democracy and the Black Metropolis: Housing Policy in Postwar Chicago* (Minneapolis: University of Minnesota Press, 2012), 109.

30. Andrew Wiese, *Places of Their Own: African American Suburbanization in the Twentieth Century* (Chicago: University of Chicago Press, 2004), 129–32.

31. Roi Ottley, "Negro's Rise Rapid as U.S. Tax Lawyer: C. E. Lomax Now Aids Regional Counsel," *Chicago Tribune,* July 30, 1960, 15; *Chicago Defender,* "Report Banks to Stay in Race for Alderman," January 19, 1963, 15; *Chicago Tribune,* "Skyles, Soubretta Powell," August 18, 2004; Maureen O'Donnell, "Expert on Foodborne Illness," *Chicago Sun-Times,* November 16, 2012.

32. Welton Taylor with Karyn Taylor, *Two Steps from Glory: A World War II Liaison Pilot Confronts Jim Crow and the Enemy in the South Pacific* (Chicago: Winning Strategy Press, 2012), 87–89, 364–65.

33. Confidential Memo from James Cassels, Aug. 19, 1952, AFSC, Box 88, Folder 9; *Chicago Report, 1957,* WBBM (Chicago, 1957), PAC; *Chicago Daily News,* "Nasty Bag of Fear Tricks Used to 'Bust Up' Blocks," October 16, 1959; *Bulletin,* "Taylor Again in Running for Chatham Council Presidency," June 2, 1960.

34. L. K. Northwood and Ernest A. T. Barth, *Urban Desegregation: Negro Pioneers and Their White Neighbors* (Seattle: University of Washington Press, 1965), 25–29.

35. Terry Sullivan, "How Marynook Meets the Negro," *St. Jude,* January 1963, 13.

36. Carl Rowan, "Why Negroes Move to White Neighborhoods," *Ebony*, August 1958, 18–19.

37. Marvin Caplan, "The Last White Family on the Block," *Atlantic Monthly*, July 1960, 56.

38. *Chicago Defender*, "Discrimination in Private Housing," January 13, 1958, 11.

39. Sel Yackley, "Tell Integration Success Stories," *Chicago Tribune*, April 2, 1967, Q7; Sel Yackley, "Integration Progresses in Rogers Park," *Chicago Tribune*, April 20, 1967, F2.

40. Arna Botemps and Jack Conroy, *Anyplace but Here* (New York: Hill and Wang, 1966), 326–28.

41. Herman Long and Charles Johnson date the Chatham Improvement Association to 1916, when the area was first developed. The first mention of the Chatham Fields Improvement Association in the *Chicago Daily News Almanac and Year-Book* came in 1926. Long and Johnson, *People vs. Property*, 51; *Chicago Daily News Almanac and Year-Book for 1927* (Chicago, 1926), 831; Gregory, *Chatham 1856-1987*, 34; *Chicago Defender*, "Chatham Paper Blessed by Bigot Patron Saint," April 28, 1956, 10; *Chicago Defender*, "Realtor Denied Cafe Service Plans to Sue," September 13, 1958, 3; *Chicago Daily News*, "Charge 'Legit' Realtors with Scare Tactics, Too," October 20, 1959.

42. Mahalia Jackson with Evan McLeod Wylie, *Movin' On Up*, (New York: Hawthorn Books, 1966), 118.

43. Laurraine Goreau, *Just Mahalia, Baby* (Waco, TX: Word Books, 1975), 210–12.

44. Jackson, *Movin' On Up*, 119–22.

45. *Chicago Defender*, "Chatham Area Homes Damaged in Race Row," May 5, 1956, 1–2.

46. Goreau, *Just Mahalia*, 212.

47. *Chicago Defender*, "Chatham Paper Blessed by Bigot Patron Saint," April 28, 1956, 10; Patricia Johnson, Letter to the Editor, *Chicago Defender*, August 13, 1957, 11; *Chicago Defender*, "Realtor Denied Cafe Service Plans to Sue," September 13, 1958, 3; *Chicago Defender*, "Find Dixie-Style Terror in Englewood," May 30, 1959, 1–2; Gregory, *Chatham 1856-1987*, 27.

48. Kermit Eby and June Greenlief, "The Furious and the Godly," *The Christian Century*, February 16, 1955, 206; Gregory, *Chatham 1856-1987*, 27; Eduardo Camacho and Ben Joravsky, *Against the Tide: The Middle Class in Chicago* (Chicago: Community Renewal Society, 1989), 45–46; *Decision at 83rd Street*, WBBM (Chicago, 1962), PAC; Terry Sullivan, "How Marynook Meets the Negro," *St. Jude*, January 1963, 10; Chicago Commission on Human Rights, "Marynook Works for Stable Interracial Area," *Human Relations News of Chicago* 6, no. 4 (July–August 1964), AFSC, Box 94, Folder 5.

49. Philip A. Johnson, *Call Me Neighbor, Call Me Friend: The Case History of the Integration of a Neighborhood on Chicago's South Side* (Garden City, NY: Doubleday, 1965), 13; Vincent Giese, *Revolution in the City* (Notre Dame, IN: Fides Publishers, 1961), 30; Arnold Hirsch, *Making the Second Ghetto: Race and Housing in Chicago, 1940-1960* (Chicago: University of Chicago Press, 1998), 59, 88–91.

50. Gregory, *Chatham 1856-1987*, 26, 65–66; Johnson, *Call Me Neighbor*, 131–32; A. L. Foster, "Other People's Business," *Chicago Defender*, April 19, 1958, 4.

51. *Chicago Tribune*, "25 Ministers to Preach on Brotherhood," February 21, 1954, SW4; Johnson, *Call Me Neighbor*, 7, 121, 126; *Chicago Defender*, "22 Made Brotherhood

Work in City," February 21, 1959, 1–2; Rev. Patrick T. Curran "A Report on Our Program and Our Progress in the Negro Convert-Apostolate," *The Catholic Church and the Negro in the Archdiocese of Chicago, Clergy Conference* (Chicago: 1960), 9–14, Archdiocese of Chicago's Joseph Cardinal Bernadin Archives and Records Center (AOC); *Chicago Daily News*, "Accept Integration, Priest Tells Flock," November 13, 1961; Rev. Msgr. Harry Koenig, ed., *A History of the Parishes of the Archdiocese of Chicago* (Chicago: Archdiocese of Chicago, 1980), 259–62.

52. Anthony J. Vader, "Racial Segregation within Catholic Institutions in Chicago: A Study in Behavior and Attitudes," Unpublished MA Thesis, University of Chicago, 1962, 18; Note from Msgr. John Egan to Rev. Hugh Anwyl, July 17, 1963, CJEG, Box 24; Giese, *Revolution in the City*, 37–39.

53. McMahon, *What Parish Are You From?* 128.

54. Minutes of Housing Committee Meeting of Catholic Council on Working Life, September 26, 1957, IAF, Folder 81.

55. *Chicago Defender*, "22 Made Brotherhood Work in City," February 21, 1959, 1–2.

56. The Church Federation of Greater Chicago, "Churches, Community Life and Community Organizations: A Preliminary Statement of Policy," March 13, 1962, TAG, Box 1, Folder 1; Stephen Turner, "High on Insubordination," in *The Disobedient Generation*, Alan Sica and Stephen Turner, eds. (Chicago: University of Chicago Press, 2005), 288.

57. Rosen, *South Side*, 94.

58. For examples, see *Chicago Tribune*, "New 'Y' Branch Is Planned for 83rd-Ellis Area: Open Fund Drive Feb. 15; Goal: $82,200," January 17, 1952, S2; *Chicago Tribune*, "Dedicate New Park Sunday in West Chatham: Program Ends 5 Year Community Drive," June 11, 1953, S1; *Chicago Tribune*, "Inclosing Wall to Mark Design of New Church," October 10, 1954, 6; *Chicago Tribune*, "Goldblatt's to Build New Chatham Unit," March 15, 1955, B7; *South Shore Commission Newsletter*, "South Shore Builds!" May 1955, IAF, Folder 388.

59. *Chicago Tribune*, "Plan Preview at New Jewish Youth Center," December 12, 1954, S4.

60. Johnson, *Call Me Neighbor*, 129.

61. Jack E. Budd, "Security A-1 in Importance to Teenagers," *South Side Courier*, November 15, 1956, Chatham–Grand Crossing Community Collection, Box 1, Folder 19, Harold Washington Library, Chicago; Peter H. Rossi, *Why Families Move: A Study in the Social Psychology of Urban Residential Mobility* (Glencoe, IL: Free Press, 1955), 22, 28.

62. Rosen, *South Side*, 29, 44.

63. *Chicago Tribune*, "New Community Group Sets 1st Public Meeting: Chatham-Avalon Pk. Unit to Aid Area," December 7, 1952, A17; Chicago Commission on Human Relations, "Proceedings of the City-Wide Conference: Solving the Problems of Chicago's Population Growth," May 29, 1957, 149–50, IAF, Folder 327.

64. Chatham–Avalon Park Community Council, "What Are We Trying to Do?" *Hi Neighbor*, May 1956, TAG, Series 1, Box 1, Folder 2.

65. *Southeast Economist*, "Fight for Civic Group Control," May 25, 1961; *South Side News-Courier*, "West Avalon Community Association Election Monday," June 8, 1961, 1–2, IAF, Folder 436.

66. *Chicago Defender*, "22 Made Brotherhood Work in City," February 21, 1959, 1–2; Hillel Black, "This Is War," *Saturday Evening Post*, January 25, 1964; Thomas Gaudette Oral History, May 15, 1990, TAG, Series 3, Box 1, Case 4.

67. Thomas Gaudette, Speech to Morgan Park Human Relations Group [1960?], TAG, Series 1, Box 1, Folder 4; Thomas Gaudette Oral History, May 15, 1990, TAG, Series 3, Box 1, Case 1.

68. Gregory, *Chatham 1856–1987*, 26, 65–66; Johnson, *Call Me Neighbor*, 131–32; A. L. Foster, "Other People's Business," *Chicago Defender*, April 19, 1958, 4; A. L. Foster, "Other People's Business," *Chicago Defender*, May 17, 1958, 4; *Chicago Tribune*, "Salem Church Will Hail 90th Year in March," February 27, 1958, S11; Roi Ottley, "Area Called Negro Showcase: Rate Park Manor, Chatham High," *Chicago Tribune*, March 30, 1958, S9.

69. *Chicago Defender*, "Mahalia Jackson Home on Ed Murrow TV Show," April 5, 1958, 18.

70. *Chicago Tribune*, "City Lures Back Some Suburbanites," January 20, 1957, A9; Hugh Brodkey, "Suburban Living Too High, Family Moves Back to Area," and Jim Cunningham, "Without Frills or Pressures," *Community Times*, December 1958, TAG, Series 1, Box 1, Folder 2.

71. Editors of *Fortune*, *The Exploding Metropolis* (Garden City, NY: Doubleday, 1958), 18.

72. *Chicago Report, 1957*, WBBM (Chicago, 1957), PAC.

73. *Chicago Defender*, "Tells Conference about Negroes as Neighbors," May 4, 1960.

74. *Chicago Daily News*, "A Middle-Class Problem," August 24, 1963.

75. Ronald Kotulak, "Chatham Integration Is Successful," *Chicago Tribune*, May 15, 1960, SW1.

76. *Chicago Daily News*, "A Neighborhood Can Integrate—and Peaceably," February 19, 1959, clipping in CJEG, Box 24; Thomas Gaudette, Address to the Fourth National Community Council Leaders Workshop, Ohio State University, 1959, TAG, Series 1, Box 1, Folder 3; *Chicago Tribune*, "Urge Oak Pk. to Welcome Integration: Move Lauded by Civic Leaders," February 20, 1960; *Jersey City Journal*, "Importance of Urban Renewal Outlined to Students at St. Peter's," September 23, 1960, TAG, Series 1, Box 2, Folder 1.

77. *Chicago Daily News*, "E. Chatham Aim: No Panic in '60," January 2, 1960.

78. *Bulletin*, "Taylor Again in Running for Chatham Council Presidency," June 2, 1960.

79. "Notes and Comments on Urban League Work in Park Manor," CUL, Series I, Folder 348; Howard Gould, "Park Manor Folk Move to Organize," *Chicago Defender*, September 29, 1958.

80. Nellie Dora, "Community Problems in Chatham," Chicago Commission on Human Relations, "The Management of Neighborhood Change," City-Wide Workshop, April 10–12, 1959, 8–10, AFSC, Box 94, Folder 5.

81. Stanley Carson Stevens, "The Urban Racial Border: Chicago, 1960," Unpublished PhD Dissertation, University of Illinois at Urbana-Champaign, 1972, 110–14; *Chicago Daily News*, "The Big 'Change' in Chatham-Avalon: Middle Class South Side Area Battles for Orderly Integration," May 8, 1959; *Chicago Tribune*, "Neighborhood Votes to Join Local Council," September 25, 1958, S13.

82. *Chicago Daily News*, "500 Taste Victory in Zoning Fight," August 21, 1958; "Neighborhood Residents Win Zoning Case," August 27, 1958, clipping in TAG, Series 1, Box 1, Folder 2; *Bulletin*, May 10, 1962, clipping in CJEG, Box 38, Folder Park Manor Neighbors; *Bulletin*, "Attacks Building Attempt," October 25, 1962, clipping in CJEG, Box 24.

83. Roi Ottley, "Community Group Sparks Drive to Shutter Taverns," *Chicago Tribune*, November 2, 1958, SW18; Robert Colby Nelson, "Negro Upsurge in Decade Vies for Chicago Housing Locations," *Christian Science Monitor*, February 18, 1960, 3.

84. Nellie Dora, "Community Problems in Chatham," Chicago Commission on Human Relations, "The Management of Neighborhood Change," City-Wide Workshop, April 10–12, 1959, 8–10, AFSC, Box 94, Folder 5; Greg Harris, "Quits Chatham Tavern Drive," *Chicago Defender*, October 1958, 2; Enoch Waters, "Good Taverns Suffer for Bad as Chatham Area Votes Dry," *Chicago Defender*, November 8, 1958; Thomas Gaudette, Speech to Morgan Park Human Relations Group [1960?], TAG, Series 1, Box 1, Folder 4.

85. Editors of *Fortune*, *The Exploding Metropolis* (Garden City, NY: Doubleday, 1958), 98–99.

86. Viviana A. Zelizer, *Pricing the Priceless Child: The Changing Social Value of Children* (New York: Basic Books, 1985), ch. 2.

87. John L. Rury, "Race, Space and the Politics of Chicago's Public Schools: Benjamin Willis and the Tragedy of Urban Education," *History of Education Quarterly* 39 (Summer 1999): 124–25; *U.S. News & World Report*, "Why a Big Northern City Faces a Crisis in the Schools," August 9, 1965, 62. Total enrollment in Chicago public schools increased by 103,609 pupils from 1959 to 1964, or 21 percent. Jan. 4, 1954, letter from Irene McCoy Gaines representing the National Association of Colored Women, writing in "appreciation for the acquisition of Dr. Benjamin Willis as superintendent of schools," IMG, Box 4, Folder 1.

88. Robert J. Havighurst, *The Public Schools of Chicago: A Survey for the Board of Education of the City of Chicago* (Chicago: Chicago Board of Education, 1964), 2; The Advisory Panel on Integration of the Public Schools, *Report to the Board of Education, City of Chicago* (Chicago: 1964), 5.

89. Mary J. Herrick, *The Chicago Schools: A Social and Political History* (Beverly Hills, CA: Sage Publications, 1971), 305–6; *Chicago Tribune*, "Big Shortage of Qualified Teachers Told: Willis Puts Number at 1,852," October 17, 1957, 14; *Chicago Tribune*, "City's School Costs Mount to New High," February 19, 1962, 1.

90. Havighurst, *Public Schools of Chicago*, 26.

91. John Gibbons Drew, "Why a Jim Crow School in Chicago?" *Half-Century Magazine*, February 1920, 17; *Chicago Defender*, "Woodlawn Race Haters Seek to Make District 'White,'" July 22, 1933, 2; Michael Homel, *Down from Equality: Black Chicagoans and the Public Schools, 1920–41* (Urbana: University of Illinois Press, 1984), 150–52, 193–94.

92. Melvin Van Peebles, *Bear for the FBI* (New York: Trident Press, 1968), 139–40.

93. Carl Rowan, "Why Negroes Move to White Neighborhoods," *Ebony*, August 1958, 18–22; *Chicago Daily News*, "Parents Told: Don't Fear Negro School: Officials Say Avalon Park Worries Are Premature," February 15, 1962; *Chicago Tribune*, "Keep School Integrated, Parents Urge," February 15, 1962, C4; Drake and Cayton, 281–84; *Chicago Defender*, "Board Orders Probe of School Bias: Study Will Check Claim of NAACP," December 14, 1957, 9; Testimony of Rev. Edsel Ammons, Pastor of Ingleside-Whitfield Methodist and President of West Avalon Community Association, to Chicago Board of Education [1962?], IAF, Folder 348.

94. Jack Mabley, "Race, Religion Spark Prep Disorders," *Chicago Daily News*, January 28, 1954, 37.

95. Kathryn M. Neckerman, *Schools Betrayed: Roots of Failure in Inner-City Education* (Chicago: University of Chicago Press, 2007), 104.

96. Vincent Giese, *Patterns for Teenagers* (Notre Dame, IN: Fides Publishers, 1956), 29.

97. Jack Schneider, "Escape from Los Angeles: White Flight from Los Angeles and Its Schools, 1960–1980," *Journal of Urban History* 34, no. 6 (September 2008): 1007–8.

98. Chatham–Avalon Park Community Council, *Chatham Newsletter*, August 20, 1960, TAG, Series 1, Box 1, Folder 4; Terry Sullivan, "How Marynook Meets the Negro," *St. Jude*, January 1963, 9; Marcia Lane Vespa, "Chicago's Regional School Plans," *Integrated Education* 1, no. 5 (October–November 1963): 25–26; *Chicago Daily News*, "City's Racial Problems in Willis' Lap," July 6, 1962.

99. George W. Reed and Stanley Drigot, "Joint Statement on Regional High School District Presented to the Chicago Board of Education Public Hearing on October 16, 1961 by the Chatham–Avalon Park Community Council and the Marynook Homeowners Association," IAF, Folder 348.

100. Andrew L. Wang, "Stanley Walter Drigot: Sued to Integrate City's Public Schools," *Chicago Tribune*, January 30, 2006.

101. R. J. Havighurst, "Schools and Social Goals," *Hyde Park Herald*, November 22, 1961, IAF, Folder 351; The Advisory Panel on Integration of the Public Schools, *Report to the Board of Education*, 11–12, 29.

102. Norton E. Long, "Education and Metropolitan Change," in *Education in Urban Society*, B. J. Chandler, Lindley Stiles, and John Kitsuse, eds. (New York: Dodd, Mead & Co., 1962), 85–87.

103. *Bulletin*, "Homeowners See Willis," June 7, 1962; Clay Gowran, "Havighurst Cites Need of Gifted Pupils," *Chicago Tribune*, November 17, 1964, 5.

104. *Decision at 83rd Street*, WBBM (Chicago, 1962), PAC; *School Integration Newsletter*, "A Study of a 'Ghetto High School' Part II," April 1962, Illinois American Civil Liberties Union (IACLU) Papers, Box 14, Folder 7, Regenstein Library, University of Chicago.

105. *Decision at 83rd Street*, WBBM (Chicago, 1962), PAC.

106. Mary Huff, "Board Places Lid on School Transfer Bid: Marynook Parents Get 'No' to Test Plan," *Chicago Tribune*, December 23, 1962, SW2; *Time*, "Cooling It in the Schools," September 11, 1964, 77; *Time*, "The Education of Big Ben," August 30, 1963, 48; Rury, "Race, Space and the Politics of Chicago's Public Schools," 126; J. Harvie Wilkinson III, *From Brown to Bakke: The Supreme Court and School Integration, 1954–1978* (New York: Oxford University Press, 1979), 172–73.

107. The Advisory Panel on Integration of the Public Schools, *Report to the Board of Education*, 11–12.

108. Marcia Lane Vespa, "Chicago's Regional School Plans," *Integrated Education* 1, no. 5 (October–November 1963): 24.

109. *New Crusader*, "Our Opinion: School Supt. Willis Vs. Negroes," November 18, 1961, 4; *Chicago Daily News*, "City's Racial Problems in Willis' Lap," July 6, 1962; Herrick, *Chicago Schools*, 333–34, 337.

110. Dorothy Shipps, *School Reform, Corporate Style, 1880–2000* (Lawrence: University of Kansas Press, 2006), 67.

111. Charles and Bonnie Remsberg, "Legacy of an Ice Age," in *America's Troubles: A Casebook on Social Conflict*, Howard E. Freeman and Norman R. Kurtz, eds. (Englewood Cliffs, NJ: Prentice-Hall, Inc., 1969), 100.

112. *Chicago Tribune*, "Unfair Criticism of Our Schools," December 16, 1961, 16; *Chicago American*, "Emotional Confusion," December 1961, 11; *Chicago Daily News*,

"Pressures on the Schools," September 30, 1961; Helen Fleming, "Cleric Chides Foes of Half-Day Class: Charges Parents View School as Educational Baby-Sitter," *Chicago Daily News*, September 19, 1961; Letter from Peter R. Scalise, president of the Joint Civic Committee of Italian Americans supporting Willis and the Board of Education, *Chicago Tribune*, January 5, 1962, 12; *Southeast Economist*, "Willis Gets Support of P-T-A Group," April 1, 1962; *Chicago Defender*, "Mrs. Green Supports Willis," April 9, 1962.

113. Philip Hauser quoted in Robert B. McKersie, *A Decisive Decade: An Insider's View of the Chicago Civil Rights Movement during the 1960s* (Carbondale: Southern Illinois University Press, 2013), 71.

114. *Chicago Sun-Times*, "Integration Is Peaceful in Dallas," September 7, 1961, 3, 6.

115. CAPCC, CORE, SNCC, "Educate Our Children Now! Our Children Are Being Shortchanged" [1959?], Cantwell Papers, Box 31, Folder 4; Dan Burley, "NAACP Misses Boat; Parents Take Over School Bias Suit," *New Crusader*, September 23, 1961, 1; *Southeast Economist*, "Lawyer Is Retained in School Test," September 17, 1961; Alan B. Anderson and George W. Pickering, *Confronting the Color Line: The Broken Promise of the Civil Rights Movement in Chicago* (Athens, GA: University of Georgia Press, 1986), 80–81. The *Taylor v. New Rochelle Board of Education* (1960) decision ruled that de facto segregation was unconstitutional and that public schools must take affirmative steps to integrate their student bodies.

116. *Bulletin*, "Burnside Area Fears Crowded Classrooms; Sets Local Meeting," December 6, 1962; *Chicago Defender*, "Call Mass Meeting over School Bias Deal," December 11, 1962, 7.

117. *Chicago Daily News*, "Renew School Sit-In with 16 Clergymen," January 18, 1962; *Chicago Tribune*, "Halt Burnside Sit-In Arrests Temporarily," January 19, 1962, 11; *Chicago Sun-Times*, January 18, 1962, 30; *Chicago Daily News*, January 17, 1962, 1, 8; *Chicago Tribune*, "Free 16, Seize 10 Others in School 'Sit-In,'" January 18, 1962, 5.

118. *Chicago Defender*, "Dumb School Principal" January 22, 1962; *Chicago Daily News*, "School Sit-In Here Is Ended," January 23, 1962, 11.

119. Anderson and Pickering, *Confronting the Color Line*, 90.

120. *Chicago Daily News*, "How School Racial Battle Has Grown," February 22, 1964, 9.

121. *Bulletin*, "Whose Government?" May 17, 1962; H. B. Law, "Summer 1963 and the Urban League," IACLU, Box 7, Folder 7; Frank Y. Ichistita, "A Neighborhood Demonstrates," in *Learning Together: A Book on Integrated Education*, Meyer Weinberg, ed. (Chicago: Integrated Education Associates, 1964), 162–66; *Chicago Defender*, "Parents Picket Slum School; Hold Mass Protest," January 30, 1962.

122. Sidney Kronus, *The Black Middle Class* (Columbus, OH: Charles E. Merrill Publishing, 1971), 51. See also Donald I. Warren, *Black Neighborhoods: An Assessment of Community Power* (Ann Arbor: University of Michigan Press, 1975), 99.

123. Seligman, *Block by Block*, 4, 41, 213–14.

124. Ronald Kotulak, "Negro Defends New Civic Organization," *Chicago Tribune*, November 29, 1959; Norris Vitchek as told to Alfred Balk, "Confessions of a Block Buster," *Saturday Evening Post*, July 14, 1962, 15–19; W. Edward Orser, *Blockbusting in Baltimore: The Edmondson Village Story* (Lexington: University Press of Kentucky, 1994); Helper, *Racial Policies and Practices of Real Estate Brokers*, 91–92.

125. *Chicago Daily News*, "Hissing Zombies Jangle Nerves of Homeowners," October 15, 1959; *Chicago Daily News*, "Nasty Bag of Fear Tricks Used to 'Bust Up' Blocks," October 16, 1959.

126. *Chicago Daily News*, "The Panic Peddlers," October 13, 1959; *Chicago Daily News*, "'Amateurs' Like Nick Cash in on Racial Change," October 17, 1959; *Chicago Daily News*, "East Chatham Unprepared for Great Racial Change," October 22, 1959.

127. *Chicago Daily News*, "The Panic Peddlers," October 13, 1959.

128. Letter from Thomas Gaudette to Mr. and Mrs. Club, Temple B'Nai Yehuda, March 26, 1960, TAG, Series 1, Box 1, Folder 4; Letter to the editor, "Hits Realty Pressures in Shifting Areas," *Chicago Daily News*, February 21, 1958.

129. Harry Swegel, "Burn 'Blockbuster' Signs in Chatham," *Chicago Daily News*, May 11, 1960.

130. William M. Dobriner, *Class in Suburbia* (Englewood Cliffs, N.J.: Prentice-Hall, Inc., 1963), 64–67; *Chicago American*, "Marynook—the Bright Side of City's Integration," August 22, 1965.

131. *Southeast Economist*, "Asks Strike in Protest over Shift," January 28, 1962, 14.

132. S. Joseph Fauman, "Housing Discrimination, Changing Neighborhoods, and Public Schools," *Journal of Social Issues* 13, no. 4 (1957): 26; *The Crisis*, "De Facto Segregation in the Chicago Public Schools," February 1958, 89; John Bartlow Martin, "The Border States Relent," *Saturday Evening Post*, July 13, 1957, 56–58; *Time*, "Civilizing the Blackboard Jungle," November 15, 1963, 86–92. For "expert" arguments that blacks lacked the same educational capabilities as whites, see Frank J. McGurk, "A Scientist's Report on Race Differences," *U.S. News & World Report*, September 21, 1956, 92–96.

133. Abrahamson, *Neighborhood Finds Itself*, 281–82; *Chicago Daily News*, "It Resisted the Irresistible and Won: How Marynook Shattered Race Myths," July 21, 1962; Author interview with Dr. Fred Malkinson, Jan. 15, 2007; Author interview with Herbert Fisher, Jan. 22, 2008.

134. The Advisory Panel on Integration of the Public Schools, *Report to the Board of Education*, 12.

135. Alvin E. Winder, "White Attitudes towards Negro-White Interaction in an Area of Changing Racial Composition," Unpublished PhD Dissertation, University of Chicago, 1952, 155–57, 162, 167, 181, 186; Vader, "Racial Segregation within Catholic Institutions in Chicago," 77, 121; Giese, *Revolution in the City*, 26–27; Marshall Sklare and Joseph Greenblum, *Jewish Identity on the Suburban Frontier: A Study of Group Survival in the Open Society* (New York: Basic Books, 1967), 278, 309, 317–19.

136. CAPCC and Marynook Homeowners Assn., "Corrective Plan for School and Community Instability," 1961, CJEG, Box 24; *Chicago Daily News*, "'We Can't Keep Running,' Chatham Residents Moan," September 21, 1959. For the fate of clustering plans, see Tracy L. Steffes, "Managing School Integration and White Flight: The Debate over Chicago's Future in the 1960s," *Journal of Urban History* 42, no. 4 (2016): 709–32.

137. Winder, "White Attitudes towards Negro-White Interaction in an Area of Changing Racial Composition" (dissertation), 127, 136, 310; *Chicago Daily News*, "How Some Realty Dealers Feed on Race Fears Here," October 13, 1959; Giese, *Revolution in the City*, 24.

138. Wini Breines, *Young, White, and Miserable: Growing Up Female in the Fifties* (Boston: Beacon Press, 1992), 10–11.

139. Milton M. Gordon, "The Nature of Assimilation" in *Human Nature, Class, and Ethnicity* (New York: Oxford University Press, 1978), 177.

140. Alvin E. Winder, "White Attitudes towards Negro-White Interaction in an Area of Changing Racial Composition," *Journal of Social Psychology* 41 (1955): 91–93; Sklare and Greenblum, *Jewish Identity on the Suburban Frontier*, 317–19.

141. Herman Long, "Facts vs. Fantasies in Integrated Housing," *Social Action* 24, no. 3 (November 1957): 13.

142. David Hollinger, "Amalgamation and Hypodescent: The Question of Ethnoracial Mixture in the History of the United States," *American Historical Review* 108 (December 2003): 363.

143. Helper, 81.

144. Murray Friedman, "The White Liberal's Retreat," *Atlantic Monthly*, January 1963, 43; Remsberg and Remsberg, "Legacy of an Ice Age," 106.

145. Author interview with Mike and Verna Dee Goren, Nov. 1, 2007.

146. Fauman, "Housing Discrimination, Changing Neighborhoods, and Public Schools," 28; Wiese, *Places of Their Own*, 97; Eleanor Wolf, "The Baxter Area, 1960–1962: A New Trend in Neighborhood Change?" *Phylon* 26 (Winter 1965): 351.

147. Robert O. Self, *American Babylon: Race and the Struggle for Postwar Oakland* (Princeton, NJ: Princeton University Press, 2003), 16.

148. John F. Lyons, *Teachers and Reform: Chicago Public Education, 1929–1970* (Urbana: University of Illinois Press, 2008), 172–73.

149. Thomas Gaudette Oral History, May 15, 1990, TAG, Series 3, Box 1, Case 4.

150. Ralph Bass, "Prejudice Won't Make Us Sell Our House!" *Coronet*, July 1959, 106; Goreau, 212; Albert J. Mayer, "Russell Woods: Change without Conflict, , Case Study of Neighborhood Racial Transition in Detroit," *Studies in Housing and Minority Groups*, Nathan Glazer and Davis McEntire, eds. (Berkeley: University of California Press, 1960), 219–20; Dan Cordtz, "The Negro Middle Class Is Right in the Middle," *Fortune* (November 1966), 177.

151. Hoyt W. Fuller, "The Myth of 'The White Backlash,'" *Negro Digest*, August 1964, 15.

152. Rosen, *South Side*, 144.

153. *Chicago Tribune*, "Hope to Add 5,000 Persons to Civic Group," April 17, 1960, S3; Rosen, *South Side*, 127.

154. For similar efforts in Cleveland, see Todd M. Michney, *Surrogate Suburbs: Black Upward Mobility and Neighborhood Change in Cleveland, 1900–1980* (Chapel Hill: University of North Carolina Press, 2017).

155. Joseph Galaskiewicz, "A Study of Racially Changing Neighborhoods in the City of Chicago" [1971?], 5–6, Morris Janowitz Papers, Box 30, Folder 11, Regenstein Library, University of Chicago. See also David R. Meyer, *Spatial Variation of Black Urban Households*, Research Paper No. 129 (Chicago: University of Chicago Department of Geography), 105; Leo Schnore, "Social Class Segregation among Nonwhites in Metropolitan Centers," *Demography* II (1965): 130.

156. *Chicago Daily News*, "Report Shows Gain in Older Home Renewals," October 16, 1964, 35.

157. St. Clair Drake, "Folkways and Classways within the Black Ghetto," in *The Making of Black America: Essays in Negro Life and History*, vol. 1, August Meier and Elliot Rudwick, eds. (New York: Atheneum, 1969), 448.

158. George Nesbitt, "Break Up the Black Ghetto?" *The Crisis*, February 1949, 52; Kerner Commission, *Report of the National Advisory Commission on Civil Disorders* (Washington, DC: U.S. Government Printing Office, 1968), 257; Seth S. King, "No Hope in Woodlawn," *Saturday Review*, August 19, 1972, 6.

159. *Chicago Defender*, "7200 Indiana Block Club Wins 'Beautiful' Prize," January 23, 1958, 14; *Chicago Defender*, "Pick 8th Ward's Best," October 17, 1970, 4.

160. *Bulletin*, "Taylor Again in Running for Chatham Council Presidency," June 2, 1960.

161. Lewis Caldwell, "Self Examination," *New Crusader*, September 8, 1962.

162. *Chicago Daily News*, "A Middle-Class Problem," August 24, 1963.

163. *Chicago Defender*, "Chatham Drys Planning New Vote Test," January 31, 1959, 3; *Bulletin*, "Tavern, Council War Heats Up: Dry Option Showdown Near," September 25, 1962.

164. Giese, *Revolution in the City*, 12; Gregory, *Chatham 1856–1987*, 22.

165. *Decision at 83rd Street*, WBBM (Chicago, 1962), PAC.

166. Letter from A. L. Foster, Chicago Urban League, to Irene McCoy Gaines, July 20, 1937; Letter from Irene McCoy Gaines to Mayor Edward Kelly, Sept. 22, 1937; Chicago & Northern District Association of Colored Women, "Findings of Conference on Taverns" in "Annual Report," 1937–1938; Letter from Irene McCoy Gaines and Joe Jefferson, Better Conduct Program, Urban League, to pastors, Aug. 3, 1938, IMG, Box 1, Folder 12.

167. Roi Ottley, "Community Group Sparks Drive to Shutter Taverns," *Chicago Tribune*, November 2, 1958, SW18, 38–40.

168. Walter Cromwell, *The Tavern in Relation to Children and Youth* (Chicago: The Juvenile Protection Association of Chicago, 1948), 2, 8; Chicago Crime Commission, "Report of the Emergency Crime Committee of the City Council of Chicago," 1952, 7–10, 22–23, MHPC, Accession 75-104, Box 6; Joe Smith, *Sin Corner and Joe Smith: A Story of Vice and Corruption in Chicago* (New York: Exposition Press, 1963), 22.

169. *Bulletin*, "WACA Seeks to Bar Area Bar," June 21, 1962, CJEG, Box 44.

170. A. L. Foster, "Other People's Business," *Chicago Defender*, November 22, 1958, 4.

171. A. L. Foster, "Other People's Business," *Chicago Defender*, October 22, 1960, 4; *Chicago Tribune*, "Store Front Churches Are Poll Subject," November 5, 1959, S6; Aldo Bechman, "Mailman Asks Route around Zoning Block," *Chicago Tribune*, February 14, 1960, SW4; *Chicago Tribune*, "Zoning Ruling Is Upheld in Circuit Court," December 8, 1960, S10.

172. Nicholas Lemann, *The Promised Land: The Great Black Migration and How It Changed America* (New York: Knopf, 1991), 77–78; James Q. Wilson, *Negro Politics: The Search for Leadership* (Glencoe, IL: Free Press, 1960), 128; *Chicago Defender*, "Cleric Admits He Ran Abortion Den: Set Up Church to Conceal 'Hospital' Abortion Den," September 25, 1954, 1–2, 5.

173. *Chicago Tribune*, "Store Front Church Hit in City Ruling," September 17, 1959, S6; *Southeast Economist*, "Community Unit Seeks Members," June 16, 1963; *Chicago Daily News*, "A Middle-Class Problem: Negro Who Moves Up Often Shows Disdain for Lower Class," August 24, 1963.

174. Thomas Gaudette Oral History, May 15, 1990, TAG, Series 3, Box 1, Case 4.

175. Adam Cohen and Elizabeth Taylor, *American Pharaoh: Mayor Richard J. Daley: His Battle for Chicago and the Nation* (Boston: Little, Brown, 2000), 533–39.

176. Thomas Gaudette, "Report on sale of land to Nation of Islam," CJEG, Box 24; *Southeast Economist,* "Rap Park Site Sale," March 27, 1960; *New York Times,* "Chicago Official Found Guilty of Mail Fraud and Conspiracy," October 10, 1974, 31.

177. Thomas Gaudette Oral History, May 15, 1990, TAG, Series 3, Box 1, Case 4.

178. Ronald Kotulak, "Park Plea Hits Temple Project on Chatham Site," *Chicago Tribune,* August 14, 1960, 1.

179. Thomas Gaudette, "Report on sale of land to Nation of Islam," CJEG, Box 24; Robert Colby Nelson, "Negro Cult Stirs Debate," *Christian Science Monitor,* May 16, 1960, 10; Thomas Gaudette Oral History, May 15, 1990, TAG, Series 3, Box 1, Case 4.

180. *Southeast Economist,* "300 Oppose Islam Plan for Area" [1960?], clipping in CJEG, Box 24; *Southeast Economist,* "Rap Park Site Sale," March 27, 1960.

181. *Chicago Tribune,* "Charges Bias, Enters Fight over Temple," August 21, 1960, 1; *New Crusader,* "400-Bed Hospital Plan in Chatham Turned Down; Temple Vows to Fight On," August 27, 1960.

182. *New Crusader,* "Negro, Catholic Fight Muhammad Hospital Program: Chatham-Avalon Group Advocates Jim-Crow Playground in Area," August 10, 1961.

183. Barbara Moffett and Jane Weston, "News from the Chicago Scene," January 4, 1961, AFSC, Box 86, Folder 29; *Chicago Tribune,* "Defer Decision in Muhammad Park Battle," August 10, 1960, 19; Open letter from Welton Taylor to George Leighton, n.d. but c. Aug. 1960, TAG, Series 1, Box 1, Folder 4.

184. *Southeast Economist,* "Five Acre Tract Stirs Hot Debate," August 11, 1960; Ronald Kotulak, "Park Plea Hits Temple Project on Chatham Site," *Chicago Tribune,* August 14, 1960, 1.

185. Alfred Borcover, "Council Asks Rezoning for I.I.T. Expansion," *Chicago Tribune,* June 25, 1959, S2; *Chicago Tribune,* "Citizens Group Asks Ban on Apartment Buildings," September 27, 1959, S2; Charles Gaines, "Chatham Man," *Chicago Daily News,* September 23, 1963; *Chicago Defender,* "Integrated Area Sought by ECO," December 4, 1967, 3. For examples of black middle-class resistance against apartments and public housing in Cincinnati and Cleveland, see Cebula, "Creating a Multiracial Community in Post–World War II Cincinnati," 36–37, 44; Leonard N. Moore, *Carl B. Stokes and the Rise of Black Political Power* (Urbana: University of Illinois Press, 2002), 100–108.

186. D. Bradford Hunt, "What Went Wrong with Public Housing in Chicago? A History of the Robert Taylor Homes," *Journal of the Illinois State Historical Society* 94 (Spring 2001): 101; Timuel D. Black Jr., *Bridges of Memory: Chicago's First Wave of Black Migration, an Oral History* (Evanston, IL: Northwestern University Press, 2003), 516; Moore, *Carl B. Stokes and the Rise of Black Political Power,* 196–97.

187. L. Alex Wilson, "Race Hate Blocks 7,300 Housing Units in Chicago," *Chicago Defender,* March 11, 1950, 2; Martin Meyerson and Edward Banfield, *Politics, Planning, and the Public Interest: The Case of Public Housing in Chicago* (Glencoe, IL: Free Press, 1955), 87; D. Bradford Hunt, *Blueprint for Disaster: The Unraveling of Chicago Public Housing* (Chicago: University of Chicago Press, 2009), 87–92; Hirsch, *Making the Second Ghetto,* 223–24.

188. Harold M. Baron, *Building Babylon: A Case of Racial Controls in Public Housing* (Evanston, IL: Northwestern University Center for Urban Affairs, 1971), 68.

189. George Nesbitt, "Break Up the Black Ghetto?" *The Crisis,* February 1949, 49; *Chicago Tribune,* "Public Housing Hearings Echo Past Debates," July 14, 1950, A13; Meyerson and Banfield, *Politics, Planning, and the Public Interest,* 233–35; Baron, *Building Babylon,*

19–20. For a subsequent example, see Mary Pattillo, *Black on the Block: The Politics of Race and Class in the City* (Chicago: University of Chicago Press, 2007), 182–84, 203–4.

190. Jeffrey Helgeson, *Crucibles of Black Empowerment: Chicago's Neighborhood Politics from the New Deal to Harold Washington* (Chicago: University of Chicago Press, 2014), 226; Meyerson and Banfield, 198; Emmett Curme, "Morgan Park, Beverly Hills Hit CHA Plan," *Chicago Tribune*, February 6, 1955, 1; *Chicago Tribune*, "3 Civic Groups Fight Housing in Morgan Park," April 3, 1955, SW8; Hunt, *Blueprint for Disaster*, 111.

191. *Bulletin*, "Group Maps Zone Fight Strategy Last Tuesday," July 16, 1959; Susan Boie, "Oppose CHA Project for Morgan Pk," *Chicago Tribune*, November 26, 1967, A1; Doris E. Saunders, "Confetti," *Chicago Defender*, November 29, 1967, 14; J. S. Fuerst, *When Public Housing Was Paradise: Building Community in Chicago* (Westport, CT: Praeger, 2003), 72–73.

192. Mrs. Hershep, "Favors Public Housing," *Chicago Defender*, May 21, 1955, 9; *Chicago Defender*, "Planning Head Resigns," October 31, 1967, 6.

193. E. Franklin Frazier, *Black Bourgeoisie: The Rise of a New Middle Class* (New York: Free Press, 1957), 228.

194. *Chicago Sun-Times*, "Jail Big Shot Owner of Slum Tenement," December 8, 1948; *Chicago Tribune*, "Raid Tenement Housing, 450 in Fifth, Arrest 3," December 8, 1948; Memo from Graham, Stevenson, and Krupp to the Metropolitan Housing and Planning Commission, "Housing Code Violations by the Hansberry Family," 1960, MHPC, Box 13, Folder 143.

195. *Chicago Tribune*, "Neighborhood Votes to Join Local Council," September 25, 1958, S13; *Chicago Tribune*, "Citizens Group Asks Ban on Apartment Buildings," September 27, 1959, S2; Statement from John Baird, President of Metropolitan Housing and Planning Commission, Aug. 9, 1962, MHPC, Box 24, Folder 291.

196. *Our People*, WTTW (Chicago, 1968), PAC.

197. Moore, 105; Bruce D. Haynes, *Red Lines, Black Spaces: The Politics of Race and Space in a Black Middle-Class Suburb* (New Haven, CT: Yale University Press, 2001), xviii.

198. Jonathan Rieder, *Canarsie: The Jews and Italians of Brooklyn against Liberalism* (Cambridge, MA: Harvard University Press, 1985), 21, 64–68; Kenneth Durr, *Behind the Backlash: White Working-Class Politics in Baltimore, 1940–1980* (Chapel Hill: University of North Carolina Press), 2, 79, 95, 113, 139; Seligman, 4, 41, 213–14; Heather Ann Thompson, "Rethinking the Politics of White Flight in the Postwar City, Detroit, 1945–1980," *Journal of Urban History* 25, no. 2 (January 1999): 166–68; Self, *American Babylon*, 16.

199. Murray Friedman, "The White Liberal's Retreat," *Atlantic Monthly*, January 1963, 43; Harvey Luskin Molotch, *Managed Integration: Dilemmas of Doing Good in the City* (Berkeley: University of California Press, 1972), 7–9; Mayer, "Russell Woods," 213; Wolf, "The Baxter Area," 348–61.

NOTES TO CHAPTER 4

1. Syl Johnson, *Is It Because I'm Black?* © 1969 by Twinight Records.

2. Charles Harrison, *A Life's Design: The Life and Work of Industrial Designer Charles Harrison* (Chicago: Ibis, 2005), 44, 49, 75; Linda Hales, "Chuck Harrison: Adding Dimension to Design," *Washington Post*, October 11, 2006, C1.

3. John David Skrentny, *The Ironies of Affirmative Action: Politics, Culture, and Justice in America* (Chicago: University of Chicago Press, 1996), 5; Paul D. Moreno, *From Direct Action to Affirmative Action: Fair Employment Law and Policy in America, 1933–1972*

(Baton Rouge: Louisiana State University, 1997); Terry H. Anderson, *The Pursuit of Fairness: A History of Affirmative Action* (New York: Oxford University Press, 2004).

4. Frank Dobbin, *Inventing Equal Opportunity* (Princeton, NJ: Princeton University Press, 2009), 2–3, 12, 42; Jennifer Delton, *Racial Integration in Corporate America, 1940–1990* (New York: Cambridge University Press, 2009), 4–5, 280–82; Stacy Kinlock Sewell, "'The Best Man for the Job': Corporate Responsibility and Racial Integration in the Workplace, 1945–1960," *The Historian* 65, no. 5 (Fall 2003): 1126; Benton Williams, "AT&T and the Private-Sector Origins of Private-Sector Affirmative Action," *Journal of Policy History* 20, no. 4 (2008): 543–45.

5. Robert W. Ackerman, "How Companies Respond to Social Demands," *Harvard Business Review*, July–August 1973, 91, 98.

6. E. Franklin Frazier, *Black Bourgeoisie: The Rise of a New Middle Class* (New York: Free Press, 1957), 24–25; Nathan Hare, *The Black Anglo-Saxons* (New York: Marzani and Munsell, 1965); Harold Cruse, *The Crisis of the Negro Intellectual: Historical Analysis of the Failure of Black Leadership* (New York: Morrow, 1967), 90, 312, 376; Manning Marable, *Malcolm X: A Life of Reinvention* (New York: Viking Press, 2011), 261.

7. Harold M. Baron and Bennett Hymer, *The Negro Worker in the Chicago Labor Market: A Case Study of De Facto Segregation* (Chicago: Chicago Urban League's Studies of the Labor Market, 1965); William Julius Wilson, *When Work Disappears: The World of the New Urban Poor* (New York: Knopf, 1996).

8. *Business Week*, "Economically the Negro Gains but He's Still the Low Man," December 18, 1954, 86; *Color*, "Top Jobs Negroes Haven't Cracked," April 1957, 28; *Chicago Defender*, "Pepsi-Cola Gives Jobs to Negroes," January 30, 1943, 22; *Chicago Defender*, "Employs Negro on White Collar Job," August 14, 1948, 13; *Jet*, "Memphis Negroes Upgraded to White Collar Jobs," May 23, 1963, 44; *Ebony*, "Big Business Names a Veep," July 1962, 25–32; John W. Work, *Race, Economics and Corporate America* (Wilmington, DE: Scholarly Resources, 1984), 40–41; Jack G. Gourlay, *The Negro Salaried Worker* (New York: American Management Association, 1965), 16.

9. Brian S. Moskal, "Ascent of the Black Manager," *Industry Week*, October 1976, 41.

10. *Jet*, "White Collar Hiring Bias Drops 75% in Chicago," January 1, 1953, 10; Ethel Payne, "Is There Job Integration on Chicago's State Street?" *Chicago Defender*, July 4, 1953, 9.

11. Frederick Pollard Jr., Acting Executive Director, CCHR, "Chicago's Human Relations Problems," April 10–12, 1959, AFSC, Box 94, Folder 5.

12. *Business Week*, "Chicago Starts Moving on Equal Job Question," May 30, 1964, 22–23.

13. *Ebony*, "Jobs for Negroes," June 1967, 81; Sewell, "'The Best Man for the Job,'" 1141; Pamela Walker Laird, *Pull: Networking and Success since Benjamin Franklin* (Cambridge, MA: Harvard University Press, 2006), 109; George F. Doriot et al., *The Management of Racial Integration in Business* (New York: McGraw-Hill, 1964), 49.

14. Judy Tzu-Chun Wu, *Radicals on the Road: Internationalism, Orientalism, and Feminism during the Vietnam Era* (Ithaca, NY: Cornell University Press, 2013), 26.

15. Wu, *Radicals on the Road*, 26.

16. Tony Bonaparte, "Problems of Black Managers in Business Corporations Today," *S.A.M. Advanced Management Journal*, January 1972, 47.

17. Albert H. Miller, "Negro in the North," *Ave Maria*, Jan. 24, 1959, 6, Daniel Cantwell Papers, Box 30, Folder 5.

18. Arvarh E. Strickland, *History of the Chicago Urban League* (Urbana: University of Illinois Press, 1966), 131–32; Lewis A. H. Caldwell, "Commentary," *Chicago Defender*, April 30, 1958, A8; *Chicago Defender*, "League Needs Money after Winning Anti-Bias Battle," May 10, 1958, 12; *Chicago Defender*, "Set Deadline for Banks to Begin Fair Hiring," May 17, 1958, 3; Doriot et al., *Management of Racial Integration in Business*, 30; *Newsweek*, "The Negro's Search for a Better Job," June 8, 1964, 79–83; Lillian Calhoun, "People's Gas Chairman Tells 'Positive Policy' on Hiring," *Chicago Defender*, August 28, 1963, 9; Mark McColloch, *White Collar Workers in Transition: The Boom Years, 1940–1970* (Westport, CT: Greenwood Press, 1983), 33, 137–39.

19. *Chicago Defender*, "NAACP Hails Bank's Action," January 17, 1962, 9; *Chicago Defender*, "Set Date for Chatham Bank to End Job Bias," July 9, 1962, 5; Chicago Commission on Human Relations, "Nine Area Firms Record 'Firsts' in Negro Hiring," *Human Relations News of Chicago* 5, no. 4 (June 1963), AFSC, Box 94, Folder 5; Edwin C. Berry, "Jobs, Poverty and Race," *Negro Digest*, September 1964, 7, 10.

20. Richard B. Freeman, *Black Elite: The New Market for Highly Educated Black Americans* (New York: McGraw-Hill, 1976), xix.

21. Monroe Sharp, Reports by the Staff of SNCC, May 1965, Student Nonviolent Coordinating Committee Papers, Box 1, Folder 17, Daley Library, University of Illinois at Chicago.

22. *The Crisis*, "PCGC's Report," February 1960, 89; *Business Week*, "The Unfinished Business of Negro Jobs," June 12, 1965, 82.

23. Operation Breadbasket, Minutes of the Meeting of the Wives of Breadbasket, June 19, 1966, Addie Wyatt Papers, Box 148, Folder 15, Vivian G. Harsh Research Collection of Afro-American History and Literature, Carter G. Woodson Regional Library, Chicago.

24. Cyrus Colter, "The Beach Umbrella," in *The Amoralists & Other Tales: Collected Stories by Cyrus Colter* (New York: Thunder's Mouth Press, 1988), 203.

25. Frank T. Cherry, "Southern In-Migrant Negroes in North Lawndale, Chicago, 1949–1959: A Study of Internal Migration and Adjustment," Unpublished PhD Thesis, University of Chicago, 1965, 6–7.

26. Sidney Kronus, *The Black Middle Class* (Columbus, OH: Charles E. Merrill Publishing, 1971), 124–25.

27. *Report of the Chicago Riot Study Committee to the Hon. Richard J. Daley*, August 1, 1968, 31, 73, 68, 123.

28. Amanda Seligman, *Block by Block: Neighborhoods and Public Policy on Chicago's West Side* (Chicago: University of Chicago Press, 2005), 216–20.

29. Donald Perkins, President of Jewel Companies, "Social Responsibility of Business," National Student Assembly, YMCA/YWCA, Chicago, Dec. 30, 1966, Addie Wyatt Papers, Box 148, Folder 15; Peter Prugh, "Chicago Executives Press Campaign to Hire More Negroes," *Wall Street Journal*, August 19, 1965, 10.

30. Margaret Halsey, "Dedicated to the Status Quo," *Negro Digest*, March 1966, 11.

31. Percy Julian, "The 'White Backlash' and Common Sense," *Chicago Tribune*, November 5, 1966, 10.

32. Dan Cordtz, "The Negro Middle Class Is Right in the Middle," *Fortune*, November 1966, 180; *Chicago Defender*, "Calif. Study Claim Middle-Class Negroes' Discontent Foments Riots," August 5, 1967, 27; *Chicago Defender*, "Showing Signs of Changing," January 18, 1968, 4.

33. John S. Morgan and Richard L. Van Dyke, *White-Collar Blacks: A Breakthrough?* (New York: American Management Association, 1970), 125.

34. *U.S. News & World Report*, "Growing Success of Negroes in the U.S.," July 3, 1967, 57.

35. Morgan and Van Dyke, *White-Collar Blacks*, 162–63.

36. Rodney Alexander and Elisabeth Sapery, *The Shortchanged: Women and Minorities in Banking* (New York: Dunellen Publishing Co., 1972), 59–60.

37. Elizabeth St. Julian, "Insight on Riots, Causes and the Results," *Chicago Defender*, August 12, 1967, 11.

38. Harold M. Baron, "Black Powerlessness in Chicago," *Trans-Action*, November 1968, 28.

39. Letter to ministers from Operation Breadbasket, Nov. 19, 1966 and Operation Breadbasket, "Covenant between Operation Breadbasket and National Tea Company," Dec. 9, 1966, Addie Wyatt Papers, Box 148, Folder 15; Chicago Seven-Up Bottling Co., "Operation Breadbasket" [1967?], Addie Wyatt Papers, Box 149, Folder 1; "A Message from Operation Breadbasket of the Southern Christian Leadership Conference: Your Ministers of Operation Breadbasket Say: Don't Shop at A&P," Flyer, [Aug. 1968?], Addie Wyatt Papers, Box 149, Folder 6; Operation Breadbasket, "Don't Shop at Walgreen's Drug Stores" [1970?], Addie Wyatt Papers, Box 149, Folder 8.

40. *Business Week*, "The Unfinished Business of Negro Jobs," June 12, 1965, 87; *Chicago Defender*, "Schlitz to Ink PUSH Jobs Pact," August 5, 1972, 1; Richard Ringer, "PUSH Targets Banking Industry for Aid Pledge to Black Communities," *American Banker*, August 13, 1982, 3.

41. Covenant between Miller Brewing and PUSH, October 3, 1973, Abbott-Sengstacke Papers, Vivian G. Harsh Research Collection of Afro-American History and Literature, Carter G. Woodson Regional Library, Chicago, Box 190, Folder 2.

42. Sharon M. Collins, *Black Corporate Executives: The Making and Breaking of a Black Middle Class* (Philadelphia: Temple University Press, 1997), 67, 129.

43. Richard P. Nathan, *Jobs and Civil Rights* (Washington, DC: Prepared for the United States Commission on Civil Rights by the Brookings Institution, 1969), 138; William H. Brown III, "EEOC Chairman Brown: 'I Submit There Is More Racial Animosity in America Today Than Ever Before,'" *MBA* 6 (1972): 12–16, 102.

44. *Business Week*, "Industry Rushes for Negro Grads," April 26, 1964, 78–81; *U.S. News & World Report*, "For Negroes: More and Better Jobs in Government," March 5, 1962, 83–85.

45. Chicago Commission on Human Relations, "Chicago Tops Nation in Negro Federal Workers," *Human Relations News of Chicago* 5:5, August 1963, AFSC, Box 94, Folder 5; Baron and Hymer, *Negro Worker in the Chicago Labor Market*, 8; Peter Prugh, "Business & Race: Chicago Executives Press Campaign to Hire More Negroes," *Wall Street Journal*, August 19, 1965, 10.

46. *Ebony*, "Many Students Still Doubt Expanded Job Opportunities," June 1967, 82; Ulric Haynes, "Equal Job Opportunity: The Credibility Gap," *Harvard Business Review*, May–June 1968, 113; *Time*, "Working in the White Man's World," April 6, 1970.

47. *Business Week*, "The Unfinished Business of Negro Jobs," June 12, 1965, 92.

48. Rev. Ed Reddick, "Research Briefs: General Foods," April 30, 1972, Addie Wyatt Papers, Box 150, Folder 12.

49. Vance Packard, *The Pyramid Climbers* (New York: McGraw-Hill Company, 1962), 178; Chester I. Barnard, *The Functions of the Executive* (Cambridge, MA: Harvard University Press, 1968), 146, 224.

50. Frederick C. Klein, "Jews and Jobs: Religious Groups Push to Get Firms to Hire Jewish Executives," *Wall Street Journal*, October 26, 1966; Frederick J. Sturdivant and Roy

D. Adler, "Executive Origins: Still a Gray Flannel World?" *Harvard Business Review*, November–December 1976, 125–32.

51. *Employee Relations Bulletin*, "The Black Manager: How He Fits into the Corporation," December 7, 1976.

52. Roland D. Zimany, "A Better Program for Employing Minorities," *Business Horizons*, December 1970, 71; *Business Week*, "The Black Message: Business Must Do More," January 22, 1972, 79–80; Eli Ginzberg, *The Negro Challenge to the Business Community* (New York: McGraw-Hill, 1964), 98; Richard F. America and Bernard E. Anderson, "Black Managers: How They Manage Their Emotions," *Across the Board*, April 1979, 8; *Time*, "'Every Negro Who Discharges His Duty Faithfully Is Making a Real Contribution,'" January 3, 1964; John P. Fernandez, *Black Managers in White Corporations* (New York: John Wiley & Sons, 1975), 80; David H. Bankston and Rudolph L. Kagerer, "Communication and the Minority Employee," *The Personnel Administrator*, June 1974, 18.

53. Robert Townsend, *Up the Organization* (New York: Knopf, 1970), 161.

54. Ethel L. Payne, "The Stores Most Afraid of Customer Reaction Seem to Be the Smallest," *Chicago Defender*, August 15, 1953, 12; *Wall Street Journal*, "'Believability Gap' on Campus: Companies Rush to Hire Negro Graduates," April 3, 1968, 34; Robert P. Quinn et al., *The Chosen Few: A Study of Discrimination in Executive Selection* (Ann Arbor: The University of Michigan Institute for Social Research Survey Research Center, 1968), 19–20; National Industrial Conference Board, *Company Experience with Negro Employment*, vol. 2 (New York: 1966), 136, 147.55. Richard Barrett, "Gray Areas in Black and White Testing," *Harvard Business Review*, January–February 1968, 94.

56. Gourlay, *Negro Salaried Worker*, 54; *Chicago Defender*, "Weaver Finds Job Openings Outstrip Negro Training," December 15, 1962, 9; Harold C. Fleming, "Equal Job Opportunity—Slogan or Reality?" *Personnel Administration*, March–April 1963, 25–28; *Wall Street Journal*, "'Believability Gap' on Campus: Companies Rush to Hire Negro Graduates," April 3, 1968, 34; Barry Newman, "Small Strides: General Electric Co.'s Hiring of Blacks, Long Company's Commitment, Proves Slow but Sure," December 10, 1974, 1; Gregory S. Bell, *In the Black: A History of African Americans on Wall Street* (New York: John Wiley & Sons, 2002), 46, 74.

57. *Race Relations and Industry*, "GE Lays Groundwork to Combat Minority Engineering Shortages," July 1974.

58. *Business Week*, "Crashing Gates to Better Jobs," June 22, 1963, 24–25; *U.S. News & World Report*, "Jobs for Negroes—Is There a Real Shortage?" August 12, 1963, 28–32; *Business Week*, "The Negro Drive for Jobs," August 17, 1963, 53, 67; *Newsweek*, "The Negro's Search for a Better Job," June 8, 1964, 79–83; *Chicago Defender*, "White Collar Jobs Open to Negroes," December 31, 1966, 21; C. R. Winegarden, "Barriers to Black Employment in White-Collar Jobs: A Quantitative Approach," *Review of Black Political Economy* 2, no. 3 (Spring 1972): 20.

59. McColloch, *White Collar Workers in Transition*, 177.

60. Fernandez, *Black Managers in White Corporations*, 86; *U.S. News & World Report*, "Jobs for Negroes—Is There a Real Shortage?" August 12, 1963, 28–32; Gourlay, 12; George Davis and Glegg Watson, *Black Life in Corporate America: Swimming in the Mainstream* (Garden City, NY: Anchor Press, 1982), 60.

61. Jackie Robinson, "The Racial Crisis," *Sales Management*, August 16, 1963, 33–37; *Business Management*, "What It's Like to Be a Negro in Management, April 1966, 60–64, 69–77; R. D. Corwin, *Racial Minorities in Banking: New Workers in the Banking Industry* (New Haven, CT: College & University Press, 1971), 56–58, 61.

62. *Wall Street Journal*, "Labor Letter," November 26, 1968, 1; Floyd Dickens Jr. and Jacqueline B. Dickens, *The Black Manager: Making It in the Corporate World* (New York: AMACOM, 1982), 100.

63. *Ebony*, "Job Consultant for Big Business," April 1965, 115; Doriot, 47.

64. *Chicago Defender*, "New Firm Sets Goal Matching Blacks, Jobs," April 2, 1970, 6; Richard Watkins and Dawn R. Jones, "Black Executive Search Firms," *Black Enterprise*, May 1975, 7–20, 56.

65. National Industrial Conference Board, *Company Experience with Negro Employment*, vol. 1 (New York: 1966), 64.

66. WFBM, *A Black Man in a White Collar*, Indianapolis, IN, 1968, PAC.

67. Morgan and Van Dyke, 16–17; Harold Eugene Byrd, *The Black Experience in Big Business* (Hicksville, NY: Exposition Press, 1977), 19.

68. Mark Kogan, "McGee Ends Long Post Office Career," *Chicago Tribune*, June 18, 1973, 20; *Jet*, "Henry W. McGee, Chicago's First Black Postmaster, Succumbs at 90," April 10, 2000, 52; *Ebony*, "Speaking of People," February 1962, 7.

69. Albert Murray, *The Omni-Americans: New Perspectives on Black Experience and American Culture* (New York: Outerbridge & Dienstfrey, 1970), 96.

70. Herbert R. Northrup and Richard L. Rowan, eds., *The Negro and Employment Opportunity: Problems and Practices* (Ann Arbor: Bureau of Industrial Relations, University of Michigan, 1965), 325.

71. Morgan and Van Dyke, 154.

72. *U.S. News & World Report*, "Growing Success of Negroes in the U.S.," July 3, 1967, 56; William Pickens III, "The Interview—The Black's Viewpoint," *Business Horizons*, October 1970, 13–14; Ulric Haynes, "Equal Job Opportunity: The Credibility Gap," *Harvard Business Review*, May–June 1968, 119; Edward W. Jones Jr., "Black Managers: The Dream Deferred," *Harvard Business Review*, May–June 1986, 109; *U.S. News & World Report*, "Blacks Find That 'Making It' Doesn't Solve All the Problems," October 14, 1974, 50.

73. Morgan and Van Dyke, 84.

74. National Industrial Conference Board, *Company Experience with Negro Employment*, vol. 1, 98.

75. Reginald Lewis and Blair S. Walker, *"Why Should White Guys Have All the Fun?" How Reginald Lewis Created a Billion-Dollar Business Empire* (New York: John Wiley & Sons, 1995), 87–88; Thomas J. Bray, "'Black Bosses': More Negroes Enter Management, but Some Find Role Frustrating," *Wall Street Journal*, May 22, 1969, 1; Stanley Penn, "Integrated Offices: White-Collar Negroes Move into Better Jobs," *Wall Street Journal*, March 17, 1965, 1.

76. Stephanie Capparell, *The Real Pepsi Challenge: The Inspirational Story of Breaking the Color Barrier in American Business* (New York: Wall Street Journal Books, 2007), 4, 82; Harrison, *A Life's Design*, 79–81.

77. Marilyn Mercer, "How It Feels to Be a Black Girl Now," *Glamour*, May 1969, 180–81; Dennis Schatzman, "Why Corporations Are Having Trouble Retaining Competent Black Professionals," *Vital Speeches of the Day*, August 15, 1979, 666.

78. Enoch P. Waters, "Were Their Faces Red!" *Chicago Defender*, October 1, 1955, 9; Bernard Sarachek, "Career Concerns of Black Managers," *Management Review*, October 1974, 19; Richard F. America and Bernard E. Anderson, *Moving Ahead: Black Managers in American Business* (New York: McGraw-Hill, 1978), 110; Theresa A. Hammond, *A White-Collar Profession: African American Certified Public Accountants since 1921* (Chapel Hill: University of North Carolina Press, 2002), 35–36, 130; Dempsey J. Travis, *Racism:*

American Style, A Corporate Gift (Chicago: Urban Research Press, 1991), 128; Brian S. Moskal, "Ascent of the Black Manager," *Industry Week*, October 1976, 43.

79. *U.S. News & World Report*, "For Negroes: More and Better Jobs in Government," March 5, 1962, 84; Arthur Shostak, "Human Problems in Improving Industrial Race Relations," *Personnel Administration*, March–April 1963, 28–31; *U.S. News & World Report*, "Are Whites Being Discriminated Against?" June 17, 1963, 8; *Wall Street Journal*, "Bias in Reverse: White Workers Claim Employers Now Show Favoritism to Negroes," August 12, 1963, 1.

80. *Business Week*, "The Unfinished Business of Negro Jobs," June 12, 1965, 97.

81. Caroline Bird, "More Room at the Top," *Management Review*, March 1963, 4–16; Davis and Watson, *Black Life in Corporate America*, 27.

82. *Business Week*, "The Negro Drive for Jobs," August 17, 1963, 52–53.

83. *Business Week*, "Crashing Gates to Better Jobs," June 22, 1963, 24–25; Eli Ginzberg, *The Negro Challenge to the Business Community* (New York: McGraw-Hill, 1964), 23; A. L. Reynolds, "Management's Search for the Instant Negro," *Industrial Management*, July 1968, 2.

84. *Wall Street Journal*, "'Believability Gap' on Campus: Companies Rush to Hire Negro Graduates," April 3, 1968, 34; Thomas J. Bray, "Black Bosses: More Negroes Enter Management, but Some Find Role Frustrating," *Wall Street Journal*, May 22, 1969, 1.

85. America and Anderson, *Moving Ahead*, 66.

86. Caitlin Deinard and Raymond A. Friedman, "Black Caucus Groups at Xerox Corporation," Harvard Business School Case 9-491-047 and 9-491-048, (Boston: Harvard Business School, 1990), 10; United States Court of Appeals, Fourth Circuit, *Equal Employment Opportunity Commission v. Radiator Specialty Company*, No. 78-1291, 1979; George Schermer, *Employer's Guide to Equal Opportunity* (Washington, DC: The Potomac Institute, 1966), 46.

87. *Chicago Tribune*, "U.S. Report Finds Area Negro Work Force to Be 13.5%," August 8, 1967, B6.

88. *Ebony*, "Many Students Still Doubt Expanded Job Opportunities," June 1967, 82.

89. Jaslin U. Salmon, *Black Executives in White Businesses* (Washington, DC: University Press of America, 1979), 92.

90. *Time*, "Corporations: Tomorrow Becomes Yesterday," December 8, 1967.

91. *Chicago Sun-Times*, "Survey Finds Discrimination in White-Collar Jobs," January 21, 1968; Stanley C. Vance, "Black Power in the Board Room," *Business Horizons*, June 1971, 81–83.

92. Jonathan Kaufman, "Rights Frontier: Black Executives Say Prejudice Still Impedes Their Path to the Top," *Wall Street Journal*, July 9, 1980, 1.

93. U.S. Department of Health, Education, and Welfare, *Work in America* (Washington, DC: National Technical Information Service, 1972), 43.

94. Stuart Taylor, "The Black Executive and the Corporation—A Difficult Fit," *MBA*, January 1972, 92; Fernandez, 15; David A. Thomas and John J. Gabarro, *Breaking Through: The Making of Minority Executives in Corporate America* (Boston: Harvard Business School Press, 1999), 74; Morgan and Van Dyke, 21, 53, 75, 76, 78, 84, 127.

95. Letter from Darrell Parrish-Johnson to Phillip Newbold and Ray Wicklander, Continental Bank, July 18, 1978, CUL, Series II, Box 63, Folder 721.

96. Jonathan Kaufman, "Rights Frontier: Black Executives Say Prejudice Still Impedes Their Path to the Top," *Wall Street Journal*, July 9, 1980, 1; *Chicago Sun-Times*, "Trailblazing Chicago City Comptroller Clark Burrus Dead at 86," June 23, 2015.

97. Regina Nixon, *Climbing the Corporate Ladder: Some Perceptions among Black Managers* (Washington, DC: National Urban League, 1985), 27.

98. Bank of America, "Performance Report–Administrative Officer," March 1973, E. Frederic Morrow Papers, Box 2, Vivian G. Harsh Research Collection of Afro-American History and Literature, Carter G. Woodson Regional Library, Chicago; Ron Howell, "Who Are the Blacks at the Top of Money Industry?" *Ebony*, November 1979, 159.

99. Edward W. Jones Jr., "Black Managers: The Dream Deferred," *Harvard Business Review*, May–June 1986, 89; Ernest Holsendolph, "Black Executives in a Nearly All-White World," *Fortune*, September 1972, 140; Thomas J. Bray, "Black Bosses: More Negroes Enter Management, but Some Find Role Frustrating," *Wall Street Journal*, May 22, 1969, 1; Jonathan Kaufman, "Rights Frontier: Black Executives Say Prejudice Still Impedes Their Path to the Top," *Wall Street Journal*, July 9, 1980, 1.

100. Ulric Haynes, "Equal Job Opportunity: The Credibility Gap," *Harvard Business Review*, May–June 1968, 116.

101. Frank E. Emerson, "You Are as Successful as You Sound," *Black Enterprise*, December 1979, 68; Susan Dentzer, "They Shall Overcome," *Newsweek*, May 23, 1983, 60.

102. Nixon, *Climbing the Corporate Ladder*, 36; Regina Nixon, *Black Managers in Corporate America: Alienation or Integration?* (Washington, DC: National Urban League, 1985), 25.

103. Orde Coombs, *Do You See My Love for You Growing?* (New York: Dodd, Mead & Co., 1972), 48–52; E. Frederic Morrow, "A Basic Plan for Bank of America to Operate Successfully in Black Communities," April 28, 1971, E. Frederic Morrow Papers, Box 2.

104. Collins, *Black Corporate Executives*, 12, 16.

105. Claudia H. Deutsch, "Black Managers Say that Washington Has Abandoned Them," *New York Times*, January 4, 1987, 2.

106. Gourlay, 57.

107. National Industrial Conference Board, *Company Experience with Negro Employment*, vol. 1, 98; America and Anderson, *Moving Ahead*, 170–73; Alexander and Sapery, *Shortchanged*, 51.

108. Robert S. Greenberger, "Up the Ladder: Many Black Managers Hope to Enter Ranks of Top Management," *Wall Street Journal*, June 15, 1981, 1.

109. *Ebony*, "The 'Acceptable' Negro," April 1966, 118.

110. National Industrial Conference Board, *Company Experience with Negro Employment*, vol. 2, 44.

111. Dickens Jr. and Dickens, *Black Manager*, 58; Davis and Watson, 3, 27.

112. Bernard Sarachek, "Career Concerns of Black Managers," *Management Review*, October 1974, 21.

113. Ernest Holsendolph, "Black Executives in a Nearly All-White World," *Fortune*, September 1972, 144.

114. Davis and Watson, 38.

115. Morgan and Van Dyke, 194–95.

116. Stuart Taylor, "The Black Executive and the Corporation—A Difficult Fit," *MBA*, January 1972, 102.

117. Brian S. Moskal, "Ascent of the Black Manager," *Industry Week*, October 1976, 42.

118. Barry Beckham, "From Campus to Corporation: The Challenge to Adjust," *Black Enterprise*, February 1980, 58.

119. Bayard Rustin, "The Middle Class in the Black Struggle," *Ebony*, August 1973, 144, 149.

120. Robert H. Boyle, "The Ways of Life at the Country Club," *Sports Illustrated*, February 26, 1962.

121. Mark S. Granovetter, *Getting a Job: A Study of Contacts and Careers* (Cambridge, MA: Harvard University Press, 1974), 22.

122. Sewell, 1130.

123. *Ebony*, "The Need to Produce," June 1961, 70.

124. Robert S. Greenberger, "Up the Ladder: Many Black Managers Hope to Enter Ranks of Top Management," *Wall Street Journal*, June 15, 1981, 1.

125. Gourlay, 89–90; Corwin, *Racial Minorities in Banking*, 90–91.

126. Jonathan Kaufman, "Rights Frontier: Black Executives Say Prejudice Still Impedes Their Path to the Top," *Wall Street Journal*, July 9, 1980, 1.

127. Roger Fox and Jerry Szatan, *The Current Economic Status of Chicago's Black Community* (Chicago: Chicago Urban League Research and Planning Department, 1977), 37.

128. Robert B. McKersie, *A Decisive Decade: An Insider's View of the Chicago Civil Rights Movement during the 1960s* (Carbondale: Southern Illinois University Press, 2013), 103.

129. Herbert R. Northrup and Richard L. Rowan, eds., *The Negro and Employment Opportunity*, 230; *Time*, "Why Companies Are Fleeing the Cities," April 26, 1971, 92. See also Louise A. Mozingo, *Pastoral Capitalism: A History of Suburban Corporate Landscapes* (Cambridge, MA: MIT Press, 2011), 24.

130. *Business Management*, "What It's Like to Be a Negro in Management," April 1966, 60–64, 69–77; Ronald Alsop, "Minority Report: Middle-Class Blacks Worry about Slipping," *Wall Street Journal*, November 3, 1980, 1; Alexander and Sapery, 147.

131. Chicago Urban League, "Marketing Careers Program for Minority Youth, Company Evaluation Form," 1980, CUL, Series II, Box 36, Folder 476. As Michael Stoll demonstrated, spatial mismatch and job sprawl continues to beleaguer African Americans. Michael Stoll, "Job Sprawl and the Spatial Mismatch between Blacks and Jobs," Brookings Institution Metropolitan Policy Program, February 2005.

132. New York State Commission for Human Rights, *In Search of Housing: A Study of Experiences of Negro Professional and Technical Personnel in New York State* (New York: State of New York, 1965), 5, 41.

133. Travis, *Racism*, 51; Susan Rugh, *Are We There Yet? The Golden Age of American Family Vacations* (Lawrence: University of Kansas Press, 2008), 69.

134. America and Anderson, *Moving Ahead*, 135; Thomas A. Johnson, "Blacks Dubious about Role in Corporations," *New York Times*, October 12, 1980, 44.

135. Ernest Holsendolph, "Black Executives in a Nearly All-White World," *Fortune*, September 1972, 142; *Black Enterprise*, "Blacks in High Finance," October 1974, 36; The HistoryMakers Video Oral History Interview with Walter H. Clark, December 21, 2000, The HistoryMakers Collection, Chicago, Illinois; Travis, *Racism*, 152–57.

136. Robert W. Brown, "The Black Tax: Stresses Confronting Black Federal Executives," *Journal of Afro-American Issues* 3, no. 2 (Spring 1975): 207; E. Frederic Morrow, *Forty Years a Guinea Pig* (New York: The Pilgrim Press, 1980), 148.

137. Herschel Johnson, "Airline Pioneer," *Ebony*, November 1976, 103.

138. Marilyn Mercer, "How It Feels to Be a Black Girl Now," *Glamour*, May 1969, 244.

139. Dickens Jr. and Dickens, 153.

140. Lewis and Walker, *"Why Should White Guys Have All the Fun?"*, 61.

141. *Time*, "America's Rising Black Middle Class," June 17, 1974.

142. Stuart Taylor, "The Black Executive and the Corporation—A Difficult Fit," *MBA*, January 1972, 92.

143. Stanley Penn, "Integrated Offices: White-Collar Negroes Move into Better Jobs," *Wall Street Journal*, March 17, 1965, 1.

144. The Proceedings of the Executive Study Conference, "The Selection and Training of Negroes for Managerial Positions," November 10–11, 1964, Long Island, New York, 145.

145. Barry Beckham, "From Campus to Corporation: The Challenge to Adjust," *Black Enterprise*, February 1980, 60.

146. Collins, 110.

147. Vincent Butler, "Negro's Climb on Chicago Job Ladder Cited," *Chicago Tribune*, May 29, 1964, 5.

148. Milton Viorst, "The Blacks Who Work for Nixon," *New York Times*, November 29, 1970, 67.

149. *Ebony*, "It's Great to Be a Negro!" March 1964, 92.

150. Edward W. Jones Jr., "Black Managers: The Dream Deferred," *Harvard Business Review*, May–June 1986, 91; Adam Herbert, "The Minority Administrator," *Public Administration Review* 34, no. 6 (November–December 1974): 557, 561–62; *Jet*, "Words of the Week," October 12, 1967, 30; Bayard Rustin, "The Militants and the Middle Class," *New York Amsterdam News*, October 14, 1967, 15.

151. Monroe Anderson, "Young, Middle Class, and Very Black," *Ebony*, August 1973, 123–29; Bernard Sarachek, "Career Concerns of Black Managers," *Management Review*, October 1974, 20–21; Herschel Johnson, "Airline Pioneer," *Ebony*, November 1976, 103.

152. George Riddick, "Operation Breadbasket as Vision, Promise, and Hope," June 1967, 9, Addie Wyatt Papers, Box 149, Folder 2.

153. Letter from Jesse Jackson to Newton Lofton [Laughlin], Chairman of the Board, Continental Baking Company, September 29, 1967; Letter from R. Newton Laughlin to Jackson, October 4, 1967, Addie Wyatt Papers, Box 149, Folder 3.

154. Operation PUSH, "This Is Operation Push" [1975?], Addie Wyatt Papers, Box 151, Folder 9.

155. Whitney Young, "The Role of the Middle-Class Negro," *Ebony*, September 1963, 67; Jean Wheeler, "Let Us All Be Black Together: A College Coed's Plea to the Middle Class," *Ebony*, January 1964, 20–21; Leroi Jones, "The Negro Middle Class' Flight from Heritage," *Ebony*, February 1964, 94; Carl Rowan, "An Answer to Youth's Challenge," *Ebony*, August 1967, 140–43; *Ebony*, "Responsibilities of the Black Middle Class," August 1973, 180; Ron Howell, "Who Are the Blacks at the Top of Money Industry?" *Ebony*, November 1979, 162.

156. *Time*, "Every Negro Who Discharges His Duty Faithfully Is Making a Real Contribution," January 3, 1964; *Ebony*, "Three State Store Chain Vice President," February 1964, 36; *Chicago Defender*, "Worker Aids Others as She Breaks Firm's Color Ban," January 7, 1969, 5; Barry Rand, "Diversity in Corporate America," in *The Affirmative Action Debate*, George E. Curry, ed. (Reading, MA: Addison-Wesley Publishing Company, Inc., 1996), 65.

157. Dan Cordtz, "The Negro Middle Class Is Right in the Middle," *Fortune*, November 1966, 180.

158. Gerald Lee Dillingham, "A Study of Class Differentiation in the Afro-American Community," Unpublished PhD Thesis, University of Chicago, 1976, 170.

159. *Chicago Defender*, "Middle-Class Negroes Are Deemed Backbone of Civil Rights Struggle," May 20, 1967, 4; Eleanor Page, "A Who's Who of Chicago Black Society," *Chicago Tribune*, March 16, 1969, 66.

160. Ellen Boneparth, "Black Businessmen and Community Responsibility," *Phylon* 37, no. 1 (1976): 38.

161. Ernest Holsendorph, "Middle Class Blacks Are Moving Off the Middle," *Fortune*, December 1969, 91.

162. Morgan and Van Dyke, 204.

163. Bruce J. Schulman, *The Seventies: The Great Shift in American Culture, Society, and Politics* (New York: Free Press, 2001), 68, 77.

164. Harrison, *A Life's Design*, 79–81.

165. Herman Belz, *Equality Transformed: A Quarter-Century of Affirmative Action* (New Brunswick, NJ: Transaction Publishers, 1991), 133, 243.

166. Robert W. Goldfarb, "Black Men Are Last," *New York Times*, March 14, 1980, 27; Carol Hymowitz, "Taking a Chance: Many Blacks Jump Off the Corporate Ladder to Be Entrepreneurs," *Wall Street Journal*, August 2, 1984, 1; Jonathan P. Hicks, "Black Professionals Refashion Their Careers: Black Executives Leaving Big Business," *New York Times*, November 29, 1985, A1.

167. *Business Week*, "Blacks Who Left Dead-End Jobs to Go It Alone," February 20, 1984, 106.

168. Harold J. Logan, "Successful Blacks Walk Own Color Line," *Los Angeles Times*, June 14, 1978, C3.

NOTES TO CONCLUSION

1. Michael Luo, "'Whitening' the Résumé," *New York Times*, December 6, 2009, WK3.

2. Marianne Bertrand and Sendhil Mullainathan, "Are Emily and Greg More Employable than Lakisha and Jamal? A Field Experiment on Labor Market Discrimination," *American Economic Review* 94, no. 4 (2004): 991–1013.

3. Michael Luo, "In Job Hunt, College Degree Can't Close Racial Gap," *New York Times*, December 1, 2009, A1.

4. Janelle Jones and John Schmitt, "A College Degree Is No Guarantee," Center for Economic and Policy Research, May 2014, http://www.cepr.net/documents/black-coll-grads-2014-05.pdf, accessed January 9, 2015; Patricia Cohen, "Arduous Job Path for Black Grads," *New York Times*, December 25, 2014, B1.

5. Louis Adamic, *What's Your Name?* (New York: Harper and Brothers, 1942), 36–39, 51, 95–100.

6. Michael Dawson, *Behind the Mule: Race and Class in African-American Politics* (Princeton, NJ: Princeton University Press, 1994).

7. Karyn R. Lacy, *Blue-Chip Black: Race, Class, and Status in the New Black Middle Class* (Berkeley: University of California Press, 2007), 220.

8. William Julius Wilson, *When Work Disappears: The World of the New Urban Poor* (New York: Knopf, 1996), xiii, 29–30.

9. Adolph Reed Jr., *Stirrings in the Jug: Black Politics in the Post-Segregation Era* (Minneapolis: University of Minnesota Press, 1999), 127–28.

10. Marwa Eltagouri, "Chicago-Area Black Population Drops as Residents Leave for South, Suburbs," *Chicago Tribune*, June 24, 2016.

11. Rachael A. Woldoff, *White Flight/Black Flight: The Dynamics of Racial Change in an American Neighborhood* (Ithaca, NY: Cornell University Press, 2011), 158–59.

12. *Ebony*, "The Black Middle Class: Where it Lives," August 1987, 40.

13. Mary Mitchell, "Changing Chatham: Neighborhood Struggles with Class Divide," *Chicago Sun-Times*, June 27, 2011. For an ethnographic study of intraracial class conflict on the South Side in the 2000s, see Mary Pattillo, *Black on the Block: The Politics of Race and Class in the City* (Chicago: University of Chicago Press, 2007).

14. Eugene Robinson, *Disintegration: The Splintering of Black America* (New York: Doubleday, 2010), 226–27; Melvin Oliver and Thomas Shapiro, *Black Wealth/White Wealth: A New Perspective on Racial Inequality* (New York: Routledge, 1997), 190–91.

15. Patrick Reardon, "Redlining Drains City, Aids Suburbs," *Chicago Tribune*, August 11, 1986.

16. Oliver and Shapiro, *Black Wealth/White Wealth*, 12.

17. Cheryl L. Reed and Monifa Thomas, "Blacks Hurt by Gap in Home Values," *Chicago Sun-Times*, November 13, 2005.

18. Mary Mitchell, "Changing Chatham: A Look Back at a Neighborhood in Transition," *Chicago Sun-Times*, June 25, 2011.

19. Bart Landry, *The New Black Middle Class* (Berkeley: University of California Press, 1987), 3, 72, 78.

20. Vernon Jordan Jr., "The Truth about the Black Middle Class," *Newsweek*, July 8, 1974, 11. For the economic parity argument, see Ben Wattenberg and Richard Scammon, "Black Progress and Liberal Rhetoric," *Commentary*, April 1, 1973, 35–44.

21. Michael B. Katz, Mark J. Stern, and Jamie J. Fader, "The New African-American Inequality," *The Journal of American History* 92, no. 1 (June 2005): 77.

22. Gary Orfield and Erica Frankenberg, with Jongyeon Ee and John Kuscera, *Brown at 60: Great Progress, a Long Retreat and an Uncertain Future*, Civil Rights Project, May 2014, 2, 10, 20, 24–25, http://civilrightsproject.ucla.edu/research/k-12-education/integration-and-diversity/brown-at-60-great-progress-a-long-retreat-and-an-uncertain-future/Brown-at-60-051814.pdf.

23. Jonathan Kozol, *The Shame of the Nation: The Restoration of Apartheid Schooling in America* (New York: Crown Publishers, 2005).

24. Jonathan Kozol, *Savage Inequalities* (New York: Crown Publishers, 1991).

25. Diane Ravitch, *Reign of Error: The Hoax of the Privatization Movement and the Danger to America's Public Schools* (New York: Knopf, 2013).

26. Donald Tomaskovic-Devey, Kevin Stainback, Tiffany Taylor, Catherine Zimmer, Corre Robinson, and Tricia McTague, "Documenting Desegregation: Segregation in American Workplaces by Race, Ethnicity, and Sex, 1966–2003," *American Sociological Review* 71, no. 4 (August 2006): 567.

27. Tomaskovic-Devey et al., "Documenting Desegregation: Segregation in American Workplaces by Race, Ethnicity, and Sex, 1966–2003," 573, 585–86; Thomas A. Johnson, "Blacks Dubious about Role in Corporations," *New York Times*, October 12, 1980, 44; Carol Hymowitz, "Taking a Chance: Many Blacks Jump Off the Corporate Ladder to Be Entrepreneurs," *Wall Street Journal*, August 2, 1984, 1; *Business Week*, "Blacks Who Left Dead-End Jobs to Go It Alone," February 20, 1984, 106; Jonathan P. Hicks, "Black Professionals Refashion Their Careers," *New York Times*, November 29, 1985, A1.

28. Nicholas McBride, "In Business and in College, Blacks Caught in a Squeeze," *Christian Science Monitor*, January 20, 1987, 3.

29. John Bound and Richard B. Freeman, "What Went Wrong? The Erosion of Relative Earnings and Employment among Young Black Men in the 1980s," *Quarterly Journal of Economics* 107, no. 1 (February 1992): 208, 215.

30. *Chicago Tribune*, "Recession, Cutbacks Hurt Urban Blacks Most," March 10, 1982.

31. Lynn Norment, "How to Succeed in Corporate America," *Ebony*, August 1987, 51–54.

32. Robert W. Goldfarb, "Black Men Are Last," *New York Times*, March 14, 1980, 27.

33. Robert S. Greenberger, "Job-Bias Alert: Firms Prod Managers to Keep Eye on Goal of Equal Employment," *Wall Street Journal*, May 17, 1982, 2.

34. Joan Rigdon and Carol Hymowitz, "For Black Men, Success Resolves Few Problems," *Wall Street Journal*, August 9, 1992.

35. Travis, *Racism*, 1–2; Russell Barta, "The Representation of Poles, Italians, Hispanics, and Blacks in the Executive Suites of Chicago's Largest Corporations," Institute of Urban Life, National Center for Urban Ethnic Affairs (Chicago, 1984), 3.

36. Elijah Anderson, "The Social Situation of the Black Executive: Black and White Identities in the Corporate World," in *The Cultural Territories of Race: Black and White Boundaries*, Michèle Lamont, ed. (Chicago: University of Chicago Press, 1999), 8.

37. Erin Kelly and Frank Dobbin, "How Affirmative Action Became Diversity Management," *American Behavorial Scientist* 41, no. 7 (April 1998): 961, 967, 981.

38. Dudley Onderdonk, Donald DeMarco, and Kathy Cardona, "Integration in Housing: A Plan for Racial Diversity," Village of Park Forest, 1977; Carole Goodwin, *The Oak Park Strategy: Community Control of Racial Change* (Chicago: University of Chicago Press, 1979).

39. *Chicago Defender*, "Praise Suburb's Compliance," January 23, 1973, 8.

40. "Why Can't We Live Together?" *Dateline*, NBC News, January 1, 1997.

41. Monifa Thomas, "No Guarantee of Opportunity," *Chicago Sun-Times*, November 15, 2005.

42. Janita Poe, "Rapidly Changing Matteson Sets a Course to Woo Whites," *Chicago Tribune*, April 17, 1995.

43. Mary Pattillo, "Black Middle-Class Neighborhoods," *Annual Review of Sociology* 31 (2005): 305–29.

44. Robert Putnam, "E Pluribus Unum: Diversity and Community in the Twenty-First Century," *Scandinavian Political Studies* 30, no. 2 (June 2007): 150–51.

45. Ta-Nehisi Coates, "The American Case against a Black Middle Class," The Atlantic.com, January 22, 2013, http://www.theatlantic.com/national/archive/2013/01/the-american-case-against-a-black-middle-class/267385/, accessed October 13, 2013.

46. Nancy DiTomaso, *The American Non-Dilemma: Racial Inequality without Racism* (New York: Russell Sage, 2013), 318–20.

47. Russell Berman, "As White Americans Give Up on the American Dream, Blacks and Hispanics Embrace It," *The Atlantic*, September 4, 2015, https://www.theatlantic.com/politics/archive/2015/09/the-surprising-optimism-of-african-americans-and-latinos/401054/, accessed February 16, 2017; Tami Luhby, "Why Blacks Believe in the American Dream More than Whites," *CNNMoney*, November 25, 2015, http://money.cnn.com/2015/11/24/news/economy/race-american-dream/, accessed February 3, 2017.

48. Ira Katznelson, *When Affirmative Action Was White: An Untold History of Racial Inequality in Twentieth-Century America* (New York: W. W. Norton & Co., 2005); Andrew Cherlin, "Why Are White Death Rates Rising?" *New York Times*, February 22, 2016.

INDEX

www.ingramcontent.com/pod-product-compliance
Lightning Source LLC
Chambersburg PA
CBHW031135270326
41929CB00011B/1639